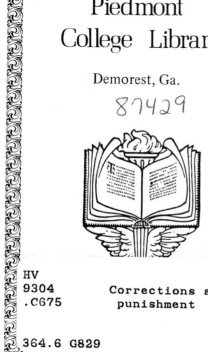

CORRECTIONS AND PUNISHMENT

Books in this series:

Volume 8. Sage Criminal Justice System Annuals

CORRECTIONS AND PUNISHMENT

DAVID F. GREENBERG, *Editor*

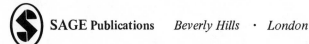

SAGE Publications   *Beverly Hills · London*

For information address:

SAGE PUBLICATIONS, INC.
275 South Beverly Drive
Beverly Hills, California 90212

SAGE PUBLICATIONS LTD
28 Banner Street
London EC1Y 8QE

Printed in the United States of America

International Standard Book No. 0-8039-0600-5 (cloth)
International Standard Book No. 0-8039-0601-3 (paper)

Library of Congress Catalog Card No. 77-79870

FIRST PRINTING

1|5|82 Beehaort Tegler 27.50

CONTENTS

INTRODUCTION

DAVID F. GREENBERG

The sociology of corrections and punishment has undergone major shifts in emphasis and perspective over the past two decades. These changes can be seen in current studies of the social *structure* of these institutions, their social *functions,* and the social *processes* through which they change.

THE SOCIAL STRUCTURE OF CORRECTIONS AND PUNISHMENT

During the 1950s, the major sociological studies of the prison were carried out within the framework of Parsonian structural-functionalism, then the dominant theoretical perspective in sociology. These studies tended to interpret the prison as a closed organization, a self-contained microsociety. The normative code which was assumed to govern inmate behavior was explained as an adaptation to the deprivations associated with involuntary confinement to a total institution. New inmates internalized this system of norms and values so effectively that the prison could be considered culturally homogeneous. The common interest of custodians and prisoners in the preservation of order maintained harmony in what only superficially appeared to be an institution in which conflict was structurally inherent. One of the contributors to this model (Sykes, 1958) argued that the introduction of a new reform-minded, treatment-oriented administration undermined the accommodation between corrupt guards and co-opted prison leaders and thus prepared the way for a prisoners' rebellion.

This *deprivation* or *adaptation* model suffered from both logical and empirical weaknesses. Although its walls and gun towers may limit access and egress, the prison is not a closed society. It is influenced in many ways by the larger society that builds and maintains it. Prison inmates and staff are both drawn from the larger society, as are the branches of government that make rules for the prison and administer it. Visitors, correspondence, and the mass media all influence what happens in prison.

Although the verbal support that inmates lend to the "prisoners' code" lends superficial credence to the claim for effective internalization, widespread violations raise grave doubts about the extent to which the entire prison population subscribes to its precepts. Although the model offers an explanation for role differentiation among inmates, it provides no explanation of how incumbents of particular roles are selected or recruited.

Moreover, a recent study of prison rebellions (Garson, 1972) failed to substantiate any link between the introduction of a reform and the outbreak of a rebellion.

The adaptation model was first challenged by Irwin and Cressey (1963) and Irwin (1970), who argued that the prison is not so overwhelming in its impact on most prisoners as to obliterate their preprison identities. These diverse identities, they suggested, reflect varying participation in the diverse criminal and noncriminal social worlds outside the prison. They insisted that the inmate code is not indigenous to the prison, but is imported by prisoners with backgrounds of professional theft and organized crime. Thus the inmate body is seen as normatively pluralistic.

Although the *importation* model had its origin most directly in Irwin's reflections on the discrepancy between his own prison experience and the key ideas of the *adaptation* model, it both reflected and was part of a wider intellectual development. In the early 1960s, symbolic interactionists were criticizing functionalism and urging the recognition of a greater degree of cultural diversity in American society. The flourishing of movements of political and cultural diversity during the 1960s lent credence to this conception and to a model in which the state's social control apparatus was less than omnipotent.

The period following the formulation of these two models has been one of refinement, synthesis, and (somewhat inadequate) empirical testing. However, as John Irwin notes in Chapter 1 of this volume, both models have been rendered somewhat obsolete by developments that have been transforming the prison society. Administrative and judicial decisions have opened the prison to outside influences to a much greater extent than was true 20 years ago or more, and inmates have been influenced by political and cultural trends that are not directly linked with their own preprison lives. The social structure of inmate society is more volatile, more fluid, and even more pluralistic than in the past. In many prisons, inmates have been able to generate a unity in opposition to the administration that transcends divisions along racial and cultural lines, but administrators have often been able to shatter that unity through repression. Where this has happened, inmates have sometimes been left divided into mutually antagonistic and predatory groups.

In a custodial institution, where inmates are not free to leave, the social structure must of course include the keepers as well as the kept. Yet, by comparison with the many studies of prisoners, little research has focused specifically on the prison staff and administration. Robert E. Doran's study of the classification of inmates in the euphemistically named "adjustment center" of a California men's prison (Chapter 2) contributes to our understanding of the means by which the administration controls prisoners. While the structural-functional studies of the 1950s placed great emphasis on the informal accommodations between guards and inmates, while barely acknowledging the existence of formal sanctions as a means of social control, Doran discusses the use of explicit and severe punishment within the prison. His study reveals the socially shared, common-sense categories used by correctional officers in reaching or justifying decisions about inmates, and he notes the essentially lawless manner in which individual prisoners are assigned to categories. His work tends to substantiate earlier characterizations of the prison as a lawless agency (Greenberg and Stender, 1972), a characterization which I believe has not been fundamentally changed by a handful of court decisions granting extremely limited rights to prisoners.

The social structure of the prison is obviously not limited to line officers who interact with prisoners; it extends into the important policy-setting levels of departments of correction and, from there, into other governmental bodies with influence or authority over the prison. Peter H. Rossi and Richard A. Berk, in Chapter 3, venture into this virtually uncharted territory in an exploratory study of patterns of influence in state corrections in three states. That the funding agency refused to permit the completion of their study despite its seemingly innocuous character suggests the high degree of sensitivity to exposure at upper levels of the punishment-corrections bureaucracy.

To date, much of the theoretical and empirical research in the sociology of prisons has been American, with only occasional contributions from other countries (notably England and the Scandinavian countries). As James H. Jacobs points out in Chapter 4, a genuinely comparative sociology of imprisonment—or punishment more generally—does not exist. Yet there are important differences among nations in the use of formal sanctions as compared with informal social controls, as well as differences in the features of the formal punishment institutions themselves. A macrosociology of punishment should be able to account for these differences. Jacobs suggests a number of promising lines for investigation.

THE SOCIAL FUNCTIONS OF CORRECTIONS AND PUNISHMENT

Over the past decade, our ideas about the functions of corrections and punishment have changed even more drastically than our ideas about the social structure of the prison.

Apart from a few studies of the deterrent effect of the death penalty, research on the functions of sanctions focused until recently almost entirely on their possible rehabilitative value. To be sure, a few sociologists had expressed skepticism about the possibility of carrying out treatment programs effectively in prison. Some had pointed to a contradiction between the rehabilitative goal and the custodial function of the prison. Others had suggested that socialization into the inmate subculture would undermine rehabilitation and that the stigmatization of ex-convicts would prevent them from going straight.

Despite these misgivings, most sociologists and reformers probably believed that it was both feasible and desirable to establish more treatment programs for inmates. Many such programs were established, and quite a few evaluations (which I summarize in Chapter 5), including a number carried out by sociologists, have suggested that most programs are not reducing the rates of return to crime of their participants to any appreciable extent.

Disillusionment over the failure of highly touted programs has been compounded by a new skepticism concerning several of the assumptions that led to the advocacy of these programs. One was that the criminal is necessarily in need of rehabilitation. An alternative assumption is that criminals for the most part respond normally to an environment in which crime is rational. Widespread disaffection from the prevailing social order during the 1960s made a large segment of the population receptive to this view, and, among some New Left circles, a tendency to romanticize criminals as rebels against bourgeois domination emerged.

A second assumption was that the state is fundamentally benign and will run the programs for the benefit of inmates. Implicit in the concept of corrections is the notion that state officials know what is correct and can be trusted to do what is correct. Since it was thought necessary to give administrators a great deal of power over prisoners in order to implement rehabilitation programs, this assumption was a crucial one.

But what if the state is itself headed by criminals? What if the social order is repressive rather than benign for major strata of the population? What if the prison staff and officials, as well as the government of which they are apart, are not merely stern or corrupt but murderous? These disturbing questions have been shown to be more than academic by the events of the last 15 years. Revelations of the killing of prisoners by guards, of lobotomies of prisoners, druggings, solitary confinement, beatings, and enforced transfers of militant prisoners have left us with a more sinister view of penal administrators, just as the war in Southeast Asia and repression of minority groups and protest movements in the United States have led us to a more terrifying view of the state.[1]

Richard Speiglman's essay (Chapter 6) reflects this new sensibility. He points out that, when penal administrators were faced with prisoner militancy, they took steps to reassert control, as we should expect they would. Finding overt violence disadvantageous because of its tendency to draw criticism, they turned to drugs and psychotherapy, which, because they could be packaged as "treatment," did not entail this disadvantage.

An obvious consequence of Speiglman's analysis is that the analytical dichotomy between treatment and custody posited by some sociologists for penal-correctional institutions can be misleading, since it takes the claims of the treatment-oriented prison at face value. Treatment programs are present in high as well as low custody institutions, and in at least some of them they are tools for achieving custodial ends. As the authors of *Struggle for Justice* (American Friends Service Committee, 1972) observed, the opposite of custody is not treatment, but liberty.

With evidence mounting that rehabilitation programs of the sort now established hold no solution to the crime problem and can have undesirable side consequences for those compelled to participate in them, greater attention is now being given to other possible crime-prevention functions of punishment, such as incapacitation or restraint (Shinnar and Shinnar, 1975; Greenberg, 1975) and deterrence.

Although the new wave of deterrence research was initiated by sociologists (Gibbs, 1968), much of the recent work has been carried out by economists. This is partly because rational models of choice based on informed assessments of costs and benefits have an occupationally derived appeal for economists and partly because econometricians are more familiar than other social scientists with the quantitative techniques appropriate for analyzing the kind of data that have been available for studying crime deterrence. Although the present state of the art is by no means definitive and although findings have not been entirely in agreement, many of these studies are consistent with the proposition that state-imposed punishment does reduce the crime rate.

In view of the methodological problems that remain in these statistical studies of crime deterrence (reviewed in Fisher and Nagin, 1976, and Greenberg, 1977), Franklin E. Zimring's study of the deterrent effect of the threat of imprisonment for bad check writing in Chapter 7, utilizing an approach that circumvents these difficulties, is of particular interest, even though it will not be applicable to all other offense categories.

Recent discussions of crime control policy reflect this same shift in emphasis. Just 10 years ago, the prestigious President's Commission on Law Enforcement and the Administration of Justice restricted its discussion of the crime-prevention function of penal sanctions to rehabilitation and how it could be carried out more effectively. The very use of the word "corrections" to characterize criminal justice dispositions—a usage that has become common over the past decade—implies that the purpose of the dispositions is "to correct," that is, to rehabilitate. Today, however, much more attention is being given to the restraining and deterrent effects of sanctions.

It is not only among "conservatives" that this is so. Some of the recent Marxist analyses of the prison have given a central role to its deterrent function. In these analyses, state coercion is viewed as being crucial to the reproduction of exploitative property relations under capitalism (Werkentin et al., 1974). Even if it is true, as I have elsewhere maintained (Greenberg, 1976), that socialist societies are likely to preserve the same abstract laws against theft as are found in capitalist societies, it may still be true that the social functions of such laws are transformed in the new social context.

Quite apart from the question of deterrence, punishment institutions as they now function individualize social problems and divert attention from their social structural sources. Selective inattention to the socially injurious activities of the upper class helps to preserve the legitimacy of these activities, while the high penalties meted out for offenses typically committed by the lower stratum of the working class help to stigmatize the entire stratum, thereby discouraging unity among the various strata of this class. As theater, state punishment institutions strengthen class relations through their constant dramatization of relationships of subordination and superordination. As Hay (1975) noted, even when the state is merciful to lower class defendants, it strengthens its dominance by directing feelings of gratitude to the state and evoking a realization of dependency on the good will of authority for continued benevolence.

Because of these collateral consequences of punishment, the policy implications of deterrence research are not so obvious for reasons quite apart from the question of whether or not punishment deters crime. Some critics of state punishment have in fact called for a restoration of the crime control function to the community for precisely these reasons (Dod et al., 1976). So far, however, popular support for community control of crime prevention has been limited.

Moreover, many neighborhoods are far from being communities; they are frequently divided into sharply antagonistic groups, and they often lack the resources to deal adequately with crime. The social structural causes of crime do not originate at the community level and cannot necessarily be dealt with effectively at that level.

PROCESS: CRIMINALIZATION AND DECRIMINALIZATION

The analysis of change in recent research represents not merely a shift in emphasis, but a new emphasis altogether. Older studies usually covered a short time span and implicitly portrayed a static, timeless world.

One development which helped to sensitize sociologists to questions of process and change was labeling theory. In taking the view that the classification of any particular form of behavior as deviant or criminal was problemmatic, labeling theory directed attention away from traditional issues of causation to the question of why the activity had come to be punishable in the first place.

Several of the early historical studies of criminalization introduced and made use of the notion of the "moral entrepreneur"—an individual or agency that undertakes a moralistic campaign to have a previously tolerated activity prohibited by the state. Scotty Embree's study of narcotics legislation in Chapter 8 suggests that these moral crusaders may not have been as crucial to the criminalization process as is sometimes suggested. Unless the sought-after prohibition is acceptable to powerful groups, a campaign waged by moral entrepreneurs may not be successful.

Although the historical studies inspired by the labeling perspective initially focused on how prohibitions are established, the recent campaigns to decriminalize various "victimless crimes" open the door to the study of the process by which an activity once punishable becomes legally tolerated again. Drew Humphries' study of the movement to repeal abortion laws (in Chapter 9) demonstrates the complexity of one such movement. At different times, different class, occupational, and status groups have campaigned for the liberalization or repeal of abortion laws for quite different reasons.

Humphries' analysis of the abortion movement points the way to a Marx-Weber synthesis which may have value for the study of other movements as well. The key idea here is that different status or occupational groups may initiate or join social movements in response to *different* social contradictions. This insight allows one to avoid the empirically false characterization of all social movements as manifestations of class conflict, yet it allows the theorist to draw on Marxian categories in explaining the existence and nature of contradictions and in accounting for the existence and ideologies of status and occupational groups.

PROCESS: CORRECTIONAL-PENAL INSTITUTIONS

It seems unlikely that any decade has witnessed as much energy devoted to the reform of penal and correctional institutions as the decade from 1965 to 1975. Now that the dust has begun to settle, we can begin to understand these efforts and their accomplishments.

By the late 1960s, the convergence of pressure from rebelling inmates, spiraling budgets, the failure of rehabilitation, criticism over scandalous conditions within the prisons and reformatories, and public concern over increased crime had led to many proposals for reform.

More prisons did not seem to be the answer. There was little reason to believe that they would do the job. They were also very expensive. What with inflated construction and operating costs, institutional expansion to accommodate the growing numbers of offenders being processed through the courts was an extremely unattractive proposition, especially at a time when increased demands were being made on state and federal budgets for military and welfare expenditures. In addition, the wave of prison rebellions raised serious doubts that prisons could continue to be managed using methods that would be acceptable to the public.

For those who had not abandoned treatment as a goal of corrections, "community corrections" was an ideal solution to these problems. The idea was that programs that were not working in prison would be relocated in the community, where offenders not considered dangerous to the public would be "treated," while some minority of "truly dangerous" and perhaps untreatable criminals would continue to be incarcerated. By thus rationalizing the selection process, costs would be kept down and the crime-prevention function of the system enhanced. Originally proposed by a "new breed" of college-educated, social-work-oriented administrators who sympathized with offenders and who did not wish to think of themselves as custodians, "community corrections" was quickly taken up both by higher level figures who perceived its possibilities for extending control more cheaply and by many liberals still under the sway of the community action ideal of the Johnson administration's so-called War on Poverty.

It is generally believed that the community corrections movement has succeeded in reducing the proportion of defendants sent to prison *and* the absolute level of the prison population. From the point of view of those who are concerned with enhancing the deterrent and restraining functions of punishment, these steps may have had the disadvantage of increasing crime. By leaving the selection process uncontrolled, it is possible that they have also increased arbitrariness and discrimination in sentencing. In providing administrators with more "carrots," these steps may have made it possible to control prisoners with less reliance on "sticks."

Leaving aside the merits of the community corrections movement, the dynamics of the reform itself may be of substantial interest. Nowhere was the community corrections model more fully implemented than in the Massachusetts juvenile justice system. Yet it now appears that some of the elements of the new juvenile system in Massachusetts are being abandoned only a short time after they were adopted. The processes by which that is happening are documented by Alden D. Miller, Lloyd E. Ohlin, and Robert B. Coates in Chapter 10.

It is too early to tell yet how far this retrenchment will go. But there is now reason to doubt that the community corrections or decarceration movements of the 1960s deserve much credit for reducing institutional populations or that their impact will be a long-lasting one. Fluctuations in the rate of admissions to prison appear to be governed almost entirely by changes in the level of unemployment, both in Canada and the United States (Greenberg, forthcoming). During the 1960s, when the American economy was expanding, prison admissions declined, as they did during previous periods of prosperity. When the economy underwent a downturn in the early 1970s, prison admissions climbed; at this writing, the per capita prison population has never been higher. Thus the movement to keep people out of the total institutions somehow failed to establish control over the mechanisms that govern the size of the prison population. On the face of the historical evidence, however, we can say with some confidence that a full employment economy would reduce the prison population more effectively than the building of any number of halfway houses.

In recent years, of course, efforts to change the prison system have come not only from above, that is, from administrators and well-funded pressure groups located outside the prison, but also from the prisoners themselves. No account of the prison in recent years could be complete that failed to take prisoners' strikes, rebellions, and unprecedented efforts at political self-organization into account. C. Ronald Huff analyzes one of these efforts, that of the Ohio Prisoners' Labor Union, in Chapter 11.

For those like the editor, who have hoped to see major penal reform grow out of such efforts on the part of prisoners, Huff's study must be sobering. There is little evidence that prisoners by themselves will be able to pressure the system into changing or that they will be able to offer outside groups the benefits that would be necessary to forge an alliance capable of doing so. The radical movement which espoused the cause of prisoners a few years ago no longer exists.

There are, moreover, serious limitations to reform from above. The occupational interests of correctional and prison employees and administrators, as well as public demands, partly instrumental and partly symbolic, for sterner measures to stop increasing crime, are likely to preclude broader change. Several states (e.g., Maine, California) have abandoned indefinite sentencing in the face of widespread criticism, but the new fixed-sentence systems being adopted may well increase the time that prisoners spend behind bars—just the opposite of what sentence reformers have been advocating. Thus, although sociologists concerned with criminal justice are now highly attuned to the study of change, the scope of the change that will be available for study is likely to be extremely limited.

This does not mean the present system will remain unchanged forever. Steven Spitzer and Andrew T. Scull, in Chapter 12, show how the English system of sanctioning was fundamentally reorganized as the result of a major change in class relations (the decline of the gentry and the rise to power of the industrial bourgeoisie). When Beccaria, in 1764, recommended far-reaching reforms in the administration of criminal justice, a French reviewer commented that such radical ideas could be implemented only by a revolutionary regime. Twenty-five years later the French Revolution took place, and many of Beccaria's ideas were, for a short time, adopted. Comparable fundamental change in the United States may well await a comparable upheaval.

NOTE

1. One might well be reluctant to grant such large powers to administrators even without believing them to be malevolent. Historically, however, few doubts were raised about doing so until a vociferous segment of the population came to believe that some administrators were malevolent.

REFERENCES

American Friends Service Committee Working Party (1972). Struggle for justice: A report on crime and punishment in America. New York: Hill and Wang.

DOD, S., PLATT, T., SCHWENDINGER, H., SHANK, G., and TAKAGI, P. (1976). "The politics of street crime." Crime and Social Justice: A Journal of Radical Criminology, 5(spring-summer):1-4.

FISHER, F.M., and NAGIN, D. (1976). "On the feasibility of identifying the crime function in a simultaneous model of crime and sanctions." Paper prepared for the Panel on Research on Deterrent and Incapacitative Effects of the Committee on Research on Law Enforcement and Criminal Justice.

GARSON, G.D. (1972). "The disruption of prison administration: An investigation of alternative theories of the relationship among administrators, reformers, and involuntary social service clients." Law and Society Review, 6(summer):531-561.

GIBBS, J. (1968). "Crime, punishment, and deterrence." Social Science Quarterly, 48(March):515-530.

GREENBERG, D.F. (1975). "The incapacitative effect of imprisonment: Some estimates." Law and Society Review, 9(summer):541-580.

——— (1976). "On one-dimensional Marxist criminology." Theory and Society, 3(summer): 611-621.

——— (1977). "Crime deterrence research and social policy." Pp. 281-295 in S.S. Nagel (ed.), Modeling the criminal justice system (Vol. 7, Sage criminal justice system annuals). Beverly Hills, Calif.: Sage.

——— (forthcoming). "Homeostatic and other punishment processes."

GREENBERG, D.F., and STENDER, F. (1972). "The prison as a lawless agency." Buffalo Law Review, 21:799-838.

HAY, D. (1975). "Property authority and the criminal law." Pp. 17-63 in D. Hay, P. Linebaugh, J.G. Rule, E.P. Thompson, and C. Winslow (eds.), Albion's fatal tree: Crime and society in eighteenth century England. New York: Pantheon.

IRWIN, J. (1970). The felon. Englewood Cliffs, N.J.: Prentice-Hall.

IRWIN, J., and CRESSEY, D. (1963). "Thieves, convicts and the inmate culture." Social Problems, 10:142-155.

SHINNAR, R., and SHINNAR, S. (1975). "The effects of the criminal justice system on the control of crime: A quantitative approach, 9(summer):581-612.

SYKES, G. (1958). The society of captives: A study of a maximum security prison. Princeton, N.J.: Princeton University Press.

WERKENTIN, F., HOFFERBERT, M., and BAURMANN, M. (1974). "Criminology as police science or: How old is the new criminology?" Crime and Social Justice: A Journal of Radical Criminology, 2(fall-winter):24-41.

PART I.

THE SOCIAL STRUCTURE
OF
CORRECTIONS AND PUNISHMENT

Chapter 1

THE CHANGING SOCIAL STRUCTURE
OF THE MEN'S PRISON

JOHN IRWIN

Several recent studies of men's prisons in the United States (Carroll, 1974; Williams and Fish, 1974; Davidson, 1974) should convince us that our current theories of the social organization of the prison and the "inmate culture" are outmoded and that we must begin work on a new sociology of the prison. Briefly, these studies suggest that currently there is more conflict among prisoners and among staff members and much less consensus or sense of purpose relative to philosophy and goals among prison administrators than existed in the past. We should expect this because the prison, like the broader society, passed through the tumultuous 1960s and was drastically rearranged. Prison populations have tilted more and more toward "minority" groups since the 1950s. The radical, critical, nationalistic, and iconoclastic ideas which spread through the general society penetrated the prison and left prisoners generally less conforming, more fractionalized, and often enraged. Simultaneously, social scientists dismantled the correctional philosophy which had prevailed for over 50 years and which had enabled correctional administrators to accomplish or disguise contradictory aspects of their operations.

In truth, the old theories were never very sound. I believe that they mistakenly treated the prison as a monolithic phenomenon and the prisoner population as too homogeneous and cohesive. This was partly a result of the limited number of studies and the fact that social researchers used the prison as a testing ground for the emerging "social system" paradigm which was being adopted from anthropology and adapted to the highly complex modern society.

In this chapter we attempt to lay the foundation for a new sociology of the prison by describing some of the social processes which are transforming the social structures of the contemporary men's prison. Before undertaking this task, however, we must build a backdrop to the present scene. Specifically we must summarize the old theories and their weaknesses and examine the social forces which impinged upon the prison during the 1960s. Then we can take the bits and pieces of new data which are available and begin constructing a new analysis of the prison. Our analysis is sketchy because our information is incomplete, and it awaits a much more complex and conflictive final analysis.

THE OLD THEORIES OF THE PRISON:
CLEMMER AND PRISON CULTURE

Tracing the development of our current sociology of the prison is like tracing the growth of American sociological theory since 1930. The progression of sociologists who entered the prison between 1935 and 1970 to study this exotic world carried with them the latest package of sociological concepts. For all intents and purposes the series starts with Donald Clemmer (1940), who analyzed the prison world with two standard concepts of that era—primary group and culture. Clemmer discovered that over half the prisoners in Menard Prison in Illinois were organized into either cliques or semiprimary groups. In cliques the members shared "each other's luxuries and secrets" and accepted, or were willing to accept, punishment "one for the other." In semiprimary groups they were "friendly" with each other, shared luxuries, told each other some of their secrets, but would not "go 'all the way' " for each other; they would not subject themselves entirely to the wishes and acts of the group as a whole, nor restrict their participation to the particular group (Clemmer, 1940:118). Clemmer also discovered a special prison culture to which all entering prisoners became oriented through prisonization. He discussed other ordering features, such as a status hierarchy and a structure of groups differentiated on race, occupational position, and criminal type, but these ideas were not developed as thoroughly as primary group and culture.

In 1951 Talcott Parsons published *The Social System* and (with several other social scientists) *Toward A General Theory of Action*. These books marked the full adaptation and expansion of English social anthropology's "functionalism" into sociology. The impact was far-reaching. It is no exaggeration to say that this elaborate paradigm conquered and then dominated sociology for the next 15 years. Its influences, as one would expect, extended to the sociology of the prison. In fact, the prison was ideally suited for "systems" or "functionalist" studies, because, unlike the complex broader society, it was relatively small, contained, cohesive, and homogeneous. It appeared to parallel the isolated tribal societies which were the subject of the first functional analyses.

The systems or functional analysis of the prison began with Gresham Sykes's study (1958) of the New Jersey prison in the early 1950s. However, two proceeding ethnographies of the prison supplied Sykes with essential components to build his theory. The first of these was a study by Hans Reimer (1937) which delineated two prisoner types—the "politician" and the "right guy"—who were leaders in the prison world. Clarence Schrag (1944), in a study of Walla Walla, expanded this classification of types or roles in the prison to include "merchants," "square johns," "outlaws," and "dings." First Sykes, then Sykes and Messinger (1960), following the Parsonian direction, tied all these and similar prison types into a "social system" which was functionally integrated. According to their analysis, the "problems" which the unique social system of roles is intended to solve divide into two classes: those of the administrators and those of the prisoners. The former have the primary problem of maintaining control over a potentially obstreperous, rebellious, and violent prisoner population who outnumber the staff at any given time more than four to one. Moreover, the administration has to maintain control without sufficient raw force. There are only a few guns, restricted to gun towers and other places inaccessible to prisoners. There are no other adequate formal systems of control. The prisoners, on the other hand, have to withstand the pains of imprisonment —the reduced level of material benefits, sexual deprivation, loss of dignity, and danger of harm from other prisoners.

The social system which has developed to solve these two types of problems is an "accommodative" one in which certain prisoner leaders are given special privileges, such as those which could be gathered by occupying a key position in the prison (e.g., captain's clerk), in return for enforcing a peaceful informal social order. This exploitative and accommodative arrangement between the prisoner leaders and the administration is implicit and appears to be one of antagonism, because the prisoner code serves as a screen hiding the true nature of the relationship. This code with its central dictum, "do your own time," gives the appearance of opposition and antagonism but is actually one which allows—in fact, promotes—exploitation of other prisoners and accommodation with the administration. The various prisoner types, such as the right guy, the politician, the punk, the merchant, and the queen are all acting out roles in the accommodative system by dividing up the scarce commodities and privileges and covertly or implicitly helping the administration maintain control.

Having argued that this special system develops within the prison, Sykes, Messinger, and other proponents of this theory were faced with a fundamental theoretical problem. Prisoners occupied other roles and carried other value systems before entering prison. These may be inconsistent with and disruptive to the accommodative system. This theoretical problem was solved by positing that prisoners, when entering prison, have their former statuses, roles, and identities stripped from them and that they begin prison life at the bottom, working their way up as they become socialized into the indigenous system.

In the early 1960s, I and a mentor (Irwin and Cressey, 1963) challenged this "indigenous," "accommodative" theory, arguing that the orientations and attributes of individuals are carried into the prison and influence the nature of the prisoner social world and that the prisoner code is actually a slightly modified version of the "thieves" code which originated and operates outside the prison. This study located a network of persons who kept their orientations toward the outside, who exercised considerable power in the prison, and who were not in an exploitative relationship to each other but, in fact, practiced mutual aid. The study also suggested that many of the types who entered into an accommodative relationship with the prison administrators and who were oriented to the prison more than the outside had long experiences in youth prisons where they had developed their exploitative and prison orientations.

I now believe that the major point of this contrasting theory was that the prison world is more complex and less solidary than the accommodative social system theory implied and that social material—concepts, information, orientations, relationships—from the outside penetrates the prison walls and influences the social activities and relationships inside.

In a later study (Irwin, 1970), I expanded the list of "social types" who enter the prison with a particular orientation which they do not completely lose and which influences their career in prison; I included (in addition to "thieves") "dope fiends," "heads," "hustlers," "state raised youths," "lower class men," and "square johns." Moreover, I discovered that a great variety of outside phenomena impinge upon the prisoner world and the prison social organization. For instance, at the time of this later study (1966-1968) the civil-rights and the radical movements were influencing prison social relationships. In addition, the vast majority of prisoners appeared to engage in planning for release, and this planning process was influenced by outside events, activities, and relationships and influenced other social relationships in prison.

At the close of my study, politically radical philosophies and activities were flourishing on the outside and penetrating the prison with more force and effect. Regrettably I captured the new trends only at their beginning and finished the study with the painful thought that it was becoming obsolete before publication.

THE TUMULTUOUS SIXTIES AND THE PRISON

Anachronistically, the superiority of one or the other of these two approaches—the indigenous and importation "models"—continues to be debated today, even when the prison situation has changed so much that neither seems to be very useful (e.g., Carroll, 1974:2-7). Now the concept of "interchange" instead of importation is more appropriate. To understand the intensity and complexity of the interchange and the shift from a more isolated to much less isolated prison world, we must review some of the events of the 1960s which opened the gate between the prison and the outside world much wider and introduced trends which are still developing today.

Black Identity and Black Radicalism

As mentioned above, the prison populations in northern and western states tipped from white to nonwhite after World War II. The northern and western migration of blacks from the South and the migration of Puerto Ricans from Puerto Rico to the northeastern United States are related to this shift. For instance, in California in 1945, two-thirds of the prison population was white. By 1960 the population had shifted to about one-half white, one-quarter Chicano, and one-quarter black. In New York in 1971, 55% of the state's prison population was black (Oswald, 1972:18); and in Statesville, Illinois, in 1972, 70% of the prison population was black (Jacobs, 1974:397).

When the Muslim and other black nationalistic and militant organizations grew in the northern and western cities, these organizations spread to the prison. Groups of Muslims with shaved heads appeared on the yards and in the cell blocks of many prisons and vehemently articulated the separatist, antiwhite Muslim philosophy. These growing inside organizations of Black Muslims attempted to hold religious meetings, receive the Muslim newspaper, obtain copies of the *Qur'an,* and receive visits from members of the local Temple of Islam, all of which were denied them. The reaction by the prison administration and staff was invariably antagonistic and obstructive—in fact, repressive. The Muslims were perceived as an extremely serious threat to the security of the prison, and their philosophy was deemed a profound threat of the beliefs and values of prison administrators and staff. For instance, in 1963 in San Quentin, California, a guard fired at a group of Muslims and other black prisoners who were fighting in the yard, and he killed one Muslim (see Pallas and Barber, 1973:245). Soon after, the prison administration established a rule that no more than two black prisoners could congregate in the recreation areas of the prison. In 1964 at a meeting of the Southern Conference on Corrections all five of the papers on "The Guts of Riot and Disturbance" dealt specifically with Black Muslims.

The era of vigorous organizing and growth of the Muslims in prisons ended in 1963 after the separation of Malcolm X from the outside organization (Pallas and Barber, 1973:247). However, the nationalistic Black Power movement and then the Black Panther Party continued to shift black prisoners toward assertiveness, pride and hostility toward the prison administration and whites in general, and organized militancy. There ensued a period of increased violence between black and white prisoners. In California, for instance (and it is appropriate to focus on California because so many trends began there and spread out across the country), the new openly expressed hostility of blacks and the enduring racial prejudices of white prisoners resulted in several ambushes by large groups of one race on smaller groups of the other in the "day rooms" at Soledad Prison. These group attacks stopped, but interracial knife fights and homicides continued. By the late 1960s whites and blacks in the medium and maximum security prisons in California were extremely hostile toward each other and practiced virtually complete voluntary segregation in all areas where prisoners commingled.

Chicanos After the Mid-1960s

Mexican-American prisoners who referred to themselves by the term Chicano followed the black prisoners and began to promote their special interests and to develop self-respect as Chicanos. This was a departure from their earlier posture, which was one of considerable ambivalence relative to their Mexican-American identity and social position. On the one hand, they had experienced extreme prejudice and discrimination in Los Angeles, Texas, and the San Joaquin Valley, where most of them had been raised, and consequently they remained deeply resentful toward whites in general. On the other hand, most were very hostile and prejudiced toward blacks, many tended to identify with whites, and quite a few had interacted and cooperated extensively with white criminals, on both the outside and the inside. In fact, in many prison racial incidents in earlier eras, Chicanos had sided with whites against blacks.

However, the ideology of racial pride and activism spread to Chicanos and moved them in the direction that blacks had been traveling for several years. In San Quentin in 1966, for instance, a group of Chicanos formed a study group to study Chicano history and culture. Out of this group EMPLEO was organized, ostensibly to promote Chicano self-help, but actually to promote the same political and nationalistic goals as the militant black organizations. The concept of Chicano as a distinguishable, honorable, cultural, and nationalistic identity took shape, and the relationship between whites and Chicanos became more hostile and that between Chicanos and blacks improved.

Whites and the Sense of Injustice

While nonwhites were becoming more and more radical and assertive, the white prisoners in the California prisons, though they were not becoming entirely "radicalized" or "politicized," were developing a deep sense of injustice related to the conditions of imprisonment, the length of their sentences, and a variety of judicial or quasi-judicial procedures which influenced these. In particular, white prisoners were increasingly resentful of the indeterminate sentence system in California, which was the most *indeterminate* in the United States. In theory, this system was adopted in many states to implement rehabilitation but, in actuality, was adopted more to promote custodial goals. After 1960 it was being perceived by prisoners as a whimsical system at best and as an unconstitutionally arbitrary one at worst. Consequently, white prisoners, though they remained somewhat conservative in their racial, economic, and political attitudes, were developing a very deep and thorough criticism of the judicial and prison systems.

The Unity Strikes at San Quentin

In the late 1960s two unity strikes which involved all racial groups occurred at San Quentin, and these set off a trend across the country. The San Quentin unity strikes followed a near race riot which had been precipitated by a series of racial incidents after an officer had disciplined a black prisoner. The near riot progressed to the point where several thousand prisoners on the prison yard at noon divided into two groups—blacks in one group and Chicanos and whites in the other. Afterwards, the prisoners were kept in their cells for several days, and, when released, many of them began to argue that they had allowed themselves to be diverted from a legitimate prisoner issue into a racial dispute. A group of prisoners began to plan a unity strike. Through the mechanism of an underground dittoed newspaper *(The Outlaw)*, the help of outside organizers, the support of a Bay Area underground newspaper (the *Berkeley Barb*), and the participation of outside pickets and rock bands, the prisoners went on strike for several days in February 1968 and then again for two days in August 1968.

The "Prison Movement"

In 1969 the "political" activities in the prisons were fused with the outside radical movement, and the "prison movement" came into being. Several significant developments drew the attention of political activists to the prisons and established links between the outside "movement" and prisoners. An important background development was that the Vietnam War as a viable issue was declining, and many activists were in need of a new issue. Their attention was drawn to the prisons first by the publication of *Soul On Ice* by Eldridge

Cleaver (1968), an ex-convict from California prisons, then by his subsequent ascension to a position of leadership in the Black Panther Party, his rise to stardom in the outside radical movement (which meant that he was the principal speaker at many rallies, was interviewed often by the press, and, when charged with a new crime, became the focus of a large defense committee) and finally his being charged and jailed after a shoot-out with the Oakland police. Then Huey Newton, the head of the Black Panther Party and one of the nation's best known activists, was imprisoned in a California prison. Finally, there were the events which ensued after a gun tower guard at Soledad fired several shots into a group of "adjustment center" prisoners who were fighting during their brief exercise period. Three black prisoners were killed, and several days later a guard was beaten and thrown to his death from the third tier in a cell block at Soledad. Three black prisoners were charged with the crime, and radical white lawyers who had been active in the civil-rights and war-protest movements formed a "Soledad Defense Committee." A year later, Jonathan Jackson, George's younger brother, walked into the Marin County Court House with guns and attempted to free three black prisoners who were appearing in the court from the San Quentin Adjustment Center. Two black prisoners, Jonathan Jackson, and the judge were killed. The only surviving prisoner and Angela Davis, a well-known radical, were charged with crimes related to the escape attempt. This interchange, ex-prisoners becoming leaders in the radical movement and radical leaders becoming prisoners, diverted many radical movement activists away from other issues to the prison and supplied them with direct knowledge about conditions in prison. The radical movement adopted the prison issue as one of its primary causes.

THE NEW IDEOLOGIES AND EVENTS OF THE 1970s

Prisoner Political Organizing

The activities stemming from the involvement of radical activists in the prison issue were for the most part restricted to organizing defense efforts for individuals involved in the more celebrated cases in California and occasionally other states. In the meantime, however, a broader based organizing movement passed through (for that matter, is still passing through) many prisons in the United States. The general pattern of this "political" trend is as follows: A group of prisoners, of varying size and racial composition, constructs a list of grievances or demands which contain a more complex analysis of the prison system and a more radical program for change than were produced by prisoners in past eras. Second, the organizing group attempts to bring together and sustain a larger organization of prisoners representing all racial groups. In addition, the organizers establish contact with outside individuals and groups from whom they seek help in publicizing their grievances and obtaining their goals. Finally, they attempt to effect strategies, such as strikes or demonstrations, which will force the administration to negotiate with them regarding their grievances. The strategies very often do not proceed as planned: at times, they are never implemented, and at other times they explode into violent incidents. However, this general pattern has been repeated many times since 1968. The 19-day Folsom strike in 1970 and the Attica riot in 1971 are two of the better known manifestations of this organizing trend.

These organizing efforts, which are still taking place, are not separate developments at each prison but are part of a national movement in which there is some degree of communication and interaction between prisoners in the same and different states. Clear evidence of this exists in the fact that the "manifesto of demands" produced by the Folsom prisoners in their strike which began on November 3, 1970, was virtually identical to the "manifesto of demands" presented to the warden of Attica in May 1971.

At least four forms of communication and interaction connect the separate organizing efforts. The most obvious is the mass media, which carry news and details of the political events in one prison to others. In addition, there have been several special newspapers or newsletters which deal primarily with news of political activities in prison and which have been distributed to many prisons in the country. Another form is the steady interchange of prisoners who are transferred from one prison to another or who are released and reincarcerated in other prisons, often in other states. Finally, there are the activities of outside organizers who maintain contact with different prisons and different prisoner organizations in different states.

The Administrative Response

In general, new political activities—the disturbances and the broader organizing efforts—have caused prison administrators across the country to display intense apprehension, fear, and hostility and to impose swift, sometimes arbitrary, repressive action. The associate warden at San Quentin after the two 1968 unity strikes delivered a paper to a meeting of California correctional administrators which warned them of the new threat and set the tone of the ensuing administrative response:

> The events of 1968 demonstrated that prison operations can be affected, almost at will, given enough publicity, by the use of rock bands and other techniques of the New Left, and the participation of dissident outside groups in conjunction with intelligent inmate leadership. [Park, 1968]

California, again leading a national trend, began to take drastic measures to prevent more of the new type of organized disruptions. Its administrators developed a conceptual category of "revolutionary" and attempted to locate prisoners who fit the category. Many persons who had been or were suspected of being involved in past disruptions, persons who revealed radical political attitudes in their censored correspondence, and persons who belonged to prisoner organizations which were suspected of planning political activities were labeled "revolutionaries" and segregated, transferred to other prisons, or sometimes released to remove them from the "mainline" prison population. Organizations such as EMPLEO and SATE in San Quentin, which were suspected of participating in the disruptions, were disbanded, and disciplinary action was threatened against prisoners who continued to belong to them. Finally, the prison system's special internal police force—the "Special Services," which was controlled from the governor's office—began investigating prisoners, employees, and outside individuals who were suspected of being involved in prison political activities.

This policy had the immediate consequence of stopping or stalling the activities of many emerging self-help and political organizations among prisoners and of removing many persons from the mainline populations. It had another, unanticipated, slower developing, but much farther reaching consequence. Many of the individuals who were removed were powerful persons in the informal prison social world. They were persons who had accumulated considerable respect through the years and occupied positions of leadership in the informal networks of prisoners or in the new formal prisoner organizations. The old social order based on the respect of prisoner leaders and an accommodative social system had already lost much of its grip on the prisoner population, but the rise of prisoner organizations headed by respected prisoner leaders was replacing the old order. However, this later trend was stopped or delayed, and another development, that of warring hoodlum cliques, spread and took over the prisons. This development is discussed below.

The Dismantling of the Rehabilitative Ideal

While prisoner political activities and their repression were occurring, social scientists were engaged in a more indirect, but eventually very damaging attack on the nation's prison systems. This was the theoretical dismantling of the rehabilitative ideal which had existed as the official ideology for many if not most prison systems. Two developments led to this. The first was a growing disillusionment and pessimism over "treatment" efforts. The foundation of the rehabilitative idea was a new approach in reforming the individual, in which the concern shifted totally from the criminal act to the individual, who was viewed as a different type, a pathological type, in need of a cure. The identification of the difference, the pathology, and the development of strategies for changing the individual were to be accomplished by social science. The disillusionment grew when the evaluation of hundreds of treatment efforts appeared to add up to no significant change in the individuals treated. Pessimism was added to this when many critical social scientists or critics of social science began to argue that the premises upon which the rehabilitative dream were founded were false. These critics contended that criminals were not different in the ways which the rehabilitative model suggested and that strategies for changing individuals in a predictable direction would never be forthcoming.

The second development which led to the dismantling of the official ideology was the discovery that the criminal justice system pursued many inadmissible, discriminatory, perhaps unconstitutional goals in the name of rehabilitation. For instance, several studies indicated that richer, more powerful persons were systematically given less punishment than poorer, less influential persons, all in the name of rehabilitation. In addition, it was argued by some observers that prison administrators used rehabilitative cosmetics to disguise punitive and severe control mechanisms.

By 1970 the growing criticism took full shape and spread among criminologists and criminal justice experts. For a short period of several years there was an intense effort to quickly substitute a new ideology—community corrections—for the old, which would leave most of the basic structures, particularly the discretionary decision-making systems, intact. However, flaws in this system were quickly recognized, and the same type of criticisms which were aimed at the rehabilitative ideal were turned toward it (see Ward, 1973; Greenberg, 1975). The movement toward community corrections still continues, but it has had its rationale seriously damaged and will probably not succeed in supplanting the dying rehabilitative ideal.

The result of the dismantling of the rehabilitative ideal is that at least two serious problems are created for correctional administrators and staff. The first is the lack of a unifying rhetoric which permits them to smooth over inherent contradictions in their undertakings and to disguise otherwise inadmissible practices. The nation's prison systems have been given a variety of tasks, some of them inherently contradictory. They have been mandated to keep prisoners under control (that is, in a state of banishment and docility), to reform them, to select the dangerous from them and keep this subgroup for long periods if not indefinitely, and to do all these things without confronting the public with the repulsiveness of the task or the perceived repulsiveness of many prisoners. Formerly, the rehabilitative ideal allowed prison administrators to employ a variety of otherwise inadmissible practices which were acceptable when given the label of rehabilitation and to make it seem that they were pursuing all the above goals.

A second problem stems from this lack of an official rhetoric and the closer, more critical scrutiny which has accompanied and produced the dismantling of the rehabilitative ideal. This is a general lowering of morale at all levels of the correctional system. The prison administrators have been criticized by social scientists, politicians, and the general public for not accomplishing all the contradictory goals assigned them and for operating an excessively brutal enterprise. The guards have been placed in an especially vulnerable position. They are seen by the more severe critics as the actual perpetuators of brutality. In addition, they are blamed by outsiders and the administration when escapes, violence, or other undesirable but inevitable events occur. They are also the focus of the heightened hostility and actual violence of the prisoners. Now they suffer all these with no justifying philosophy to give their work purpose or dignity. As would be expected, they are revealing the symptoms of extreme demoralization and resentment (see Carroll, 1974).

THE STATE OF THE PRISON: 1976

This is the backdrop. What forms or structures have taken shape on the new stage? Needless to say, there is no single "inmate culture" or "inmate social system." Nor is there an overreaching inmate code. The variety of cultural and subcultural orientations (ethnic, class, and criminal), the variety of preprison experiences, and the intense, open hostility between segments of the prison population preclude this. The general climate is much more threatening, both to prisoners and staff, and there is more prisoner-to-prisoner and prisoner-to-guard violence. It is not total chaos, however. New systems of order have emerged (or old systems have reemerged).

The Rise of the Small Cliques

At present the principal structural feature in the prisoner social world appears to be the small clique. With the impossibility of participation in a larger, more encompassing social system, most prisoners form small friendship groups and, to a great extent, restrict their social interaction to members of their own "tip." These friendship groups are the vehicles for accomplishing whatever goals the prisoner must pursue through interaction and cooperation with other prisoners. For instance, these cliques supply the satisfaction which derives from group interaction, and they are the mechanism for cooperative task performance which cannot be accomplished individually or through other channels. Some of those tasks are the provision of mutual protection from theft and physical assault, the conduct of gambling or other "wheeling and dealing" activities, and the learning of crafts or academic subjects. These cliques are formed among persons of the same race, with friends from the outside, among persons who share criminal orientations, or among persons who work or cell in the same area. They range from groups of two or three persons to large "gangs" of several dozen. In fact, some of the cliques are tied together into very large loose affiliations or gangs of several hundred, such as the "Mexican Mafia" in California and the "Blackstone Rangers" in Illinois, which span an entire prison system (Jacobs, 1974). The cliques range from loosely committed groups of friends who share leisure hours together to tightly knit organizations in which the members cooperate in rackets, thefts, and violence, share each other's materials, protect each other from attacks, and avenge each other when attacked. In between these extremes there are a wide range of small to large and more or less cohesive groups.

The "Ordered Segmentation"

The relationship between the groups and the social order which has emerged among prisoners resemble greatly the "order segmentation" that Gerald Suttles (1968) discovered in a slum area of Chicago. In this system of group relationships there is a generally low level of trust between inhabitants of a given area and considerable hostility between members of different social categories, particularly racial categories. Prisoners living together in the same restricted areas now interact only with members of their own clique and a few other persons with whom perhaps they share racial and other social characteristics. There are some exceptions. A few prisoners who have maintained friendships among different groups and who have general respect in the prison are able to cross the barricades of hostility and maintain ties with "alien individuals." However, the vast majority confine their associations to their own group or persons of their social category and maintain social distance from all others even though they physically commingle. This is made possible by considerable voluntary segregation in the public areas, cell blocks, and work settings.

This hostile accommodation has been reached in some states after a period of extreme intergroup violence. In fact, it is this violent phase which creates or greatly enhances the atmosphere of distrust, destroys any incipient or existing prison-wide social organizations, and produces the ordered segmentation.

In California the period of extreme "gang" violence began in 1968 with the appearance of a small, tightly knit clique of young Chicanos from Los Angeles who were aggressively muscling in on the drug dealings and other illegal activities of other prisoners, particularly other Chicano prisoners. This group earned a reputation for aggressiveness and success in taking other persons' drugs and money and was approached by many young new Chicano prisoners for membership. The rumor which circulated in San Quentin at that time was that a person first had to commit a random murder to be admitted into the Mafia (which was the name that the clique acquired). Whether this was true or not, considerable fear was generated by the belief and by the actual strong-arm tactics of this aggressive group. Other Chicanos conspired to eliminate this clique by murdering all known Mafia members. The Mafia was not eliminated, but gained strength. Its opponents formed another organization—La Familia. Both groups grew rapidly. The Mafia drew mainly from Los Angeles, and La Familia from Texas and the "Valley" (the San Joaquin Valley). There had been a long-enduring enmity between Chicanos from these different locations.

The emergence of the Mafia and then La Familia was occurring when the attention of the administration was focused on political activities. This is not to say that they did nothing about the violence related to the gang fights, but they remained more concerned about "revolutionaries" and took more action against persons suspected of political activities. This had the consequence mentioned above of removing those persons who might have maintained alternative social structures and prevented the total dominance of gang violence.

Groups like the Aryan Brotherhood and the Black Guerrilla Family began to grow because of the threat that white and black prisoners faced from the Chicano group; their recruitment came especially from "low-riders," prisoners who engaged in petty rackets, stole from other prisoners, and threatened violence or committed violence against other prisoners, particularly other racial groups. Many prisoners who had disapproved of, had disliked, and would not associate with these groups now affiliated with them for protection. Eventually the Black Guerrilla Family formed an alliance with La Familia, and the Aryan Brotherhood allied with the Mafia. Moreover, the prison officials systematically separated Chicanos on the basis of their gang affiliation, sending members (or persons who stated that they leaned toward one gang or the other) to different prisons. By 1974, although there were still occasional assassinations and disputes over rackets, a hostile detente had been reached between all the gangs.

Similar events have occurred in other prisons, and, because of them and because of the general hostility and distrust between prisoners and groups of prisoners, variations on the California version of order segmentation have emerged (Carroll, 1974; Jacobs, 1976).

The Sub-rosa Economic Life

Though interaction between hostile groups and general segmentation prevails, there is one form of activity which bridges the gaps between the hostile groups. This is the vigorous sub-rosa economic activity among prisoners which has increased greatly in recent years (see Williams and Fish, 1974). In this world of scarcity—the prison—there has always been a considerable amount of "wheeling and dealing," that is, trading in contraband, and gambling. However, in the last decade there has been a marked increase in the amount of legal and illegal commodities and a corresponding increase in the sub-rosa activities involved in the exchange of these commodities. The primary explanation for the increase in commodities (and money) in the prison is the increase in the standard of living in society in general. Prisoners come to prison with more money and more access to money. Friends and relatives have more money and give more (legally and illegally) to prisoners. In addition, there has been a general increase in the commodities that prisoners can legally obtain through the canteen or the catalog purchasing systems or from friends and relatives. Consequently, there are more goods and cash in prison (most prisons will not allow prisoners to have cash in their possession, but many prisoners have money smuggled to them).

There is also much more illegal contraband, particularly drugs, which are smuggled into the prison by friends and family or by prison employees who are paid with the increased flow of cash. The general demoralization of the guard force and the influx of younger urban guards who are more tolerant of drugs are related to this increase in smuggling on the part of guards and other staff.

The net result of the greater availability of such things as money, drugs, cigarettes (and other tobacco products), television sets, typewriters, stereo sets, books, magazines, furniture, craft and art materials, clothes, and other goods is that it is possible to live on a higher standard of living in prison than in past eras and to leave prison with a sizable cache of money. Consequently, wheeling and dealing is more widespread at present.

The two main forms of sub-rosa economic activity are gambling and distributing contraband commodities. In former years, most of the contraband was of internal origin—e.g., food from the kitchen, drugs from the hospital, and material from the shops—and the "money" used was cigarettes. But in this era of greater prosperity, real money has become part of the economic system, and much more contraband from the outside, particularly drugs, is available.

The sub-rosa economic activity has a dual relationship to the ordered segmentation. On the one hand, wheeling and dealing activities cross the lines of hostility. The relative scarcity of goods encourages individuals and groups to interact with others whom they may dislike and distrust, and some ties and norms are established between hostile individuals and groups. However, many violations of the general rules governing the exchange of goods (e.g., "double crosses," "burns," and "thefts") increase the hostility and precipitate violence. These violations occur with some frequency because of the conflicting sets of definitions governing exchange between individuals and groups. The traditional definitions prohibit cheating and theft among prisoners, at least among a subset of prisoners who are collectively defined as "all right" or as "regulars." However, in recent decades, with the growing diversity of racial and criminal types and with the intensification of hostility between different segments, a new set of definitions built upon the idea of "might or guile makes right" has emerged, and stealing and cheating are acceptable if one succeeds. The result is that persons engaging in the sub-rosa economic system must be ready and able to protect themselves from attempts to steal from or cheat them. Few prisoners have enough individual power to accomplish this and must be affiliated with others for successful operation of wheeling and dealing activities. Consequently, gangs and cliques control most of the sub-rosa activities, particularly those involving cash and drugs. Individuals may become involved to the extent that they purchase goods for their own consumption, but lone individuals seldom engage in distribution for profit.

The Prison Guards

The second most prominent actor in the prison world—the guard—has been almost totally neglected in studies of the prison. The general view has been that guards are uneducated, undertrained, unskilled, rural in background, racially prejudiced, politically conservative, and too often brutal. There has been little attention to verifying these impressions or to studying the special skills and systems which have developed in the guards' world to accomplish their difficult, contradictory, poorly rewarded work. There have been a few studies which have pointed to the contradictions in the guards' tasks, particularly the contradictions between maintaining security and pursuing rehabilitation. In one ethnography of the guards' world, Jacobs and Retsky (1975) verified that the guards' work is contradictory and dangerous and that at present guards are demoralized.

Two new developments among guards and the middle-range staff of the prison are making them a much more prominent force in the prison enterprise and should inspire students of the prison to look more closely at this understudied segment. The first is the trend toward developing separate occupational identities and forming organizations to work for their particular interests. Some guards are forming "professional" organizations, but the largest organizational movement is toward unions, a movement led by the Teamsters Union.

Generally guards' organizations are a relatively conservative force in the prison system. Along with the traditional labor goals of increased pay and other job benefits, they have consistently promoted more punitive measures to control prisoners. For instance, in recent years, guards' organizations have staged picket lines at prisons to protest leniency in custody routines. In Walpole prison in Massachusetts, after several weeks of difficulties with the prisoners, the guards' union called for a walkout until the prison administration allowed them to use more force to control prisoners. In California, the head of the guards' organization, along with members of the "Special Services," attempted to frame an ex-prison psychiatrist considered sympathetic to militant prisoners by getting him charged with complicity in the murder of a prison guard. Later in California this organization threatened to strike if the administration allowed prisoners to establish "representative prisoner organizations" which would represent prisoners in disciplinary matters and meet regularly with prison administrators in "meet and confer" types of proceedings.

The other development which is taking place in the guards' world and converting them to a much more active force in the prison system is the influx of young urban, often nonwhite, recruits. As earlier mentioned, guards in the past were predominately rural and white. Now with the disappearance of other job opportunities in the city, the upgrading of guards' salaries, and "affirmative action," many more urban and nonwhite guards are entering the prison. At some locations where there is a heavy influx of this new social type, such as at Statesville, Illinois, a strong conflict between the "old guard" and the "new breed" is developing. Some of the senior guards have indicated in interviews at Statesville that they believe that the new guards from urban settings are less loyal to the prison system, poor as disciplinarians, too friendly with the prisoners, and too often involved in smuggling to prisoners. On the other side, several of the new guards have revealed that they do feel somewhat closer to the prisoners with whom they often share more in terms of culture and experience than they share with the older guards.

Considerable tension exists between these two segments. In fact, at Statesville some old guards have argued that the "new breed" are a more serious problem to them than the prisoners—which gives some indication of the seriousness of the conflict between the two groups.

In some prisons this division is mainly a racial one and sometimes becomes formalized in separate guards' organizations.

The prisoners are aware of these divisions within the guards' world and play upon them. They sometimes are friendlier to the younger guards and attempt to sway them toward their interests by implicitly or explicitly reminding the guards of shared characteristics, such as racial identities or "hip" orientations.

These divisions are going to remain and continue to play an important role in shaping the prison social world. They must be included in any sociological examination of the contemporary prison.

The Administration

At present, prison administrations are faced with the new levels of prisoner-to-prisoner violence and conflict and the increase in sub-rosa economic activities, which involve considerable smuggling. These events have diverted most of their attention away from the "political" organizing activities, which have died down (temporarily at least). It is my impression that the administrators are not as troubled by the new violence in prison as they were by the disturbances and violence which derived from political activities, even though the level of violence from cliques and gangs is much higher. There are several explanations for this. In the first place, the threat of violence toward guards and staff is now less. But I think more important is the fact that the new violence poses no threat to the administrators' values and self-respect. In the political activities there was the persistent implicit or explicit accusation that the administrators were evil and blameworthy. This message is of course totally repulsive to administrators, and to a great extent it precipitated a response which was often incommensurate with the threat presented by the political activities.

The new violence, on the other hand, is not threatening to their values and, in fact, encourages the belief that prisoners are morally inferior and deserve their punishment, a belief which makes the task of holding other human beings in an oppressive situation less psychologically disturbing. In addition, the new violence seems to demand more traditional methods of control, such as lock-downs and segregation of persons suspected of gang activities—methods of control with which administrators are more familiar and which outside critics object to less when they are employed against sub-rosa economic activities and gang violence.

Though the criticism from outside has abated considerably and though the violence has shifted to more understandable and less threatening forms, the life of prison administrators has not become less troublesome and problematic. Two factors have increased their difficulties. The first is the organizing tendency of guards, middle-range staff, and other employees in the prison. The prison used to be organized much like the military, with the lower ranks displaying considerable discipline and loyalty to the organization. Now they are becoming assertive and, in fact, demanding in the pursuit of their own self-interests. At present, consequently, administrations have to consider, even negotiate with, many different organizations representing the separate interests of different categories of employees while attempting to solve other difficult administrative problems.

The second factor which makes the administrators' situation problematic is the loss of a guiding philosophy to give their enterprise justification, meaning, and importance. As mentioned earlier, the old philosophy which accomplished this has been dismantled, and nothing has emerged to replace it. Many administrators are adopting punishment and deterrence as their primary objectives. For instance, Norman Carlson, head of the vast federal prison system, listed the three goals of the prison as "deterrence, retribution, and rehabilitation," but he suggested that, if rehabilitation is the goal, "it ought to be done in the community," and he thereby indicated that he had eliminated it as a primary goal of imprisonment (quoted in Serrill, 1975).

However, to explicitly embrace punishment and the subsidary task of custody as the primary objectives of imprisonment is not going to lead the administrators out of the difficulties caused by the loss of the rehabilitative ideal. For at least a century in most states, prison administrators have been constructing an image of themselves as humanitarians and professionals. The archaic stereotype of the tough, perhaps even mean, prison warden is one which persists but is not popular among actual administrators, and they are not likely to feel comfortable in adopting a punitive prison philosophy that fosters this image.

REFERENCES

CARROLL, L. (1974). Hacks, blacks, and cons. Lexington, Mass.: D.C. Heath.

CLEAVER, E. (1968). Soul on ice. New York: McGraw-Hill.

CLEMMER, D. (1940). The prison community. New York: Holt, Rinehart and Winston.

DAVIDSON, T. (1974). Chicano prisoners. New York: Holt, Rinehart and Winston.

GREENBERG, D. (1975). "Problems in community corrections." Issues in Criminology, 10(spring):1-34.

IRWIN, J. (1970). The felon. Englewood Cliffs, N.J.: Prentice-Hall.

IRWIN, J., and CRESSEY, D. (1963). "Thieves, convicts and the inmate culture." Social Problems, 10(3):142-155.

JACOBS, J. (1974). "Street gangs behind bars." Social Problems, 21(3):395-409.

——— (1976). "Stratification and conflict among prison inmates." Journal of Criminal Law and Criminology, 66(4):476-482.

JACOBS, J., and RETSKY, H.G. (1975). "Prison guard." Urban Life, 4(1):5-19.

OSWALD, R.G. (1972). Attica—My story. New York: Doubleday.

PALLAS, J., and BARBER, R. (1973). "From riot to revolution." Pp. 237-261 in E.O. Wright (ed.), The politics of punishment. New York: Harper and Row.

PARK, J. (1968). "Power to the people." Unpublished manuscript.

PARSONS, T. (1951). The social system. New York: Free Press.

PARSONS, T., and SHILS, E. (eds., 1951). Toward a general theory of action. New York: Harper and Row.

REIMER, H. (1937). "Socialization in the prison." Pp. 151-155 in Proceedings of the Sixty-Seventh Annual Congress of the American Prison Association.

SCHRAG, C. (1944). "Social types in a prison community." Unpublished M.A. thesis, University of Washington.

SERRILL, M.S. (1975). "Is rehabilitation dead?" Corrections Magazine, (May/June):3-12, 21-32.

SUTTLES, G. (1968). The social order of the slum. Chicago: University of Chicago Press.

SYKES, G.M. (1958). The society of captives. Princeton, N.J.: Princeton University Press.

SYKES, G.M., and MESSINGER, S. (1960). "The inmate social system." Pp. 5-19 in Theoretical studies in social organization of the prison. Social Science Research Council pamphlet.

WARD, D.A. (1973). "Evaluative research for corrections." Pp. 184-206 in L.E. Ohlin (ed.), Prisoners in America. Englewood Cliffs, N.J.: Prentice-Hall.
WILLIAMS, V.L., and FISH, M. (1974). Convicts, codes and contraband. Cambridge, Mass.: Ballinger.

Chapter 2

ORGANIZATIONAL STEREOTYPING:
THE CASE OF THE ADJUSTMENT CENTER
CLASSIFICATION COMMITTEE

ROBERT E. DORAN

The study of organizations has focused on a variety of interests. This has included studying interpersonal relationships within the organization, control structures, communications within organizations, authority, influence, and leadership (March, 1965). It is the argument of this paper that one of the most meaningful ways to study organizations is to study the decision-making process, that is, the bases upon which the organization makes decisions about the actual work that it is charged with doing. It is the purpose of this paper to explore the process of stereotyping in the decision-making function of a bureaucracy. Stereotyping is important since it can facilitate organizational processes, make organizations run more smoothly, and perhaps ensure a steady supply of persons who "need" the organization's services.

Perhaps the most salient work in the area of organizational stereotyping has been done by Scheff (1962, 1964, 1966). It is his contention that stereotyping plays an important part in the business conducted by treatment, control, and welfare bureaucratic agencies. He found that much of what is subsumed under the title "mental illness" is independent of the behavior or condition of the person being processed by the organization—e.g., a court. In 196 cases out of 196, court examiners (psychiatrists) found evidence of "mental illness" and recommended treatment (Scheff, 1964). This finding, coupled with diagnostic interviews averaging about 10 minutes, strongly suggests a prejudgment on the part of the psychiatrists—that is, a mental illness stereotyping which may be invoked after, in most cases, a person in the community has referred the individual to the court (thus activating the formal social control apparatus of the community), the court has accepted the case, and the psychiatrist has been called upon to participate in the ceremonial process since he (the psychiatrist) has special knowledge and tools (and the all-important status) to legitimate the "mentally ill" label.

Sudnow (1965), in his study of a public defender's office, also found that the stereotypes which the public defenders had about their clients greatly determined the kind of action that they took in regard to these cases. Apparently the stereotyping was implicitly agreed upon by the district attorney's office and by other actors in the system, such as the judge. The "understandings" about what constituted a normal crime of, for example, burglary were constituted within the action between the defendant and the public defender and between the public defender and the district attorney. It should be noted that the goal of stereotyping was to obtain a guilty plea, thus minimizing the time spent in processing "this kind of case." The stereotype acted as a set of criteria against which the defendant's offense could be compared; the plea bargaining process could then commence in earnest. This entire process was greatly facilitated by the belief of the public defender's office (and shared by the district attorneys) that the defendants were guilty (Sudnow, 1965:167). This belief was based on two interrelated "facts": the fact that the defendant had been charged with an offense, and the faith in the arrestor (city police) to arrest people who have in fact committed something. Also important to this process is that the public defender, the police, the district attorney, the judge, et al. are employed by the same organization (local government). The only outsider in the process (in the sense that he has no organizational ties) is the defendant.

In addition, Piliavin and Briar (1964), in their study of police encounters with juveniles, found that the stereotypifications which the police had of what constituted a potential (or actual) troublemaker greatly determined—and therefore made predictable—police decisions regarding the detention of juveniles. One police department's juvenile officers in a city of 450,000 were observed for a nine-month period as they performed their regular tours of duty. These officers had a great deal of discretion in the decision to arrest or detain or not to detain. What then helped to determine which course of action the officer might follow? Delinquent stereotypes based first on appearance and then on "recalcitrant demeanor" as corroborating "evidence" constituted the basis upon which officers answered the questions, Is this juvenile delinquent? and Should I detain him? The point is that police case dispositions "were based on the youth's personal characteristics and not their offenses." The work of these juvenile officers was carried out largely on the basis of the stereotypes that they carried around in their heads about which juveniles were "delinquent" and which were not.

The empirical data cited above support the idea that people in organizations respond to and make official decisions about their clients based on shared understandings of who is "mentally ill," a "burglar," and a "juvenile delinquent."

Apparently stereotyping is an integral part of social interactions as found in everyday life. What Scheff and others have contributed is the idea that these stereotypifications are relied upon in organizations whose work is processing people. Furthermore, these stereotypifications have real consequences for those being processed and for the organization itself—the consequences being whether or not to commit an individual to a mental institution, prosecute him as a felony check writer, or arrest him for possible juvenile delinquency.

A STUDY OF FOUR CALIFORNIA PRISONS

In order to explore the process of organizational stereotyping, a study was conducted in four state prisons of the California Department of Corrections. In the following sections, the research site and the sample are described, the study method discussed, the findings and results given, and the staff justifications for organizational stereotyping enumerated.

Setting

The research was carried out in four prisons of the California Department of Corrections: namely, San Quentin, Folsom, Deuel Vocational Institution, and California Training Facility-Central. These four are all large, medium to maximum security prisons, housing some 8,000-plus inmates, employing over 1,500 staff, and costing something in excess of $20,000,000 per year to operate.[1] They represent, therefore, large governmental, bureaucratic organizations. The adjustment centers (i.e., segregated housing units) within these four institutions were the specific foci of the research.

The adjustment centers represent in a very real sense "prisons within prisons."[2] They are units with maximum physical control and are each segregated from the rest of the prison in a separate building. Each of these particular four units has an average daily population of about 150 inmates. The staff typically consists of a program administrator (who is in charge of the unit), a supervising counselor, two line counselors, a lieutenant, two sergeants, and 10 correctional officers. This staffing arrangement represents a ratio of staff to inmates three times greater than the general population staffing ratio. Inmates are placed in these units because the staff cannot tolerate their behavior (involving everything from murder to possessing contraband) in the general population or because the general population cannot tolerate the inmates (especially the prison rats, i.e., inmates who tell the staff about real or imagined rule violations by other inmates).

This type of research setting was suggested by Scheff (1962:147), since prisons are concerned with processing people, i.e., moving people from one status to another status; at least this is an oft-quoted manifest function. And one can hypothesize that stereotyping is the predominant method by which such status changes are effected; that is, the mental images of "what kind of people we process" will determine the status-altering decisions made by the staff.

Method

The key decision-making body for inmates in the prison is the classification committee. It is in this committee that all official decisions are made, such as the inmates' housing, their work or school assignment, their custody classification, and their transfer consideration.[3] In the adjustment center, inmates appear before the classification committee perhaps four to six times more often than the average inmate in the prison general population. Adjustment center inmates must, according to the *Classification Manual* of the California Department of Corrections, be reviewed at least once every 90 days; general population inmates, once a year. Apparently the "special" type of inmate found in the adjustment center necessitates his being reviewed more often. Perhaps two-fifths of the unit administrative staff's time is spent in these committees.

Each committee is composed of a unit supervisor, a unit sergeant, a unit supervising counselor, and an inmates' counselor. Others may also participate, such as a lieutenant from the general prison cadre. In addition, officers assigned to the unit who escort the inmate to the classification room may participate in some cases, such as when asked for their opinion.[4]

As part of the committee process, official records are available to the committee members. These records contain extensive accounts of the inmate's behavior and, in some cases, prognostications of his future behavior.

The author, as a participant observer, observed 174 inmates appearing before the four prison adjustment center classification committees. Although this is not a random sample, one may argue that, since the purpose of this paper is to learn about the process of stereotyping, a random sample is not essential. What is essential is how the committees go about the organizational task of deciding what happens to each inmate based upon the alternatives available and "what kind of case" the committee believes the inmate to be.

Sample

The sample included adjustment center inmates who appeared before the classification committees during the months of June and July 1970. These inmates seemed to be fairly representative of inmates in the adjustment centers. Of the 174, 66 were white, 58 were black, and 50 were Mexican-American. This ratio represented a higher proportion of blacks and Mexican-Americans than the ratio in the general prison population, which was approximately 50% white, 28% black, and 22% Mexican-American.[5] It may be that, even in prison, blacks and Mexican-Americans are likely to be "arrested," "convicted," and "imprisoned" out of proportion to their numbers—as is the case in the outside community.

Many of the sample had long histories of "getting into trouble," and perhaps a third had been in the adjustment centers for long periods of time (i.e., over six months). Many were long-termers with a range of time served of about one to 20 years, with the average around six years. Eliminating the extremes, the average would be slightly higher, indicating the longer periods of time served by these inmates.

Generally, the inmates were often disheveled, sleepy, and in various states of dress and occasionally appeared to the writer to be sullen and disinterested. It should be noted that the committees meet in the units, which are self-contained (feeding, housing, recreation, etc. are all done within the unit). Inmates are escorted directly from their individual cells to the committee room. Sometimes they must be awakened and, with hair awry, eyes swollen, and clothes not always completely on, stumble before the committee. According to the staff, adjustment center inmates quite often stay up very late at night—yelling, talking, reading—and consequently sleep late in the morning, which "explains" how they appear physically (disheveled) and attitudinally (sullen, disinterested). Another explanation might be that the inmates are expressing their cynicism about the committees; i.e., their opinions will not be listened to or be the basis for any action taken. In fact, the latter explanation seems to be more plausible in light of the data which are presented in the following sections.

It is within this context that the drama is played out week after week in the adjustment center classification committee meetings.

Results and Findings

It is important to keep in mind that the average length of appearance before the classification committees for each of these 174 inmates was about 10 minutes. Although several minutes before and after the committee appearance were also devoted to the inmate, the inmate himself had approximately 10 minutes in which to make his views and opinions known. Although the staff, in casual conversations, talk a great deal about individual attention to and consideration and programming for inmates, it is apparent from the committee sessions themselves that this is truly not the case. The staff is actually more concerned about placing the inmate in one of several possible categories so that they can make their decisions. These several categories seem to be the following:

1. *Inmates with Racial Problems.* The staff belief is that many of the current prison problems revolve around the inmates' commitments to various militant ethnic groups such as the Mexican Mafia, the Nazis, and the black militants. If the inmate is Mexican or black especially, a line of questioning to determine his involvement is always pursued.

2. *Pressure Artists.* Part of the staff folklore about prisons is that there are predators roaming the prison who prey upon others, usually weaker than themselves. These so-called pressure artists demand everything from sex to cigarettes.

3. *The Weak and Pressured.* According to staff belief, these are inmates who often because of their youthful appearance are ready victims of Pressure Artists and become sexual partners or dupes of one kind or another for one or more of the predators.

4. *The Prison Rats.* These are the inmates who habitually inform on other inmates about offenses ranging from escape plots to murder to minor infractions of the rules, such as having illegal hobby materials. One of the problems with this group is that they are often well known among the inmate population and frequently must ask for adjustment center status in order to protect their lives.

5. *Inmates in the Residual Category.* If an inmate cannot be fitted into one of the above four categories, then there is a residual category reserved for "other kinds of problem inmates." Generally speaking, these are not seen as "tough cases"; that is, these are fairly minor offenders who can be dealt with fairly quickly, not only in the classification committee, but in terms of the amount of time that they spend in the adjustment center. For the most part, these residual category cases spend less than 90 days in the adjustment center, perhaps averaging around 15 to 30 days. Two major groups appear under this category: (1) escape risks (or ones who have escaped and have returned to the institution) and (2) inmates with fairly minor, but persistent disciplinary problems, e.g., home brew, pills. The staff's belief is that a short period of time in the adjustment center will stop these inmates' minor disciplinary problems.

One other residual type should be commented upon—the "mentally ill." There are a few of these "types," which usually are "mixed types," since the problems of some or any combination of the other types may be a part of their "problem."

The overriding assumption of the classification committee is that, even if they cannot substantiate or get a confession of guilt, each inmate must in fact be guilty of something—that is, that the folk belief that where "there's smoke, there's fire" especially pertains to adjustment center inmates. As evidence of the strength of and commitment to this belief, in almost every initial appearance observed, the inmate was retained for at least a short period of time (a few weeks) even though one alternative was immediate release. Further, in cases of disciplinary hearings, all but a few either pleaded guilty or were found guilty. Even when charges were dismissed, the reports were retained in the file for future reference. Appearance before the committee, coupled with the fact that the inmate was already in the adjustment center, was used as prima facie evidence that placement in the adjustment center was appropriate and, in the case of disciplinary reports, that the inmate was "guilty."

The task of the committee, then, is to fit each inmate into one of the five stereotypes so that action appropriate for the stereotype may be taken. The staff frequently anticipate the kind of appearance that the inmate will make, perhaps setting up a kind of self-fulfilling prophecy: 'This next guy's no trouble," or "This guy's going to snivel." The anticipatory rehearsal for inmates goes something like this: "They won't really listen or consider my case," or "Maybe if I say as little as possible, they'll give me some consideration."

And, as a number of staff members remarked, "For half the inmates appearing, we already know what we are going to do. The inmate knows, too." Question: Then why see them? Answer: "To meet the *Manual* requirements and to make them feel better, if that's possible."

The work of the committee is to somehow fit each and every inmate into one or another of the preconceived categories that the staff is at the moment entertaining. Inmates help maintain the process by sometimes quickly accepting whatever stereotype the staff places on them;[6] more often, inmates are not very communicative and are extremely cynical about the committee meetings. Inmate behavior serves to reinforce what the staff already knows: that inmates have certain kinds of problems (different than the staff's), are irresponsible and immature, cannot be trusted, and need to be corrected and adjusted.

Since, in general, the staff's belief is that most if not all of the inmates in the adjustment center are somehow dangerous, typically the error in judgment will be on the side of conservatism. That is, if there is any doubt about what an inmate may do if released back into the general institution population, release will not be granted. Supposedly this provides the staff with more time during which an appropriate decision may be made. It is the thesis of this paper that this time will more probably be used to extend the negotiation with the inmate to accept, in the staff's viewpoint, a reasonable stereotypification about what the inmate's trouble is.

In order to better understand the work of the committee, we should take a closer look at each of the five categories: inmates with racial problems, pressure artists, the weak and pressured, the prison rats, and inmates in the residual category. As stated before, the work of the committee is to place each inmate into one of these categories.

INMATES WITH RACIAL PROBLEMS

As a Chicano inmate stated to this writer outside the classification room:

The staff think that just about everything you do has to do with racial pressure. It's their way of getting it off their own back. If they can blame it on the blacks and the browns or anyone else having that kind of trouble, then they [the staff] don't have to take the responsibility for all this goddamn trouble that's happening in prison nowadays.

And from a staff member who made the following remarks after the committee appearance of six Chicano inmates who had been charged with assaulting a staff member:

As you can see, the problems in the prison business are different nowadays than they used to be. Used to be that the inmates got along a lot better. But now, it's not uncommon for a bunch of one ethnic group to get together and cause a lot of stuff like these guys beating on Officer ———. I get the idea that they're being influenced by outside people and what's happening on the streets. They seem to think that they're martyrs or something. As you see in front of the committee, one at a time, they play a lot different role than when you get a gang of them together. Then they think they're really something and have to get it on.

The inmates account for the category of racial problems as an attempt by the staff to put the blame for current prison turmoil on "racial pressure." This implies that there is something "wrong" with the inmates, when, in their view, it is the staff's responsibility. Also implied is that the staff exaggerate racial problems as a major source of trouble. The staff's belief, on the other hand, includes a conspiracy element; there are racial problems which inmates participate in but which are really part of a (planned) conspiracy taking place in the outside community. If inmates take part in the "racial problems conspiracy," then there is "something wrong" with the individual inmate. Several other aspects of the staff's belief regarding racial problems are apparent: it is a gang activity; outside the gang (i.e., alone) the inmates are "no trouble"; the gang activity is frequently assaultive; inmates think "they're martyrs" or innocent (therefore, the staff is guilty?).

The staff's beliefs can especially be detected in the following committee appearance by a black:

Staff: This is your initial review. You've been here about 10 days?

Inmate: Yeah, I guess so.

Staff: [Looking at inmate's file] You were part of the racial trouble on the 13th.

Inmate: No, sir! I was in the lower yard when the shit came down, tried to get out of there, and the cops arrested me. I'm clean.

Staff: Do you know ――― [an inmate who was convicted of stabbing another inmate in the incident of the 13th]?

Inmate: May have talked to him once or twice. [Long series of questions regarding inmate's associates and a review of "other disciplinary" problems, most of which were relatively minor.]

Staff: Well, we'd better see you again in 90 days. OK?

Inmate: Hell, no! I ain't done nothin'. Why don't you charge me with something? . . . [led out by an officer still talking, getting more angry].

The inmate was black, already had had some disciplinary problems, knew an inmate seriously implicated in the "trouble," was in the area, and obviously (from the staff's viewpoint) had a bad attitude. Several other "facts" subtly assist the staff in their stereotyping of this inmate. First, he *is* in the adjustment center, which in a circular, circumstantial way, designates him as one in trouble, apart from the fact the staff placed him in the adjustment center. Second, his anger, especially at the end of his appearance, provided the staff with firsthand "evidence" of a troublemaker symptom [7]; i.e., as one committee member noted, "He sure has a lot of anger inside him, couldn't even control himself in front of the committee." Other committee members silently nodded agreement.

He fitted the category of inmates with racial problems; the staff discussed the interview after the inmate had been escorted out, and this was their diagnosis. Official action based on this stereotype included retention in the unit so that he could not cause further racial trouble in the general population, careful movement within the unit so that persons of other races and he would not cause problems, and the entering of appropriate notations in the official records so that the staff would all know "who he is."

PRESSURE ARTISTS

Appearing before the adjustment center classification committee are inmates known as pressure artists. These inmates are considered dangerous to other inmates because they pressure for canteen articles, sex, and favors. This is especially the case if the inmate being pressured works in a position in which he has access to "wealth" (e.g., works in the canteen), information (e.g., is a captain's clerk) or privileged treatment (e.g., is a clerk who maintains lists for dental treatment).

As an adjustment center inmate explained it:

Yeah, there are some guys in the yard who pressure other people, usually weak individuals for all kinds of things. All you have to do to make it is to stay away from these guys and just generally be a man. [Q: What does that mean?] Well, you know; that means if someone drives on you, you got to put up or shut up. Usually if you fight back or stay with your homies (people who are from your home town and share your interests), then most guys will leave you alone. If you show any weakness around a joint, you're sure to get gobbled up.

And an adjustment center staff member:

There aren't a lot of inmates roaming the yard who want to get things from other inmates, such as cigarettes or sex or favors of one kind or another. But, there are enough that it makes it real bad for some inmates, especially those guys who are kind of young and sweet and innocent. And, of course, there are just some inmates who don't have any backbone. These weak guys very often don't have any backbone. These weak guys very often don't have much to do except run to us and ask for lockup. As often as not, it's their own fault.

The inmate seems to be saying that there are inmates who pressure others but that it is only inmates who are not "men" who receive the pressure. This explanation is not unusual in that inmates frequently call upon manhood to explain how men do or do not get along in prison. In a situation such as the prison, where many of the conventional methods of achieving and maintaining dignity, self-esteem, and moral worth are denied, about the only thing left is what the inmates call manhood. This encompasses having dignity, self-esteem, and moral worth usually based on how one observes the "convict code" in relations with other inmates and the staff.

It is also important to be a group member for mutual protection. A "man" can do this and maintain his dignity; no "man" would go to the staff for protection, i.e., tell the staff that a particular inmate was pressuring him.

The staff's response is very similar to the inmates'. The message seems to be that the "weak and pressured" have the problem.

In the committee appearance that follows, the inmate has apparently already been stereotyped.[8] The committee appearance serves various functions: first, to maintain or reestablish the "fact" that this inmate is a pressure artist; second, to apply the official agency's social control measure to the "deviant"—that is, officially place the inmate in the adjustment center.

Staff: How many times you been in here now?

Inmate: Oh, I don't know, quite a few times.

Staff: Seems like every time we let you out of here, six other people come running to us to be locked up because they're afraid.

Inmate: That's their problem. What's their names?

Staff: Don't get smart. Seems like the only thing we can do with you is to keep you locked up, and maybe sometime you'll learn that we're serious.

Inmate: Hey, look, you keep talking about people are afraid of me, but you never charge me with anything or tell me who they are. I never put the arm on anyone in my whole life; just take a look at my record. What do you think I'm in prison for, anyway; robbery, rape, murder? No, I'm in on burglary and checks, usually.

Staff: Well, apparently when you're on the outside you don't get into violence, but what's that got to do with what happens in the joint?

Inmate: Just no convincing you people. Sure I've loaned a few things, who hasn't? And I get mad if someone doesn't pay me back. But I don't go around threatening to stick 'em or anything like that.

Staff: That's not what we've been told. We have it on good authority that you threaten lots of people and even on occasion are the muscle for other guys to collect their debts.

Inmate: Like I said, there's just no convincing you people. How long am I going to be in this time?

Staff: You know the routine; we take a look at your case every 90 days and then make some kind of decision. You usually behave yourself when you're in the adjustment center. Maybe that's the kind of housing you need. So we'd appreciate it if you'd behave yourself this time too.

Inmate: I not only behave here in the adjustment center; I take care of business out there, too.

The negotiating or bargaining is apparently about the "degree" of the deviance. According to the staff, it is a serious situation; according to the inmate, it is a relatively harmless situation which happens to almost everyone. However, time is on the side of the staff. They can wait until the inmate "understands" his problem better, and this seems to be the intent in this case. Indeed, in the situation of organizational stereotyping as seen in the adjustment center classification committee, time is the most often used means of securing the inmate's acceptance of a given stereotype. There is no effective appeal for the inmate from the committee's actions.[9] And the committee presents a united front; seldom do members disagree, and, if they do, the disagreement is discussed backstage. That is, the inmate will be sent out of the room during the discussion. The few disagreements that do occur generally concern what to do with the inmate: is he ready (or does he deserve) release from the unit? The stereotype never seems to be in doubt. The staff always seem to know "what kind of case" they are processing.

Here is an example of the kind of documentation that follows a committee appearance of a "pressure artist":

> ——— has been preying on other inmates, according to the file, ever since he came to prison. He has at least three disciplinary reports to this effect and has been suspected on at least seven other occasions, as documented in file memorandums. His MO seems to remain about the same. He loans things at exorbitant interest and, then, on several occasions has been known to beat inmates who would not, or could not, pay him, and on another occasion he apparently stabbed an inmate over a three-carton cigarette debt. The staff has to be exceptionally alert to any indication that this inmate is persisting in this behavior, such as possessing an unusual amount of canteen in his cell.

As is well known in total institutional situations, official case files are more often used to record unsuccessful attempts to deal with life situations. The much greater number of successful copings are typically not recorded. In addition, from the above recording, several other important facets emerge. First, a great deal of hearsay evidence is used to initiate and perpetuate the stereotype. References to "the file" would almost indicate a reference to an unimpeachable source. Not so. The file is an accumulation of all kinds of information compiled from many sources. Many of these sources are the staff's personal opinions of events in the inmate's life history, intuitive remarks about what the inmate is like psychologically, and sometimes grave forecasts about what the inmate may do in the future.[10] The inmate's future must be made more predictable; he must be successfully stereotyped, and social control measures must be applied. These are part of the same process, and in prison they may occur concurrently or consecutively with either the stereotype or social control measure coming first.

The authority of the classification committee makes its official case recordings the key point at which an inmate can be stereotyped.

THE WEAK AND PRESSURED

The pressured represent the "victims" of pressure artists. Who are they?
An inmate version:

A lot of inmates just don't know how to do their time. They get in over
their heads, and before they know it some guy's running around ready to
kill them. For almost nothing, like a pack of cigarettes or something like
that. Sure, and sometimes an inmate has two guys fighting over him for
sex. These real weak guys should never be placed in joints like Quentin and
Soledad. Sometimes I think that the staff do this on purpose just to get
people hurt and have a little excitement.

The staff version:

We have people coming to us and asking for lockup all the time. We don't
lock every man up who comes and asks for it. But it's kind of hard to
know who's really in trouble and is going to maybe be hurt and who's just
sniveling [unreasonably complaining]. Of course, if a guy demands to be
locked up and just won't go back to his unit and seems to have some basis
for going to the adjustment center, then the probability is that he will be
put in. It's a bad thing to do because once these kind of guys get going
around in the adjustment center system, it's very hard to get them out of
it.

For one thing, according to inmates and the staff, "the pressured" do exist.
Inmates can cite many examples of inmates who are placed or place themselves
in a position to get more than their share of "trouble." For many inmates, this
has to do with not knowing how "to do one's time." To develop a style which is
constructive, minimizes trouble, and perhaps increases the possibility of serving
the minimum amount of time for one's crime is the ideal. Maintaining a "manly"
image with other inmates may help ensure that one will not be pressured. There
is also an inmate belief that the staff sometimes deliberately place weak inmates
in "tough joints" (for example, inmates call Soledad the "gladiator's school") to
get them hurt and "have a little excitement." In this view, there is an assumption
that something is wrong with "weak inmates" which the staff and inmates are
aware of and which the staff can do something about—namely, place them in
better institutions rather than "joints like Quentin and Soledad."

The staff's ambivalence about whom to place in the adjustment center is
evident in the above quotation. Apparently, the inmate must make a case for
being locked up.[11] It is not automatic. The consequences of being locked up
are commented upon in the last sentence of the staff member's quote. Of course,
it also provides a part of the stereotype of "the pressured" and affects the time
that "the pressured" needs to spend in the adjustment center.

Inmate: Why don't you let me go back to the main yard? I can't get down with any programming in here, and I'm going to the [parole] board in just a few months.

Staff: We know that. And we'd like to see you get out of prison and go back to the community and behave yourself and live a good life just as much as you would.

Inmate: Then why won't you at least send me to another institution if you don't think I can make it here.

Staff: With the way you dress, comb your hair, and pluck your eyebrows, we don't think you'd make it almost anyplace.

Inmate: I don't think you're right. I didn't have any trouble when I was in YA [a Youth Authority institution].

Staff: That may be true, but those guys are a lot younger than the guys in state prison. Besides, the guys [in state prison] see a cute thing like you coming down the tier; it's just too much to resist.

Inmate: I think you're making a big thing out of nothin'. I'll admit that I have had several problems, but I sure am not gonna comb my hair different or wear my clothes any different; I'm going to just be me.

Staff: Well, as long as you are just yourself, that's what we're trying to tell you; it's a big problem. But you don't seem to realize that it is a problem.

Inmate: I admit that I've had a couple homosexual experiences in prison, but it's no big thing with me now. If you put me back on main line somewhere, I can promise you that there'd be no problem.

Staff: It's not your promises that we're worried about. There are other people around, and it's those other people that we're concerned about.

Inmate: I can take care of myself. I can fight if I have to.

Staff: Well, for your own good, we're going to keep you here a while longer, and then maybe we can consider another institution's main line.

Inmate: You won't regret it, and I tell you this: I really appreciate the chance to get out there and be in a full program before I hit that [parole] board.

This inmate had originally asked to be placed in the adjustment center and participated in his own stereotyping to the point that the staff were now thoroughly convinced. The inmate now wanted to renegotiate the stereotype, so that he would be allowed placement in the general prison population. His appearance and demeanor and, perhaps, his reinterpreted file information made it difficult for the staff to undo the current mental image that they had of him. This brings up a major point about stereotyping. A stereotype can be constructed in moments,[12] particularly when something very dramatic happens (such as a murder); undoing the stereotype always takes considerably more time. For one thing, "evidence" accumulates; current and past events are interpreted in light of what "we now know about the inmate"; the official files are filled with pronouncements of the newly discovered status; and mental images are distributed among the staff and inmates—all these and, in addition, the inmate's own version of who he is must be dealt with. Social "facts" so constructed and distributed to a variety of persons die hard.

As a stereotype progresses, many persons assist in the "care and feeding." Inmates and the staff are extra attentive to details which they might, under other circumstances, either ignore or at least not think of as important, and these details are communicated to committee members for their consideration in deciding how to program the inmate. The frequent committee appearances and the subsequent recordings have the effect of keeping the stereotype alive and well even under difficult circumstances. These difficult circumstances occur when, during the interims between committee appearances, the inmate seemingly does nothing to nourish the stereotype. The committee appearance is time to remind everyone (not the least of whom is the inmate) of what happened last March, or three years ago, and how the inmate may be faking his "real" feelings and intentions. An oft-heard remark during these periods is, "Sure he's clean since we last saw him [at committee] , but don't forget; this is the guy who tried to do in ———." To which another staff member may apologetically reply, "That's right, I *almost* forgot."

THE PRISON RATS

In the outside community, if you see someone beating up your neighbor, you call the police. It is your duty. In the prison, if the same situation occurs, you either make some attempt to assist your neighbor or look the other way. You do not call the cop (the custodial staff).

From an adjustment center inmate in a private interview:

Sure, I tell staff what they want to know, and for a long time it worked out pretty good. But, this last time around, I got myself really jammed up. Now I'm waiting to go to court to be a witness about an assault. If the guys who did it ever get their hands on me, I'll be in real big trouble. About the only thing I can do is to stay in the adjustment center and maybe go home from here someday. Or maybe sometime in the future, I could go to minimum custody where people aren't getting hurt all of the time.

From an adjustment center administrator:

We have quite a few inmates in the adjustment center who have maybe snitched off one too many inmates. The word gets around that "so and so" is telling tales to staff, and then his life isn't worth a nickel. We don't want to keep him in the adjustment center, but what are you going to do? If we let him go, maybe something will happen, maybe something won't happen. So we just keep him in, usually for a long time, and then maybe sometime he can go to the yard at one of the institutions where he won't have any enemies. But some of these guys wear out their welcome at all of the institutions, and then we don't have anyplace to send them. They're also one of our biggest headaches. They sure do whine a lot.

The inmate apparently had witnessed an assault by other inmates and was going to be a prosecution witness. He now faced indefinite placement in the adjustment center because of what he feared might happen. Somewhat ironically, those who had committed the assault were probably also "doing time" in the same adjustment center. In this particular case, the inmate and the staff, by mutual agreement, were retaining the inmate in the adjustment center.[13] Whether he was in fact a "rat" or a good citizen doing his duty is a matter of audience definition.

Staff: How are things going?

Inmate: [Remains silent, looks at the floor.]

Staff: What would you like to do?

Inmate: Go back to the yard [return to the general prison population].

Staff: Out of the question.

Inmate: I know I can make it now. Give me a chance. All them guys are transferred now.

Staff: [Discussion of where the "enemies" are, what kind of programs the inmate would participate in.] OK. We'll put you on the yard—if things get too tough, you'll let us know?

The inmate was a prison rat who had been in the unit for 18 months. The staff's view about potential harm to rats—that they are essentially weak and need the staff's protection now and in the future—contributed to the decision that perhaps now the inmate might be released after sufficient time had elapsed (18 months) and those ratted on had been transferred. The staff would need to be kept informed about and to maintain, close surveillance of the inmate, and also proper entries had to be made in the official records.

There is very little bargaining or negotiating in the committee. The staff does have total power.[14] This probably contrasts with less authoritarian settings, such as a tuberculosis sanitarium or the office of a private physician (Roth, 1962). Obviously, the adjustment center offers a unique opportunity for successful staff stereotyping of inmates.

When the committee documents "who the inmate is," the stereotyping process is in full swing.

——— is one of the inmates, along with [several other inmates are listed here], who are willing to testify in the case of ———, who escaped three months ago. He says he can make it on the yard if released; however, it is this committee's opinion that the friends of ——— [the escapee] might take some action against him. It should be noted that, on at least one other occasion in ——— [another prison named], the inmate had volunteered to be a witness at a trial which never came off. He had to be placed in the adjustment center of that institution also. He was transferred to this institution's adjustment center and placed on the main line. Due to his problems, extreme care should be taken in with whom and how he exercises, escorted to the visiting room, and who is placed in the cells immediately in his area.

INMATES IN THE RESIDUAL CATEGORY

In addition to inmates with racial problems, pressure artists, the weak and pressured, and the prison rats, there is a group of inmates who do not fit easily into the other stereotypes. They range from minor, persistent disciplinary offenders to returned escapees.

An adjustment center inmate:

If you do something, then you should take what's coming to you—like a man. But if they just lock you up and keep you indefinitely, that's not right. I was caught with two pills. So I'm where I should be [in the adjustment center]. But after two weeks, they should put me back on the yard. [Q: Does it help to put inmates in the adjustment center for short periods of time?] Sure it does. Makes you stop and think. And that's about all you can do in here. But, after a while, you're sure to get worse.

A staff member:

There are some men who get into fairly minor trouble. A short jolt in here [the adjustment center] can help get their attention. [Q: Does it help?] Maybe not, but you can't ignore someone breaking the rules. You have to do something. What we do is based on the individual and what we think he needs.

The last sentence of the staff quote perhaps summarizes why there even *is* a "residual category." There is a belief in doing *something,* and this usually means something in addition to talk (called counseling when the talk is from the staff to the inmate).[15] When loss of privileges, custody reduction, visiting restrictions, and other sanctions seem to "fail"—i.e., when the "undesired behavior" persists—then adjustment center may be tried. Many of those placed in this category would more often be stereotyped as "nuisance cases."

Staff: You are charged with having three Seconal pills in your possession. How do you plead to that charge?

Inmate: Yeah, I had them, but I want to explain.

Staff: Yeah, you'll get your chance to explain in just a minute, but, first of all, are you saying that you are guilty?

Inmate: Yes, I had the pills.

Staff: Okay, we'll note that. Now tell us what happened.

Inmate: Well, I was just kind of down in the dumps, and this guy offered me a couple of pills. If you look in my jacket, you'll notice that I'm not a hype or a pill head, or anything like that. But doing all this time—I've been in about six years now—started to get to me. I was going to take those pills, and that was it. I wasn't giving them to anyone else, selling, or anything like that.

Staff: We're not so sure about that. You've been in some other trouble before.

Inmate: Yeah, but it wasn't too serious.

Staff: Yeah, we'll agree with that, but we think you'd better spend a little while in the adjustment center. We'll talk about it and let you know.

In this particular case, the staff decided that the inmate should be released at the end of 45 days. Apparently the time would have been about half, had he not had several other disciplinary problems. The staff commented favorably on his deference to the committee. However, one committee member did remark somewhat sarcastically, "It seems like each time we talk to him about one of these things, he's usually very sorry and cooperative."

Staff: How long has it been since they brought you back from that escape.

Inmate: About six weeks now.

Staff: You didn't have any problem on the yard before, did you?

Inmate: No, only that I got tired, and when I finally got minimum custody and went to the ranch, I took off.

Staff: Yeah, well, it's harder to take off from inside the walls.

Inmate: Yeah, I know that, but you don't have to worry about me. I've learned my lesson. I'm just going to stick and do my time this time.

Staff: OK. We'll put you back on the yard.

The prejudgment of the staff—i.e., the stereotypical image of the average nonviolent escapee who simply walks away from minimum custody—is that he is not dangerous, that he can be typically trusted in a secure perimeter situation with adequate supervision, and that, over a period of time, such as one to two years, he can probably even be trusted back in minimum custody.[16] There are perhaps only two reasons why he is placed in the adjustment center upon return from escape. One has to do with the staff belief that, if an inmate does something, especially something as serious as an escape, then something should be done, such as placing him in the adjustment center for a period of time. Second, the institutional policy is that, when a man is initially brought back from an escape, he should be placed in the adjustment center until the staff can find out what the circumstances of the escape were (for example, whether he escaped from another institution) and what, if anything, he did while out on escape. But if he did in fact escape, as the inmate in the above action did, and did not apparently commit any crimes while out on escape, he will probably be returned to the main institution in a relatively short period of time.

The official recording reflects this stereotype:

——— was returned from escape approximately six weeks ago, having left the ranch while on a work assignment. The committee notes that there was no violence involved in the escape; it was in fact a walkaway. Also noted that, in the interest of justice, the district attorney declines to prosecute. Also, that while in escape status in the community, he apparently did not commit any new crimes. Prior record in the institution has been outstanding, programs well, does what he is told, and is just generally no trouble. Committee can find no reason not to return ——— to the general population at this time.

This recording is fairly typical of many which are written "on behalf" of men assigned to adjustment centers. That is, it seems an unwritten rule that there must be established that the committee has carefully reviewed any and all background material which might suggest that the inmate should be retained in the adjustment center. If none is found, a rather reluctant phrase often found at the end of the recording is: "No contra-indications appearing, subject is recommended for the general population."

The importance of official records cannot be overemphasized. As many inmates have stated in informal conversations with the writer, "the pen is mightier than the sword." That is, the inmates are quite aware, probably much more than the staff, of the official documents which the staff use to stereotype inmates and make official decisions about them. The most poignant example from the observations of these committees came in seven of the cases in which official records were not available at the time of the committee proceedings. Without hesitation, and in each case, the committee decision was to postpone the proceedings until the records would be available.[17]

The combination of "what's going around," the official record, the decision alternatives available to staff, and the ipso facto seeking of appropriate symptoms—all in combination stereotype and determine what official action will be taken in any given case. The *coup de grace* is the entering of the stereotype and accompanying "evidence" in the official recording.[18]

THE DECISION TO RELEASE:
AN EXTRA TREATMENT FACTOR

Adjustment center placement and release are determined on some occasions by "space requirements." There are, after all, only a certain number of cells available. No observation was made of placement in terms of space requirements, but release under such conditions was observed.

Just prior to one of the committee meetings, the committee chairman received a call from the associate warden. He then reported to the committee:

> The Associate [warden] called, said he wanted us to have at least 10 vacant cells by Friday. Expecting some problems over the weekend, wants to be sure there's some room. We have three right now, think we can cut loose 7 on committee this morning?

As it turned out, the quota was not met from those appearing before the committee. In order to complete the "order," the committee reviewed in absentia every inmate in the adjustment center. This was done from picture cards maintained in the adjustment center office, which also served as the committee meeting room. The only information available, therefore, was the inmate's name, his cell assignment, and his prison picture and the staff's images and beliefs about "who these inmates are." The main criterion seemed to be which inmates presented the "least" risk; that is, their current stereotypes indicated that they had served time commensurate with their stereotype, perhaps had had some "progress" recordings, and had a recent disciplinary-free history.

Several of the inmates who were released after screening from the picture board had recently appeared at committee and had been retained for 90 days.

The paradox of the two actions was not recognized by the staff. How did the staff think that the inmates would perform? "Probably will do no better or worse" was the response. Apparently, the system allowed committee members to stereotype each inmate in front of the committee and take action based on "what everyone knows" about people who fitted the type. Then, under an order from above, they released inmates who presented the least risk.

CONCLUSIONS

Some of the consequences of the stereotyping process will now be discussed. Several things are apparent from the discussion: each consequence is a justification or rationale for stereotyping; each is most directly related to making a smooth-running organization; and each in its own way may facilitate the process of stereotyping. These were offered as organizational rationales in use at the time of the study. In a dynamic system, where change is the rule, one would expect these rationales to change completely or at least be modified over time. No doubt, this has happened. They are offered, therefore, as being indicative of the kinds of organizational consequences which may occur as a result of the process of stereotyping.

Facilitate Organizational Goals

In order to realize the goal of isolating dangerous inmates from the general prison population into the adjustment centers, the staff feels it necessary to have some kind of categorical stereotypes. These stereotypes are the basis upon which the staff can meet the organizational goals and objectives of demonstrating to the general staff and inmate population that, in fact, the organization has taken precautionary steps to make the general prison situation less precarious. By having ready-made categories for inmates (perhaps as few as four or five), the staff can more readily classify thousands of inmates into these few types and not have to undertake the insurmountable task of actually treating each inmate as an individual and facing perhaps 8,000 "types."

Create Areas of Shared Understanding

It is important, in order to speed up any function or process, to have areas of shared understanding—i.e., to have what we all know to be the truth regarding certain kinds of inmates. It is in these areas that one can, in an economical way, talk and write about such stereotypes as black militant, Mexican Mafia, bike rider, and so on.

Enable the Administration to Be Responsive and
Able to Make Quick Decisions

This is especially true in times of general trouble in the prison. If the administration wants to know who are the potential troublemakers or who may have helped start the trouble in process, it is highly functional to be able to consult a list of stereotyped inmates who meet the criteria of being Mexican, having a history of institutional troublemaking, etc. Very rapidly, the staff may then round up all those appropriate categorical stereotypes and isolate them in the adjustment center. The function of the roundup is to minimize or forestall a general prison disruption.

Maintain Sharp Distinctions Between the Staff and Inmates

By stereotyping inmates, the staff is able to perpetuate the idea that there is something different between the staff and inmates and that inmates are typically this or that, for most typifications imply that something is wrong with the inmates, either morally or mentally. The staff can more easily maintain their role of authority, minimizing their own role conflicts and maintaining role distance.

Delimit the Number of Alternatives to Be Considered

If one were to consider the actual decision possibilities for each and every inmate, the number would be great and perhaps unwieldy. Certainly 10 minutes before a classification committee is not ample time to explore all these alternatives, much less make a decision. By having only a few organizational stereotypes, the organization can at the same time routinize and thus make easier the decision-making process and limit the number of alternatives to that number which can actually be considered in each and every case requiring a decision. The job, then, becomes one of matching one of several stereotypes to one of several alternate causes of action.

Make Official Action More Predictable

By dealing with only a few stereotypes, the staff has more control over the official outcome, and these outcomes are more understandable based on the shorthand of typing. The understanding of other staff members who may be the implementers of the particular decisions is increased, and the action follow-up is less problematic.

The Stereotyping Process in the Situation of the
Adjustment Center Classification Committee

Although the central focus of this study is the adjustment center classification committee, a few comments are needed to place the committee in proper perspective within the total prison scene. The committee may initiate a stereotype, but more likely the process commences some time prior to the committee appearance. The activities associated with stereotyping fall into three areas: initial events in the general population, appearance before the adjustment center committee and concurrent action in the adjustment center, and subsequent events in the general prison population.

The initial events in the prison which may lead to adjustment center placement involve several uncertainties. One is that at least one staff member will be involved in the placement of any inmate in the adjustment center. How this will come about is uncertain; it will, however, be a prison inmate (at that prison)—no other is eligible. A report of some kind will be written setting forth what the "problem" is. The five categories used by the adjustment center committee are well known and are used by the staff who work outside the adjustment center. The probability is high that some reference will be made to one of these categories in the report—inmates with racial problems, pressure artists, the weak and pressured, the prison rats, inmates in the residual category. This often will be discussed with the inmate so that he is now aware of a prospective label. Since the initiation of adjustment center placement always occurs in the general prison population, how this is accomplished would seem to be of great influence on later events in the stereotypification process.

Events subsequent to the adjustment center placement may reinforce the stereotype or allow it to be extinguished through lack of care. Stereotypes never really disappear completely; they may always be revived. The official case record may at any time remind the staff about "who this inmate is." Whether or not the stereotype will stick depends on a great many contingencies, such as his housing, the availability of programs for him, the influence of his peers, and many more.

The committee may initiate or facilitate stereotyping. It is in the committee that the stereotype is decided upon and recorded officially in the individual's case file.

It was discovered from observing the four adjustment center committees at work that there were five categories to which they assigned or stereotyped inmates. These categories were a product of the staff's belief in "what was going around" during that period of time. These categories are subject to change or modification at any time; they are not static. The point is that committee members will know "what's going around" and will have helped produce it.

The power of the committee cannot be overemphasized. This is where any and all decisions about the inmate's prison conditions are made—housing, programs, and physical constraints. Because the parole board, caseworkers, administrators, and others in positions of authority over the inmate will often refer to the committee's reports, the consequences of its version of "what kind of case this is" can be enormous. Moreover, there is usually no effective appeal from the committee's actions; in almost every case, the committee's decisions are followed.

The one-sided character of the hearings is manifested in territorial arrangements and in the procedures followed. The business of the committee is carried out in the staff's territory, i.e., the adjustment center office, which is ordinarily out of bounds to inmates. There are four, sometimes more, staff members present representing the organization; the inmate appears alone representing his own view of himself and his behavior. The rules governing his appearance are all staff products; the inmate is told when to enter and when to leave. These conditions all serve to place the inmate at a severe disadvantage in all aspects of the committee proceedings. No doubt, they also serve as cues to the inmate about his chances to bargain about the nature of his "problem" (stereotype). Coupled with the committee's power, the frequent committee appearances have the effect of perpetuating the stereotype. In the cases observed, stereotypes were never reconsidered. The inmate might be considered to be "making progress," but the original stereotype was not questioned.

Although the inmate cannot, under these circumstances, effectively bargain or negotiate his stereotype, there are strategies which may affect the committee decisions. Two such strategies seemed to be especially effective. The first was for the inmate to accept the committee's stereotype or, more frequently, not to protest. The second was for him to show remorse. If the inmate carried through with both these strategies, his chances of receiving favorable comments in the official recording were good. Further, the committee usually wanted to reward this "improvement" in the inmate's "condition" with adjustment center release immediately or in the future (contingent upon "continued improvement").

The committee also functioned as an agent to collect "evidence" on the intended stereotype. Much of this "evidence" appeared to be based on three "facts." The first was the fact that every inmate was in the adjustment center; second, that every inmate was presumed guilty of something; and, third, that the demeanor of the inmate during his committee appearance was "evidence" of the kind of person he was. Therefore, if the inmate was in the adjustment center, had a staff report citing some institutional offense (especially fighting), and became angry in committee, these three "facts" may have been interpreted that (1) the inmate was properly placed "for the kind of person he appears to be," (2) the staff report was correct because "the staff have no reason to lie," and (3) his anger "reveals" a "basically hostile person who must learn to control his temper—he may even be dangerous."

The shared understandings among the staff members about "what kind of inmates we process here" enabled the committee to present a united front to each and every inmate. The inmate always faced four or more "authorities" who "knew" his "problem." Occasionally, some differences would arise between committee members regarding what action to take; these were usually of a minor nature, e.g., whether to consider adjustment center release this month or next (perhaps the inmate had already been in the adjustment center for 18 months). Time was always on the staff's side and was perhaps their greatest single device for securing the inmate's agreement with, or silence about, the stereotype that they had chosen for him. It was not accidental that the 90-day interims between committee appearances were referred to by the staff and inmates alike as "a program." And a program, among other things, was a time to consider sharing the staff's version of one's stereotype.

Official documentation—that is, the faithful recording in the case file for every committee appearance—played a vital role in the stereotyping process. It is the staff's version of the inmate stereotype. The consequences of this recording are widespread and crucial. For example, every time the inmate appears before the parole board, he will be talked to on the basis of his file and its accumulation of recordings—all reflecting what the staff think the inmate to be. And in the adjustment center committee the file is constantly referred to. The inmates' words count for much less. And the official file is the major obstacle to be overcome. There are those inmates who do participate with the staff in overturning their official file stereotypes. Overturning one's stereotype, however, is difficult. If hours are required to establish the stereotype, perhaps years are required to get proclaimed "as someone else." And the official file remains, lurking in the shadows, ready to be brought out and used as part of the "evidence" that the inmate really has not changed after all and is what the staff has known him to be all along.

NOTES

1. The sources for these data are California Department of Corrections (n.d.), *Weekly Population Control Document,* and *State Budget, 1969/70.*

2. "Incorrigible unit" was the name used by Richard McCleery (1961). It should be noted that these units are called "adjustment centers" by the California Department of Corrections.

3. See Irwin (1970:36-50) for some very cogent remarks about prison classification. Because his study was done in the California Department of Corrections during the 1960s and specifically in several of the institutions included in the present study (Soledad, San Quentin, Folson), Irwin's comments are especially relevant. Basically, he views classification as one of the ways in which inmates are controlled by manipulating where they live, the custody grade they are given, and generally the programs they are assigned to.

4. This procedure differs from that of the general prison population classification,

which almost never has inputs from the custodial staff on the line, i.e., those who deal wtih the inmate in his day-to-day activities.

5. Source: "California Prisoners," annual report of the Research Division, California Department of Corrections. See the report for 1969.

6. Lemert (1967:44) has pointed out that the first step that a deviant must often take on the "road to recovery and change" is to accept a bad stereotype (such as prison troublemaker)—even though, as Lemert has stated, this stereotype may be "an anomolous conception of himself."

7. Judging suspects by their demeanor, police officers "in the field" often come to the same kind of conclusion, as Piliavin and Briar (1964:141) have noted. Conclusions based on visual cues such as those cited by Piliavin and Briar probably are not as relevant in the adjustment center committee since there is not the great difference in dress.

8. The initial or first steps toward official stereotyping are taken in many cases sometime prior to the actual annointing ceremony which the committee represents. The guard who wrote the original report which eventually resulted in the inmate's adjustment center placement will influence the stereotype finally decided upon. The committee will believe without reservation whatever the "arresting officer" (guard) wrote. Implicit in Sudnow (1965) is the same kind of initiation and influencing process between the police (guards) and the public defenders and district attorneys (committee).

9. Agencies and officials of agencies working "in behalf of their clients" are granted great measures of discretion. This is done so that individual considerations will take precedent over other kinds of consideration. The unintended outcome is, however, that almost anything the agency or officials do is "legitimated." See Piliavin and Briar (1964:139) for conditions of discretion for juvenile police officers and, later in the article, the actual payoff of sanctioned discretion, i.e., arrest and detention often based on stereotypes of offenders.

10. All of which makes official case files suspect. They are, after all, one version; a version maintained by the inmate or his fellow inmates might be quite different. Scheff (1964) seems to have made this same point throughout his study of the psychiatric screening of mental patients for the court; that is, official versions are not always "the only or the true reality."

Public defenders and district attorneys associate certain kinds of social behavior with images of what the person who engages in that kind of behavior "is like" (e.g., the possible circumstances which "typically" 'lead' to a certain kind of behavior), and they match these images with various offenses (Sudnow, 1965). The prison staff similarly carry around mental images of prison troublemakers. Sudnow quotes a public defender: "But we often get fathers charged with these crimes. Usually the old man is out of work and stays at home when the wife goes to work, and he plays around with his little daughter or something. A lot of these cases start when there is some marital trouble and the woman gets mad." And from an adjustment center committee member: "This inmate is irresponsible—he doesn't give a damn. If he did, he wouldn't go around doing this kind of stuff. He may not be technically crazy, but no one in his right mind would ———."

11. The psychiatrists in Scheff's (1964) study took only a few minutes to establish the "fact of mental illness." In the situation of the adjustment center committee, only 10 minutes (on the average) was needed.

12. Even though juvenile officers depended on stereotypes for arrest and/or detention purposes at the station, "the distribution . . . of decisions . . . revealed that in virtually every category of offense, the full range of official disposition alternatives available to officers was

employed." The reason cited for this use of many alternatives was the recognition of the possible consequences of stigmatization; e.g., it might reinforce or initiate juvenile delinquency (Piliavin and Briar, 1964:139). Conversely, the adjustment center committee apparently had no such belief and certainly did not use its full range of alternatives.

13. Scheff (1962, 1963, 1964, 1966), Sudnow (1965), and Piliavin and Briar (1964) made no mention of the possibility of a mental patient, defendant, or juvenile delinquent "volunteering" for processing (and possible programming) by the official agency. The implication is that the clients whom they refer to are either reluctant or passive participants in their own stereotyping. This seems improbable, especially in view of some of the findings in this study which suggest that an adjustment center inmate may actively participate in establishing his stereotype.

14. See Lemert's (1967:44) discussion of "total institutional" settings and the consequences for stereotyping.

15. Psychiatrists also have a difficult time in not discovering treatment needs in many different populations. See Scheff (1963:101) for a discussion of his own and others' findings in this regard. The prison staff are not unlike psychiatrists in "discovering" inmates who "need" staff services.

16. The magnitude of the deviance will influence the stereotyping process (Piliavin and Briar, 1964). And in the above case, there is "little" deviance, i.e., one nonviolent escape; therefore, the inmate is "not dangerous," etc.

17. In four cases apparently a mistake had been made in placing the inmates in the unit. They had been transferred from another institution where there was "trouble." Their transfers, it turned out, had been unrelated to the "trouble." At the committee, the inmates made good appearances; i.e., they were respectful and cooperative. Committee members made repeated attempts to find the stereotypifications which would justify unit placement. Almost reluctantly, the committee action was to immediately release the inmates based on file stereotypes of "good worker, no problem, participates in program."

18. As Goffman (1962) pointed out, the case record is used more often to record unsuccessful attempts to cope with life situations.

REFERENCES

California Department of Corrections (n.d.). Classification manual. Sacramento: Author.

GARFINKEL, H. (1956). "Conditions of successful degradation ceremonies." American Journal of Sociology, 61(March):420-424.

GOFFMAN, E. (1962). Asylums. Chicago: Aldine.

IRWIN, J. (1970). The felon. Englewood Cliffs, N.J.: Prentice-Hall.

LEMERT, E.L. (1967). Human deviance, social problems, and social control. Englewood Cliffs, N.J.: Prentice-Hall.

MARCH, J.G. (1965). Handbook of organizations. Chicago: Rand McNally.

McCLEERY, R. (1961). "Authoritarianism and the belief systems of incorrigibles." In D. Cressey (ed.), The prison. New York: Holt, Rinehart and Winston.

PILIAVIN, I., and BRIAR, S. (1964). "Police encounters with juveniles." American Journal of Sociology, 69(September):206-214.

President's Commission on Law Enforcement and Administration of Justice (1967). The challenge of crime in a free society. Washington, D.C.: U.S. Government Printing Office.

ROTH, J. (1962). "The treatment of tuberculosis as a bargaining process." In A. Rose (ed.), Human behavior and social processes. Boston: Houghton Mifflin.

SCHEFF, T. (1962). "Typification in the diagnostic practices of rehabilitation agencies." Chap. 8 in M. Sussman (ed.), Sociology and rehabilitation. Cleveland: American Sociological Association.

――― (1963). "Decision rules, types of error, and their consequences in medical diagnosis." Behavioral Scientist, 8(April).

――― (1964). "The societal reaction to deviance: Ascriptive elements in the psychiatric screening of mental patients in a midwestern state." Social Problems, 11(spring).

――― (1966). Being mentally ill: A sociological theory. Chicago. Aldine.

SUDNOW, D. (1965). "Normal crimes: Sociological features of the penal code in a public defender's office." Social Problems, 12(winter):255-276.

Chapter 3

THE POLITICS OF STATE CORRECTIONS

P E T E R   H.   R O S S I   a n d
R I C H A R D   A.   B E R K

To change our prison systems means to change the relevant portions of state criminal codes and to institute new administrative procedures within the prisons that correspond to the changed legal code. These are political changes in the sense that the state political machinery—executive, legislative, and administrative branches—is necessarily involved.

In the voting booths where the elections of public officials are decided, it is one vote per voting citizen. On the level of changes in corrections legislation or administrative procedures, there is hardly a comparable simple formula. Persons vary in their ability to influence the outcomes of issues partly because their opinions carry more weight with those who officially make decisions. A public opinion poll which counts every opinion equally can be a misleading predictor of political outcomes outside of popular elections.

Properly to assess the potentials for changes within each state requires that one take into account the established patterns of authority and influence that have grown up in each state around the settlement of issues concerning corrections. The state political elites are the "gatekeepers" of change, passing some suggested changes into law and administrative practice while preventing others from becoming part of local institutional norms and practices.

METHOD

This chapter describes the political elites of three states and attempts to assess the influences that certain groups among such elites were able to bring to bear upon corrections changes. The data base for our chapter consists of interviews made in 1973 with members of political elites in three states—Florida, Illinois, and Washington. The purpose of the study was to gauge the receptivity of elites to changes in the prison systems of their states. Part of the study attempted to assess the elites' level of discontent with their prison systems as well as the specific content of their dissatisfactions. (A full account of these findings can be found in Berk and Rossi, 1977.)

The main reason that we needed to know the patterning of influences concerning corrections reforms was to measure the propensity of each state elite to accept prison reforms—an assessment in which members of the elites would have their opinions weighted according to their abilities to influence the course of legislative activity and administrative practices. We needed to know precisely how much inequality there was in the influencing of corrections legislation and administrative practice in order to apply appropriate weights to respondents' opinions, thereby constructing a more realistic assessment of the viability of corrections reforms.

The first step in such an enterprise is to uncover the patterning of influence. It is this task to which this chapter is devoted. We are concerned here not with uncovering the patterning of influence in general but with finding those patterns which have been established with respect to formulating, initiating, and validating changes in corrections systems.

The respondents in our study were selected because their opinions on corrections were likely to have some significant impact on policy making in the area of corrections. In constructing our lists of people to question, we deliberately erred on the side of including as many persons and groups as could be reasonably expected to be concerned vitally with the issues involved.

We defined a member of a state elite as a person who held a position either as an officially defined "decision maker" (governor, chairpersons of relevant legislative committees, etc.) or as a "partisan," one who has a position of leadership within an organization having an interest in correctional legislation but who is without decision-making powers (law enforcement officials, state bar association officials, mayors, police union leaders, etc.). Within each state a total of approximately 110 positions were so identified. (A full listing of the positions is given in Berk and Rossi, 1977).

A. Official decision makers (governors, appointed corrections officials, state legislative leaders, etc.)
   (N = 33)

B. Partisans: law enforcement officials and lower-level corrections officials (wardens, parole board members, police chiefs and sheriffs)
   (N = 24)

C. Partisans: judiciary, states attorneys, and members of legal professions (state bar association officials, criminal court judges, states attorneys)
   (N = 30-36)

D. Partisans: other public officials (mayors and county officials)
   (N = 9)

E. Other Partisans: American Civil Liberties Union officials, leaders of police and corrections unions, citizen crime commissions)
   (N = 11)

The sampling plan in the three states was not completely fulfilled. A total of 266 persons were interviewed, somewhat short of the 330 intended. For reasons that we are not able to fully ascertain, our study was abruptly terminated by the funding agency—the Law Enforcement Assistance Administration (LEAA)—before the fieldwork had been fully completed. Indeed, our original plan had been to sample 20 states, for which the present three, Florida, Illinois, and Washington, were to serve as a pretest.

Over the past decade, considerable controversy has agitated the fields of political sociology and behavioral political science over appropriate methods for studying patterns of influence in political decision making. On the one hand, there are those who insist that the most appropriate way to proceed is to study a number of concrete decisions and to induce from such instances what are the customary patterns of influence. There is much to say for this position, especially its close attention to actual practice. On the other hand, the opposing point of view claims that the study of specific decisions obscures the important overall patterning which can be best uncovered by studying the reputations that individuals and organizations enjoy as influential and powerful social units. As is often the case with such controversies, there is some merit on both sides. Even more important, however, studies employing one or the other method are often not as far apart in their findings as protagonists claim. Reputations are not manufactured out of whole cloth: they have some basis in practice. Specific decisions are often influenced not only by those with reputations but also by others whose interest in a particular decision may be very high. Thus, one may find that the governor's office is usually regarded as extremely influential with respect to state legislation. Yet, one may also find that, in the case of a particular piece of legislative action, the governor's office may have no influence on the outcome.

Properly to interpret our findings is to regard them as outlining the *potentials* for influence in each of the three states. The reputations are based upon the collective experiences of our elite respondents with decision making in the past—an informal average over the years prior to 1973. It is problematic how much decision making in the future might depart from the practices of the past. We can safely wager, however, that, while some states may show marked deviation from the patterns as described by reputations, the overall patterning of the past will tend to persist at least into the proximate future. We advance this prediction mainly out of regard for the remarkable persistence of customary behavior.

The survey was undertaken in a time period when there was little active movement in each of the three states to change the state's correctional system. The reputations we obtained, therefore, obtain for "normal" times in which such issues are not near the top of state political agendas.

WHO IS ACTIVE ON CORRECTIONS ISSUES?

The first question to raise on the way to uncovering the configuration of influence is, Who usually participates in corrections policy making and legislating? Respondents were asked to rate the activity levels of a number of groups and persons on corrections issues in their state. The resulting data are shown in Table 1, all three states combined.

The percentages indicate wide variability in the degree of perceived participation across groups and persons. For example, governors were assessed as quite active, while associations of lower level corrections personnel were relatively inactive. Sixty-five percent of the respondents said that the governors of their state were "always active." In contrast, only 21% said that associations of corrections personnel were "always active." The most active "groups"[1] were the governor, the corrections committees of both houses, the head of the state department of corrections, and the state parole board.

Some of the groups listed in the bottom four rows of Table 1 also showed high levels of activity. However, these were groups or persons which some respondents—usually a small number—volunteered as additions to a standard list of 19 groups. The percentages involving these groups are based on a very small number of ratings; hence, we do not refer to these groups any further in this chapter.

It is also instructive to note those groups/persons who were not particularly active in corrections legislation. The state bar associations, corrections unions, police officials, criminal lawyers, and ex-offenders associations were all considered to be relatively inactive in political decision making. In part, these findings may represent the absence of some of the organizations on the local scenes, particularly ex-offender organizations and corrections unions. The lower levels of activities for police officials or for criminal lawyers may suggest that these are groups that become active only when their interests are very closely engaged.

Table 2 contains average activity levels for each group in each state, calculated by forcing the categories of activity into a four-point scale ("no role" = 1, "rarely active" = 2, "sometimes active" = 3, "always active" = 4). A mean of 3, for example, would indicate that a group was given an average rating of "sometimes active."

Averages over 3.5 appear in boldface in Table 2. In general, the groups with high mean ratings in each state were the same groups that were active as shown in the percentage distributions of Table 1. However, there were some state differences. In particular, Illinois had the lowest relative average for its governor and the highest mean for its corrections head. In contrast, Washington had the highest mean for its governor and the lowest for its corrections head.

It should be noted that Illinois Governor Daniel Walker, a Democrat, was elected in 1972 against the opposition of the "regular" Democrats and was then confronted in early 1973 by a senate and lower house in which Republicans predominated. Shortly thereafter, the legislature refused to confirm Governor Walker's candidate for head of corrections and overrode his veto of some extraordinary financial aid for the Chicago Transit Authority. In short, Governor Walker was a governor at odds with strong groups in his own party and faced by a legislature dominated by the opposing party. His was not a position that could be called one of great power.

Another way to evaluate these data is to examine the extent to which respondents differed one from the other in attributing to groups more or less activity in corrections legislative matters. Since the elite members were supposedly reacting to these questions as informants, the major differences among respondents should arise out of their positions and the states in which they reside, with small differences among respondents according to educational level, age, and other purely biographical characteristics. To test out these expectations, we computed regressions of activity levels of the groups in Table 2 on the state, positional, and biographical characteristics of the respondents.

The results of these regressions are too tedious to report here. In none of the regressions were significant results obtained: in only one case, involving the activity level of the governor, did any one of the variables attain close to conventional levels of statistical significance. As we might anticipate from the results of Table 2, Illinois elite members were more likely to attribute a lower level of activity to the governor of that state. In other respects and in the cases of activity levels for the other major actors shown in Table 2, respondents hardly

Table 1. GROUPS PERCEIVED AS ACTIVE ON CORRECTIONS ISSUES
    (3 States Combined)

Person/Group	Plays No Role	Rarely Active	Sometimes Active	Always Active	100% =
Governor	0	3	32	65	[257]
Citizens' crime commission	13	12	42	33	[227]
Democratic leader in state senate	7	20	51	22	[237]
Republican leader in state senate	8	21	51	20	[238]
Democratic leader in lower house	6	21	52	21	[235]
Republican leader in lower house	6	21	52	21	[232]
State senate corrections committee	2	3	27	69	[233]
Lower house corrections committee	2	5	27	66	[234]
LEAA state planning agency	8	10	38	43	[224]
Head of state corrections department	0.4	2	14	84	[248]
State attorney general	2	7	44	47	[248]
State bar association	4	24	51	20	[249]
Police chiefs of large police departments	6	19	51	24	[249]
American Civil Liberties Union	4	8	40	48	[246]
State parole department and staff	2	14	28	56	[246]
Ex-offenders organization	28	25	30	17	[210]
Associations of corrections personnel	16	23	39	21	[218]
Prominent criminal lawyers in state	13	29	46	13	[238]
Associations of police personnel	12	26	48	14	[241]
Prison reform groups	4	0	35	62	[26]
Public defenders	0	10	47	43	[30]
Other public officials and agencies	3	10	49	38	[39]
Other private persons and groups	0	12	62	26	[34]

Activity Level

Table 2. AVERAGE PERCEIVED GROUP ACTIVITY LEVELS, BY STATE

	Average Activity Levels for Each State					
	Florida		Illinois		Washington	
Person/Group	$\overline{X}$	N =	$\overline{X}$	N =	$\overline{X}$	N =
Governor	**3.6**	[101]	**3.5**	[74]	**3.8**	[82]
Citizens' crime commission	2.7	[85]	3.1	[64]	3.2	[78]
Democratic leader in state senate	2.9	[71]	3.1	[42]	2.7	[81]
Republican leader in state senate	2.8	[91]	3.1	[66]	2.7	[81]
Democratic leader in lower house	2.9	[92]	3.0	[64]	2.8	[79]
Republican leader in lower house	2.9	[92]	3.0	[63]	2.7	[77]
State senate corrections committee	**3.7**	[94]	**3.7**	[65]	**3.5**	[74]
Lower house corrections committee	**3.7**	[97]	3.5	[62]	**3.5**	[75]
LEAA state planning agency	3.2	[87]	3.0	[62]	3.3	[75]
Head of state corrections department	**3.8**	[99]	**3.9**	[67]	**3.6**	[82]
State attorney general	**3.5**	[100]	3.1	[67]	3.4	[82]
State bar association	2.9	[97]	2.8	[70]	2.9	[82]
Police chiefs of large police departments	2.8	[98]	2.9	[69]	3.2	[82]
American Civil Liberties Union	3.2	[96]	3.3	[67]	3.4	[83]
State parole department and staff	**3.6**	[99]	3.2	[66]	3.4	[81]
Ex-offenders organization	2.0	[81]	2.5	[58]	2.7	[71]
Associations of corrections personnel	2.4	[68]	2.8	[62]	2.9	[70]
Prominent criminal lawyers in state	2.5	[91]	2.7	[68]	2.5	[79]
Associations of police personnel	2.5	[94]	2.7	[68]	2.8	[79]

differed one from the other in any systematic way that could be captured by biographical, experiential, or positional characteristics evidencing consensus among themselves.

WHO IS REPUTED TO WIELD POWER?

In order to understand which bills are likely to pass, one must know far more than who typically is active in corrections matters. It is crucial to know which parties have the "clout" to impose their goals on legislation. Our interviews examined this issue in several ways.

One way to discover who wields power on corrections matters is simply to ask. Though this reputational approach has known weaknesses, it is a useful first approximation, especially when checked against other kinds of data. One reputation item was, "If you wanted to get a piece of corrections legislation through the state legislature, which of these groups or persons[2] would be very important to get on your side?" A second item asked, "Whose opposition could make it impossible or very difficult to get corrections legislation passed?"

Table 3 indicates that on several individuals and groups there was high consensus. The governor, the Democratic and Republican leaders of both houses, and the corrections committees of both houses were seen by at least 40% of the respondents as very important for passage *and* also having the ability to stop legislation.

Comparing these results with Table 1, governors and corrections committees were both seen as always active and very powerful, but the Democratic chamber leaders were viewed as, at best, moderately active but very powerful. This suggests that although Democratic leaders were not typically involved and active in corrections matters, they must be won over for a bill to pass.

Table 3. REPUTATIONS FOR POWER ON CORRECTIONS ISSUES (N = 266)

Person/Group	Proportion Claiming Group Very Important for Bill Passage	Proportion Claiming Group Can Stop a Bill
Governor	74	79
Citizens' crime commission	25	17
Democratic leader in state senate	62	61
Republican leader in state senate	51	47
Democratic leader in lower house	62	59
Republican leader in lower house	49	45
State senate corrections committee	59	53
Lower house corrections committee	56	52
LEAA state planning agency	16	7
Head of state corrections department	55	36
State attorney general	35	34
State bar association	20	18
Police chiefs of large police departments	17	18
American Civil Liberties Union	12	10
State parole department and staff	22	13
Ex-offenders organization	6	1
Associations of corrections personnel	10	7
Prominent criminal lawyers in state	10	9
Associations of police personnel	9	11

In general, groups who were seen as essential for passage were also seen as able to stop passage, the correlation between the two columns of Table 3 being .95. There are several interesting exceptions to this pattern. The LEAA state planning agency was seen by a few respondents (16%) as important for passage, but by virtually no one (7%) as able to block corrections legislation. A similar pattern appears for the state parole department and staff; more people believed that this group was important for passage (22%) than felt it could block legislation (13%). The most striking example of this perceived ability to aid passage of legislation but not to prevent it was the head of corrections: 55% believed the corrections head to be very important for support of a bill, but only 36% felt that he could stop a bill. One may think of these three groups as performing "staff functions": they were probably very important in the development and writing of corrections legislation, but exercised little direct power in the legislature. If they are not prepared to work on a bill's development, it may never get into the legislative process. However, once a bill is submitted, they apparently can do little to affect its passage.

Table 4 presents data on the perceived power of groups within states, taking advantage of the .95 correlation between perceived ability to aid and perceived

Table 4. REPUTATIONS FOR POWER IN CORRECTIONS ISSUES IN EACH STATE
(Proportions Saying Group/Individual Important in Getting Legislation Passed)

Person/Group	Florida (N = 107)	Illinois (N = 76)	Washington (N = 83)
Governor[a]	78	69	81
Citizens' crime commission[a]	13	20	45
Democratic leader in state senate[a]	62	67	59
Republican leader in state senate[a]	39	70	48
Democratic leader in lower house[a]	59	67	60
Republican leader in lower house[a]	38	68	46
State senate corrections committee[a]	64	51	57
Lower house corrections committee[a]	62	50	54
LEAA state planning agency	18	12	18
Head of state corrections department[a]	52	57	57
State attorney general[a]	37	20	46
State bar association	18	22	22
Police chiefs of large police departments[a]	52	57	25
American Civil Liberties Union	37	20	17
State parole department and staff[a]	26	7	30
Ex-offenders organization	2	4	13
Association of corrections personnel	3	11	19
Prominent criminal lawyers in state	10	11	8
Associations of police personnel	4	9	16

a. Person/Group for which at least 25% of a state's sample said they were very important for passage of corrections legislation.

Table 5. INTERSTATE CORRELATIONS IN RATINGS OF GROUPS AS "ESSENTIAL FOR AID" IN PASSAGE OF CORRECTIONS LEGISLATION

	1	2	3	4	5	6	7	8	9	10	11	12
Democratic leader in state senate	1	78	87	80	14	−99	−03	−58	−45	−99	−30	−90
Republican leader in state senate	2		98	99	72	−86	−03	−96	−90	−80	−46	−96
Democratic leader in lower house	3			98	59	−93	−19	−89	−82	−89	−33	−91
Republican leader in lower house	4				70	−87	−05	−95	−89	−82	−35	−90
Head of state corrections department	5					−27	66	−88	−95	−17	−43	−35
Governor	6						57	68	57	99	74	99
Citizens' crime commission	7							−25	−38	61	87	57
State senate corrections committee	8								98	60	32	60
Lower house corrections committee	9									48	11	63
State attorney general	10										81	98
Police chiefs of large police departments	11											69
State parole department and staff	12											

ability to block and using perceived ability to aid passage as the index of perceived power.

To aid in making comparisons in Table 4, we have indicated with superscript "a" those individuals or groups in a given state designated by at least 25% of state respondents as very important for passage. Focusing on these 12 groups, we find some provocative differences between states. The governor, leaders of the senate and lower house, corrections committees, attorneys general, and parole departments were seen as considerably less likely to be essential in Illinois than in the other states. In contrast, the party leaders of both houses (especially Republicans) were seen as more essential in Illinois than in the other states.

Following this lead, we computed a correlation matrix using the state as the unit of analysis and the proportion saying a given party was essential for passage as each observation (see Table 5). The correlations cluster strongly and can be arranged so that two very distinct blocks (outlined with triangles) of ratings are formed, each block primarily containing variables which correlate positively with each other but negatively with ratings that involve the groups contained in the other block. States that had a governor perceived as powerful also regarded as powerful the crime commission, the legislative corrections committees, the attorneys general, the parole departments, and the police chiefs of large cities. Further, when the governor was seen as more powerful, party leaders in both houses along with the head of corrections were seen as far less powerful.

Because only three states are involved, these correlations must necessarily be regarded quite tentatively. However, the consistency of the signs in Table 5 apparently indicates that the configurations of reputational power around corrections issues fell into two broad types. First, some states apparently possessed an "administrative coalition" in which there existed close connections between the governor, the corrections committees, and most criminal justice agencies. Though not part of state government, police chiefs of large city departments and citizen crime commissions were linked to this network, possibly through the governor and the attorney general's office.

The second type of state was dominated more by legislators than by executives. Here the power resided in the leaders of the political parties. For our three states, however, the pattern is not as neat as one might like. Although party leaders all tended to be powerful together in a given state, when they were more powerful the corrections committees were less powerful. Hence, in legislative-dominated states, not all relevant actors in the legislature shared dominance.

In summary, one can think of two "ideal types" of configurations of power around corrections issues—executive- and legislative-centered coalitions. Illinois was apparently closest in our example to legislative dominance, and Florida and Washington were examples of executive coalition domination.

Table 6. EXTENT OF PERSONAL CONTACT ON CORRECTIONS MATTERS, BY STATE

Person/Group	Proportion Knowing Group Well Enough to Call			Proportion Who Have Contacted Person/Group		
	Florida	Illinois	Washington	Florida	Illinois	Washington
Governor	50	32	46	30	29	30
Citizens' crime commission	15	22	35	13	21	26
Democratic leader in state senate	40	30	40	24	25	17
Republican leader in state senate	31	30	41	23	26	16
Democratic leader in lower house	40	29	39	23	24	17
Republican leader in lower house	31	30	36	24	24	14
State senate corrections committee	42	32	32	31	26	28
Lower house corrections committee	44	28	31	36	22	24
LEAA state planning agency	28	28	43	22	26	32
Head of state corrections department	47	40	46	38	37	40
State attorney general	54	32	59	23	22	43
State bar association	36	28	39	17	16	6
Police chiefs of large police departments	28	29	40	12	16	23
American Civil Liberties Union	19	18	29	8	14	19
State parole department and staff	38	30	45	26	21	35
Ex-offenders organization	8	14	28	3	10	17
Associations of corrections personnel	12	18	31	8	9	20
Prominent criminal lawyers in state	29	18	25	8	10	12
Associations of police personnel	16	18	26	8	10	13
$\overline{X} =$	32.0	26.7	37.4	19.9	20.6	23.9
SD =	13.1	6.3	8.1	10.1	7.2	8.8
N =	[107]	[76]	[83]	[107]	[76]	[83]
	Grand Mean = 32			Grand Mean = 20.2		

How much consensus is there over attributions of power to influence legislation? If these reports of influence are to be regarded as having some validity, we should find that there were few differences among elite respondents in their opinions about which groups are powerful, except for those opinions that may have been generated by interstate differences. Biographical differences resting on such characteristics as educational attainment should in contrast have been relatively slight. To test these expectations, we ran regressions on major biographical, positional, and state variables, using the attributions of influence to the major actors as the dependent variable.[3] None of the regressions turned out to be significant, and only residence in Illinois came close to attaining a statistically significant regression coefficient. While consensus, so defined, is hardly proof that we have captured the essence of the configurations in influence surrounding corrections legislation, such findings do bolster this assertion.

WHO KNOWS WHOM?

The exercise of political influence requires communication. Some interaction is necessary not only for the transmission of information but also for the negotiation processes that go on in all decision making. Hence, the next step in our examination of the configuration of influence around corrections was to trace out the interpersonal networks that function within each state capital.

Two interview items were aimed at assessing the amount of contact with various groups on corrections issues. One asked, "Are there any groups in which you know some key members well enough to call them about something concerning corrections issues?" A second item asked, "Have you ever contacted any of these individuals or group members about corrections issues?" In answering these questions, respondents had before them the list of 19 groups and individuals.

Table 6 shows the percentages of respondents in each state who claimed contact with each group on the list. Thirty-two percent of the respondents claimed to know the "average" group included on the list well enough to call them on corrections matters, and 21% claimed to have actually made such contacts (see the averages at the bottom of Table 6). Focusing on the left-hand columns, we see a tendency for Illinois respondents to know each of the groups less well. Note that the standard deviation for Illinois was also lower, suggesting that not only did Illinois respondents know fewer people but the variability from group to group was not as large. Comparing the Illinois patterns with the other two states suggests why the standard deviation and mean were lower. The head of corrections plus several persons that we have identified earlier as part of the executive coalition tended to have fewer respondents who knew them well enough to call. This makes sense, since many new appointments were involved. However, these lower percentages relative to other states did not substantially change the *ordering* of groups and individuals in Illinois relative to the other states. Correlations between the three columns of percentages were of the order of .75.

The state of Washington presented a different, almost cozy, pattern. Not only did more respondents claim to know each group, but the low standard deviation suggests a rather even distribution of interpersonal networks.

In contrast to Illinois and Washington, corrections politics in Florida seemed more atomized. The mean percent was considerably lower than Washington's, while the standard deviation was by far the largest of the three. In short, there were fewer interpersonal networks more unevenly distributed among political actors.

The means for the three right-hand columns ("have contacted") were virtually identical. Hence, in spite of a lower proportion of respondents in Illinois claiming to know important persons and groups, in practice it did not seem to matter too much at the aggregate level. All three states showed an approximately equal overall amount of actual contact. Correlations between the three columns of percentages showed consistently high positive values of approximately .70, suggesting that the states showed roughly the same *percentage orders* of magnitude of contacts with groups within each state.

In summary, on the average, the persons and groups were well enough known to be contacted on corrections matters by 32% of our respondents. The average level of actual contact with groups was smaller, 20%. Apparently some persons and groups were more central to communication networks than others. In general, the governor and his executive departments who worked in the criminal justice field were likely to be more familiar to the respondents than to the other groups listed. In Illinois, this tendency was less pronounced, and the patterns of actual contact showed somewhat less selectivity.

PATTERNS OF GROUP INFLUENCES ON ELITES

In an earlier section of this chapter, our attention was focused on the reputations of each of the 19 groups concerning their abilities to facilitate or impede the passage of legislation affecting corrections. The "power" reputations uncovered in that section referred to power wielded in a particular important arena, legislative changes in corrections.

But there is another face to influence, possibly a step or more removed from legislative change, involving influencing the views of key actors. Thus an official in the corrections system might have had little leverage to *directly* affect corrections legislation, yet through his ability to persuade and convince, he may have been able indirectly to affect changes. To tap this different form of influence, we asked our elite respondents which of the 19 groups had influenced them on corrections matters and, conversely, which of them had been able to exercise influence on others. We were especially concerned with this "influence" aspect to power since our respondents are considerably more important politically than ordinary citizens, and hence the groups that exercise some influence over their views are especially important in the understanding of how change comes about. Since influence is usually a two-way street in which persons who are influenced by someone are often in turn influential with that person, our measures of this form of influence took that reciprocity into account.

Two items were used in the questionnaire: The first item read, "For which groups or individuals (on this list), if any, do you feel you have significant influence on the positions they take?" The second read, "Which of the groups of individuals, if any, do you feel have a significant influence on the positions you take?"

The results of these influence questions can be seen in Table 7 in simplified form. We selected the 12 groups noted earlier as those for which at least 25% of the sample in one state said they either were very important for passage or could block it. The means and standard deviations (bottom of Table 7) show essentially the same pattern as could be shown for the total number of groups and persons, a finding which suggests that by limiting our analysis to the groups who were reputationally important we do not change the overall patterns of summary statistics. We appear to have retained the same pattern of central tendencies and variabilities.

In Table 7, a number of patterns appear: first, overall, people were more likely to say that they were influenced than to say that they exercised influence. We would have been surprised had it come out the other way since the persons and groups selected here represented the most powerful actors among the 19, whereas our sample of respondents included many relatively unimportant persons.

Second, the columns of percentages show some interesting differences. Governors, for example, stood out in two of the three states (Illinois being the exception) as the most powerful influencers while not especially different from other persons and groups in the amount that they were influenced by others. In all three states, the head of corrections stood out as an influencer but not especially as someone who was influenced. Since there are a very large number of such comparisons, we have reduced some of the complexity by presenting the correlations in Table 8 between the patterns of influence from state to state, in this case correlations between the columns of percentages in Table 7.

Table 7. PATTERNS OF INFLUENCE, BY STATE (For Most Powerful Persons Only)[a]

Person/Group	Florida (N = 107)		Illinois (N = 76)		Washington (N = 83)	
	Have Influenced	Influenced By	Have Influenced	Influenced By	Have Influenced	Influenced By
Governor	22%	37%	18%	16%	19%	41%
Citizens' crime commission	11	8	13	16	19	24
Democratic leader in state senate	16	17	17	10	14	7
Republican leader in state senate	12	11	16	8	12	7
Democratic leader in lower house	15	18	17	12	14	8
Republican leader in lower house	12	10	13	10	10	5
State senate corrections committee	20	21	14	13	20	19
Lower house corrections committee	22	24	13	12	17	14
Head of state corrections department	17	28	25	33	28	37
State attorney general	11	23	8	16	24	34
Police chiefs of large police departments	5	10	8	12	18	12
State parole department	16	16	17	16	19	24
$\overline{X} =$	15.9%	15.9%	17.1%	15.8%	19.3%	24.1%
SD =	4.7	8.2	4.4	6.1	4.8	12.1

a. Person/Group for which at least 25% of a state's sample said they were very important for passage of corrections legislation.

Table 8. CORRELATIONS BETWEEN INFLUENCE PATTERNS, BY STATE
(Computed over 12 Most Powerful Person/Groups)[a]

			Florida		Illinois		Washington	
			1	2	3	4	5	6
Florida	Have Influenced	1	X	72	56	18	15	32
	Influenced By	2		X	43	47	53	72
Illinois	Have Influenced	3			X	59	20	28
	Influenced By	4				X	82	75
Washington	Have Influenced	5					X	84
	Influenced By	6						X

a. Person/Group for which at least 25% of a state's sample said they were very important
for passage of corrections legislation.

Table 8 shows the correlations between the patterns of influence based on the
12 most powerful groups and persons.[4] All of the correlations are rather high
and positive, though the highest correlations (in boldface) tend to occur for the
two types of influence within a state.

Probably the most obvious pattern involves the high correlations which
reflect the associations within a given state. Groups who influence are also those
that are influenced. Note that one could have expected quite the opposite, a
pattern that does hold true for a few actors in some states, usually the governor
and the head of the corrections department.

The matrix of Table 8 contains quite low correlations involving cross-state
comparisons. Looking first at the correlations involving "have influenced" across
the three states (variables 1, 3, 5), Florida and Washington have the most
different (though still positively associated) pattern. The correlation between
variables 1 and 3 is .56, between 3 and 5 is .20, and between 1 and 5 is .15. The
states tended to show idiosyncratic patterns of influence.

We can also examine the pattern of correlations between the percentage of
people in each state who claim to have influenced others, the correlations
between variables 2, 4, and 6. It is not especially clear which of the pairs of
states were more alike. The correlations are all fairly high: however, Florida and
Washington appear to be slightly more alike. The states' elites are more alike in
their patterns of *whom* they claimed to have influenced than in *who* influenced
themselves.

ELITE VARIATION IN INFLUENCE

The influence attributions discussed in the previous section can also be used to differentiate among elite respondents. We can anticipate that some will claim to be quite influential across a rather wide range of the 19 groups, whereas others may attribute to themselves the more modest position of not having influenced any. The same range of variation may be anticipated with respect to having been influenced by the 19 groups. Those who were seemingly influential to our respondents can be viewed as participating especially strongly in the networks of personal contacts that define decision making involving corrections legislation and administrative practice.

Almost half (46%) of our respondents did not claim to have influenced any of the 19 groups, although, on the average, 2.6 groups were claimed as the recipients of respondents' influence. This finding suggests that there were some respondents who claimed to have influenced a large proportion of the groups: indeed, those who claimed to have influenced *any* group made that claim for an average of 4.8 groups.

An "influencer score" was computed for each respondent summing the number of groups that each respondent claimed to have influenced. This score was regressed on a number of respondent characteristics—e.g., age, position, education. A very modest amount of variation was captured by the regression analysis, R^2 being +.28. Only two of the variables used in the regression reached statistical significance. Being a state elected official had a regression coefficient of 2.45, indicating that persons in that position influenced about twice as many groups as the average elite member.[5] Elite members' educational attainment also affected their claims to influence, .64 additional groups being claimed for each educational level.

It appears that state elected officials were most likely to claim influence along with those who have better-than-average educational attainment. State elected officials and lawyers are those elite members who are most likely to be close into the network of contact and mutual influence surrounding legislative activities in general and concerning corrections in particular.

"Influenced scores" were also calculated for each respondent by summing the number of groups who influenced the respondents. While this score might be thought of as an index of the willingness of respondents to be influenced by others, in fact the index turned out to be an alternative expression of being part of the communications network surrounding political decision making. The correlation between influencer and influenced scores was rather high, +.63, indicating that persons high in influencing others were likely to be high on the receiving end of influence relationships.

Fewer respondents (35%) claimed not to have been influenced by anyone of the 19 groups, the average number of groups from whom influence was claimed being 2.8.[6] Being influenced was apparently a more common phenomenon than being an influencer.

Using the influenced score as a dependent variable, respondents' characteristics accounted for a small 25% of the variance in these scores. Only one respondent characteristic achieved a significant regression coefficient. Once again, state elected officials are more likely to claim to have been influenced as compared to the average elite respondent. No other characteristic reaches statistical significance, although educational attainment approaches conventional standards.

In sum, influence means to be a part of the decision-making scene, with the state elected officials being apparently in a good position both to influence others and to be influenced in turn.

CONCLUSIONS

What are the potential policy implications of such findings? First, the data have shown that groups and individuals were not equally active in corrections matters. Further, there appeared to be a division of authority so that across states some groups define corrections as their "turf" while others do not. The same groups were not equally active in all states: rather, each state showed clusters of active groups peculiar to that state.

Second, states differed in the degree to which the configuration of influence was based on personal contact between actors. Some states appeared to have rather "clubby" structures in which a large proportion of interested people were in touch with one another. Other states either were less politically integrated or coordinated activity through different techniques. One would suspect that the "clubby" states might have been more efficient in bringing about corrections reform. Once several key members of the dominant coalition are sold on a given set of reforms they can more easily coordinate their efforts.

Third, states differ in the coalitions dominating corrections issues. Obviously, persons interested in lobbying should know which people can most easily implement their programs. To understand who supports which reforms is of little use without knowing which supporters have "clout."

Fourth, being a member of the state elected officials brings one far into the network of reciprocal influence that surrounds decision making on the state level. (Indeed, it would be surprising if we found to the contrary.) Elite members who were especially well acquainted with powerful groups, who had contacted them and who had either influenced their stands on corrections or been influenced by them tended to be state elected officials and the better educated among our respondents. Since being better educated in our sample means to have some training beyond the B.A. level, this probably means that state level decision making surrounding corrections is dominated by elected officials and lawyers.

NOTES

1. For convenience, we refer to all the categories in Table 1 as "groups" even though some—e.g., a governor—are individuals. Although the groups listed here are ones that we thought might show up typically in most states, we also allowed respondents to add to the list. Groups added by the respondents are shown at the bottom of the list (the last four categories) in Table 1.

2. On the list shown in Table 1.

3. Regressions were run with both "essential support" and "veto power" as dependent variables. As one would expect from the high correlation (.95) reported between these two measures, results of the regressions were only marginally different from each other. In neither case were the regressions significantly different from zero.

4. Correlations are computed across the columns of Table 8. A high correlation between "have influenced" and "been influenced" means that groups with high percentages of respondents claiming to have influenced such groups were also groups for which high percentages claim to have *been* influenced.

5. The average number of groups influenced was 2.62.

6. For those who claimed to have been influenced by any group, the average number of such influenced groups was 4.4.

REFERENCE

BERK, R.A., and ROSSI, P.H. (1977). Prison reform and state elites. Cambridge, Mass.: Ballinger.

Chapter 4

MACROSOCIOLOGY AND IMPRISONMENT

J A M E S   B.   J A C O B S

Prisons do not exist in a vacuum: they are part of a political, social, economic, and moral order. Besides the intervention of the military to maintain internal order, imprisonment is society's most important instrument of coercive control. Who is sent to prison, the deprivations which are imposed, and the authority vested in the custodians reveal much about a society's values, its distribution of power, and its system of legal rights and obligations. Thus, many of the most important characteristics of a society can be inferred from an examination of its prisons. In part, this insight is captured in the famous observation that the level of a society's civilization can be judged by the state of its prisons.

Prisoners are not drawn randomly from a population. On the contrary, the character of the prisoner population reflects the stratification system of the larger society. The social and occupational origins of the prison staff, especially when compared with the employees of other state bureaucracies, mark the status of the penal institution. A comparison of the residuum of legal rights left to the prisoner with those rights held by society's members-in-good-standing illumi-nates the meaning of both citizenship and criminality. The extent to which

AUTHOR'S NOTE: *I am grateful to Professors Rose Goldsen, Joseph Kahl, and Ian MacNeil for their very helpful comments on the manuscript of this chapter.*

prevailing humanitarian norms and values apply to prisoners, the most peripheral members of society, indicates a great deal about the overall moral order.

Therefore, the prison is an important institution for those who seek to understand the way in which society is organized. Moreover, a macro analysis is essential for explaining the organizational life of the prison and its segments. Living and working conditions, the legitimacy or illegitimacy of various disciplinary mechanisms, and the structure of punishments and rewards all depend upon how the prison articulates with the political, economic, and legal systems of the whole society. In this chapter I attempt to direct attention beyond the prison's walls to the society in which the institution is lodged. The theoretical lens that I find most valuable is found in political sociology, more specifically in macrosociology.[1]

A LEGACY OF POLITICAL SOCIOLOGY

Despite a few useful exceptions (Clemmer, 1958:xi; Sykes, 1966:8), most sociological studies of prison reflect an organizational perspective which stresses the day-to-day details of prison life for inmates and staff. Therefore, to discover a macrosociological analysis of the prison, one must cast a wider net. For example, in 1833 Gustave de Beaumont and Alexis de Tocqueville (1964), perhaps the first students of the American penitentiary, linked this penal innovation to the culture, social structure, and political system of the young nation. The French travelers compared the institutions of social control in the American and French societies of the period. They emphasized such differences as (1) the philanthropic and religious traditions giving rise to the American penitentiary movement, (2) the egalitarianism of American society responsible for the absence of class privileges inside the penitentiary, and (3) the effect of public opinion in America in setting limits on prison policies and conditions. They hypothesized that it was easier to maintain order in the American penitentiary because of the more pervasive commitment to law and order in American society generally, lamenting that

> this spirit of submission to the established order does not exist in the same degree with us. On the contrary, there is in France, in the spirit of the masses, an unhappy tendency to violate the law, and this inclination to insubordination seems to us to be of a nature to embarrass the regular operation of the [prison] discipline. [de Beaumont and de Tocqueville, 1964:121]

A second classic comparative macrosociological study of imprisonment is Georg Rusche and Otto Kirchheimer's (1939) analysis of the evolution of punishment in Europe from the 12th to the 20th centuries. The two German emigré sociologists showed the integral relationship between the institutions of punishment and a society's economic system. They argued that the emergence of the modern prison was linked to the transformation of the European economic system (from feudalism to mercantilism to industrial capitalism) and to demographic changes, which by the 19th century had established a situation of chronic surplus labor. By the mid-19th century, the economic function of the precursors of the modern prison (workhouses) was undermined, and the prison's role of keeping the working poor in the labor market became more explicit.

By the late 19th and early 20th century, the masses were participating more fully in the material advantages of modern society. In addition, according to Rusche and Kirchheimer, there was a wider acceptance of a "sociological" understanding of criminality, which emphasized society's responsibility for crime as well as the need for "scientific treatment" of the criminal. These trends supported the ideology of "rehabilitation." It is impossible to understand what is at stake in most debates about penal policy inside and outside the prison without appreciating the history of rehabilitation as an ideology since the founding of the American penitentiary.

Rusche and Kirchheimer stressed that the way in which prison articulates with the economic system has crucial implications for penal practices and conditions. They pointed to the near universal acceptance of the principle of "less eligibility" as setting limits to the potential for penal reform. This is said to be true because, if prison conditions were made preferable to the circumstances of the next-best-off segment of the population, the working poor would cease to be deterred from dropping out of the work force and joining the ranks of the criminal lumpen proletariat.

No recent scholars have approached the topic of imprisonment from as broad a comparative macrosociological perspective as de Beaumont and de Tocqueville or Rusche and Kirchheimer.[2] Selected research on the German concentration camps and on prisoner-of-war camps, however, constitute important contributions to a prison tradition in political sociology. The ways in which the concentration camps articulated with the race ideology of National Socialism and the economic requirements of the German war economy demonstrate the bases for both slave labor and genocide. One student of the camps, H.G. Adler (1958:514), explicitly embraced political sociology:

One may look at the concentration camp within the system of contemporary society, especially within the authoritarian and terroristic states. In a world made vulnerable, or at least strongly influenced, by the ideas of enlightenment, the purely secular state, the new democracy, and secular socialism, the fate of the man who dissents from the guiding principles and idea of the ruling group has become important: how he is to be rendered innocuous as soon as the ruling group feels threatened by him and how, under whatever pretense, that group discards all protections granted by the constitutional state and the democratic guarantees for personal inviolability. The dissenter is excluded from the community of those who conform, sent to the concentration camp, or killed. This approach to the study of the concentration camp would begin with the position of the ruling group, paying particular attention to political and economic conditions.

The concentration camp research illustrates the most complete exclusion of the imprisoned from the rights of citizenship. It demonstrates the convergence of political, economic, and social circumstances which make it possible for a society to destroy its prisoners without contradicting law, public opinion, or political leadership.

Studies of prisoner-of-war camps also show how institutions of confinement and control articulate with the political and military objectives of the state. In his analysis of Chinese prisons of the early 1950s, Edgar Schien (1960) pointed out that the techniques of coercive persuasion used on Western prisoners were an expression of a cultural emphasis on unanimity and that the treatment of Western prisoners was merely an extension of the policy used to "convert" Chinese peasants to the communist cause.

Albert Biderman (1968) has argued that the administration of prisoner-of-war camps is an extension of broader military and political conflict. The treatment afforded the enemy's prisoners of war will depend upon the captor power's sensitivity to international opinion and its concern for the treatment of its own prisoners. Of more general significance for all prison studies is Biderman's observation that the degree of control exerted over prisoners of war has fateful implications for the type of social system which will develop among the prisoners. The more unlimited (by law, public opinion, etc.) the captor's recourse to coercive sanctions and the more repressive the organizational regime, the more likely it is that predatory relations will develop among the prisoners. Where administrators are constrained by national or international law, it is more likely that the captives will be able to maintain the structure of military or criminal organization imported from the outside (see Jacobs, 1976).

This tradition of prison studies in political sociology emphasizes comparative study at the level of the nation-state. While the research constituting this tradition has been important, it suffers from several limitations. The Rusche and Kirchheimer book stressed materialism at the expense of almost all other variables. No room was left in their analysis, for example, for the role of religious thought in the evolution of institutions of social control. De Beaumont and de Tocqueville stressed cultural variables, but their study was cursory and limited to a comparison of America and France. While instructive, neither the concentration camp nor the prison-of-war research has been integrated with sociological studies of society's more typical penal institutions. In the rest of this chapter I suggest ways to extend the tradition which now exists.

PUNISHMENT AND SOCIAL STRUCTURE

From the perspective of political sociology it is important to trace how each prison segment (inmates, guards, administrators, treatment personnel, etc.) articulates with society's systems of stratification. The social origins of the staff, prisoners, and interest groups serve as indicators of the prison's status in a particular society.[3] It makes a difference whether the management of the prison is entrusted to people who share elite status with those who administer other state bureaucracies or whether it is entrusted to members of nonelite groups who cannot get better jobs.[4] It is a worthy hypothesis that, where prison administrators are drawn from the same groups as other bureaucrats, the prison will tend to be run more like other state agencies. On the other hand, we should not overlook the possibility that the powerful constraints impinging on prison management might limit the impact of a change in the social class background of the administrators.

Not only the social status of the prison's leadership, but its occupational status as well, is of utmost importance (see European Committee on Crime Problems, 1963). Whether a country has turned over the administration of its institutions of punishment to the clergy (as in some Latin American countries), or to the top levels of the civil service (as in Austria), or to the national police (as in the Soviet Union), or to the mental health professions (as in some cases in the United States and Western Europe) will have important implications for the formulation of penal policy, the maintenance of discipline, and the promotion of humanitarian objectives.

Just as significant for explaining the day-to-day operation of the prison is the origin of the front line staff. In his classic essay "Good People and Dirty Work," Everett Hughes (1964:33) stated that "it is likely that the individuals recruited to run the Nazi concentration camps were *gescheiterte Existenzen,* men or women with a history of failure, of poor adaptation to the demands of work and of the classes of society in which they had been bred." But what is problematic, according to Hughes and to my analysis as well, is not the existence of such elements, but the process by which certain segments of the population are recruited to staff the institutions of punishment and control. Whether the guards are drawn from the ranks of the unemployed, military service veterans, displaced farm workers, or aspiring law enforcement officers and bureaucrats should help to explain day-to-day behavior.

Where the organization's rank and file and the prisoners are drawn from dissimilar and antagonistic segments of a society one would expect the same culture conflicts that occur on the streets to be imported into the prisons. Hostility between rural white guards and urban black prisoners, while frequently exaggerated, has been so often pointed to as a key source of conflict in American prisons that to ignore it would surely be a significant oversight. On the other hand, almost no attention has been paid to conflicts which occur between guards and inmates presumably drawn from the same classes, a common situation in large metropolitan jails in the United States.

Class conflict may also occur between the penal organization's rank and file and its administrative elite. J.E. Thomas' thorough study (1972) of the English prison officer reported how members of the educated middle class gradually dominated the top positions in the prison service, leading to the alienation and demoralization of the guard force. The prison officers perceived (with much justification) that an "alliance" existed between liberal administrators and prisoners, both groups blaming the guards for the "failures" of the prison system.

My own case study of Stateville Penitentiary (Jacobs, 1977), Illinois' largest maximum security prison, is consistent with Thomas' research. In 1970 the Stateville warden who had risen through the ranks and who shared a background and ideology identical to the rank and file was replaced by a young college-educated professional oriented toward treatment. The new warden's first expressions of empathy with the plight of the prisoners convinced the guards that he was "for the cons." The subsequent estrangement of the rank and file from the growing number of professional administrators resulted in a deterioration of the prison's ability to provide food, showers, clothing, mail, and other basic services. Ultimately the breakdown of administration led to more and more violence and a "crisis in control."

The trend toward bureaucratizing and professionalizing the prisons in Great Britain and the United States has been strong, at least since the mid-1960s. (Indeed, John Conrad, 1965, has suggested the existence of a professional cadre of prison administrators throughout Western and Eastern Europe.) Whether this trend will continue and whether the same trend is evident in societies with different political, economic, and social systems and at different "stages of development" are questions worthy of extensive empirical research.

The prisoners themselves, of course, do not represent a cross section of an entire societal population, but may be drawn disproportionately from racial, ethnic, religious, or regional minorities. Whether the prisoners are members of groups of higher than marginal status on the outside will partly determine the parameters of the conditions and policies of confinement. What penal deprivations are defined as legitimate substantially depends on the social, economic, and political status of those who are imprisoned.

Almost one hundred and fifty years ago de Beaumont and de Tocqueville observed that the egalitarianism of American society prevented social status from being recognized inside the penitentiary. This was in sharp distinction to the equivalent French institutions, where a prisoner with sufficient wealth could supplement substantially his diet and living conditions. The issue of whether social class differences are explicitly or implicitly recognized in prison continues to be important.[5] It is reported that Mexican prisoners can rely on their personal resources to purchase better food and other benefits (*New York Times,* May 23, 1976:22). The same is true in Pakistan, where the laws prescribe different entitlements for prisoners drawn from different social strata. Prisoners in the higher tax brackets and those with higher education are provided "better class" accommodations.[6] Social class penetrates the prison more indirectly in Colombia, which designates separate penal facilities for violators of traffic laws (including vehicular homicide) who are drawn disproportionately from the members of the urban sector, including chauffeurs.[7]

THE PRISONER AND THE RIGHTS OF CITIZENSHIP

The definition of who is a member of the community and what rights and obligations membership entails are central issues for understanding the emergence of mass society and the welfare state. In his seminal lectures on "Citizenship and Social Class," T.H. Marshall (1964) distinguished three aspects of citizenship—civil, political, and social. Civil citizenship meant "the rights necessary for individual freedom—liberty of person, freedom of speech, thought and faith, the right to own property and to conclude valid contracts and the rights to justice." Also included was the right to bargain collectively over the conditions of employment. He defined political citizenship as "the right to participate in the exercise of political power, as a member of a body invested with political authority or as an elector of the members of such a body." Social citizenship designated "the whole range from the right to a modicum of economic welfare and security to the right to share to the full in the social heritage and to live the life of a civilized being according to standards prevailing in the society." All three aspects of citizenship are problematic for those convicted and punished for violating the criminal laws (see Cohen and Rivkin, 1971).[8] How modern societies have accommodated notions of citizenship with criminal jurisprudence is an important distinguishing characteristic of different types of contemporary regimes.

Civil Rights of Citizenship

In a recent judicial opinion (*Miller* v. *Twomey*, 1973) Judge (now Justice) John Paul Stevens wrote for the 7th Circuit Court of Appeals:

> Liberty protected by the due process clause may—indeed must to some extent—coexist with legal custody pursuant to conviction. The deprivation of liberty following an adjudication of guilt is partial, not total. A residuum of constitutionally protected rights remains. . . . The view once held that an inmate is a mere slave of the state is now totally rejected. The restraints and the punishment which a criminal conviction entails do not place a citizen beyond the ethical tradition that accords respect to the dignity and intrinsic worth of every individual. Liberty and custody are not mutually exclusive concepts.

Precisely this question, whether imprisonment is necessarily incompatible with the rights and obligations of society's members-in-good-standing leads us to compare the juridical systems of different modern states. In those societies not ensuring freedom of speech and religion to members-in-good-standing, of course, there is no need to enquire whether those liberties are held by felons. What is important is to identify the rights of citizenship withdrawn from the convicted criminal. Does the prisoner lose the rights to contract, marry, divorce, inherit property, and use the courts?

In Argentina, for example, an individual sentenced to three years of imprisonment or more suffers *inhabilitación* (absolute disqualification), forfeiting paternal rights *(patria potestas),* the right of administering his estate, and the right of disposing of it by *inter vivos* transactions. He is placed under the creator-guardianship system of the civil code.[9]

In the United States, much has been written about the extraordinary post-World War II legal changes extending the civil rights of citizenship to minorities, criminal defendants, servicemen, students, women, the mentally ill, and, more recently, the mentally retarded. The momentum generated by the expansion of civil rights and liberties inexorably penetrated the prison's wall. The same trend toward the extension of substantive and procedural rights to prisoners, although to a more limited extent, is evident also in Great Britain (see Williams, 1975) and Canada. In West Germany and Japan recent legal developments have broadened the opportunity of prisoners to formally object to the way in which they are being treated.

The Scandanavian countries have gone furthest in providing that the rights of prisoners are coextensive with those of society's members-in-good-standing. One recent student of the Swedish penal system (Solomon, 1976) has observed:

There is a sense of oneness of community, that pervades Swedish society. Perhaps best expressed by the former Swedish prime minister, Per Albin Hansson, "the nation was seen as a home—folkhemmet—with its citizens as members of a single family." In terms of crime, *Swedes regard convicted persons as citizens who have broken the law, but nonetheless as citizens.* [emphasis added]

In Denmark and Sweden the governments have recognized prisoners' unions and have bargained over living conditions, wages, and prison policy (Ward, 1972). What limits there are on how fully prisoners can enjoy the rights of civil citizenship without sacrificing the moral component of criminal jurisprudence is a crucial sociolegal problem for the modern welfare state.

That there are limits is suggested by recent shifts in public opinion in the direction of more punitive attitudes toward those who break the law. In addition, at some point the assertion of individual rights and liberties by prisoners conflicts with the administrative discretion required to successfully manage such volatile institutions as prisons. The intrusion of juridical norms into Illinois' Stateville Penitentiary (Jacobs, 1977) exposed the administrative deficiencies of the old authoritarian regime which operated according to tradition rather than by written rules and regulations. For example, the authoritarian regime was unable to justify in court why it treated Black Muslims differently from members of traditional religions, despite the prison leadership's certainty that First Amendment claims were only a facade for "troublemakers" intent on their own self-aggrandizement.

By demanding some form of rational decision-making process, the courts hastened the demise of Stateville's old regime. But the professional treatment-oriented administrators who next assumed command were only marginally more capable of fending off the increased legal challenges of prisoners and their public interest counsel. For a system of decision making based upon custom and tradition, the professional treatment-oriented administrators substituted a system based on "professional" judgment and discretion. State laws, court decisions, and the central department's own regulations were not followed consistently.

A breakdown of control and of the provision of basic services finally led to the emergence of a more rational legal bureaucracy, whose leaders were explicitly committed to rationalizing and making visible the processes and justifications for institutional decision making. But the strain caused by the intrusion of juridical norms has not dissipated entirely. While the actual substance of the federal court decisions have generally not directly attacked the basic needs of prison administration, the recognition of prisoners' constitutional rights continues to have important indirect effects. The fear of being sued, and particularly of being held personally and financially liable, has demoralized the staff. The substantial administrative burden of responding to lawsuits and providing "due process" (hearings, appeals, etc.) strains an organization chronically short of resources and constantly facing the threat of individual and collective violence.

Political Prisoners

In many countries, the civil as well as the political and social rights to which a prisoner is entitled depend upon whether he is defined as a political prisoner. It is an open question how political prisoners will be treated. They are not universally granted fewer rights than common criminals. Political prisoners can be separate but equal, separate but unequal, or integrated on an equal or unequal basis with common criminals. In political systems in which the change of leadership is fluid, the imprisonment of political opponents may be a regular part of the political process, and the conditions of such prisons may not be as repressive as those housing run-of-the-mill offenders. Adolph Hitler, for example, wrote *Mein Kampf* while serving a prison term in the Landsberg fortress, a special facility for political prisoners, to which he was sentenced after the abortive Beer Hall Putsch of 1923. During the struggle for independence on the Indian subcontinent, such political prisoners as Gandhi and Nehru were treated almost as plenipotentates. As the struggle expanded and demonstrators began to flood the prisons, the government decided to treat lesser political prisoners the same as common criminals in the hope of deterring them (Barker, 1944). [10]

American law does not recognize political crimes, although other Western democracies like France have explicit designations for political crimes and special prisons for political prisoners (La Santé in Paris). In the United States it is assumed that the political institutions of society are flexible enough to resolve all legitimate political conflict. This is not to say that there have not always been American prisoners who have preferred to define themselves and have been defined by their fellow prisoners as political (e.g., Jackson, 1970, 1972; Flynn, 1972; Wright, 1973). The prison in the Anglo-American system is not explicitly defined as a *political* institution. The prisoners are not defined as enemies of the state and as offenders against the political order, but rather as actors opposing the social order. Perhaps as a result, the political system can more easily accommodate reform efforts aimed at "helping" the prisoners and justify the prison as an institution of rehabilitation.

To either explicitly recognize or deny the prison's political purpose has important implications for the day-to-day treatment of those who are confined. Where, as in the Soviet Union, the prisons are used to enforce political and economic orthodoxy, one would expect the relationship of the staff to the prisoners to be quite different from what it is in those societies in which the prisoners are offenders against life and property but are seen as victims of the system. Because political prisoners in the Soviet Union are enemies of the state, the officials need not be accountable for their survival (Cressey and Krassowski, 1958; Solzhenitsyn, 1973, 1975). Aside from the few prisoners with an international reputation, no interest groups exist committed to protecting their rights. In the Soviet labor camps the common criminals are offered some advantages in exchange for their repression of the political prisoners. Another extreme example is the Nazi concentration camp, where the inmates were granted no rights of citizenship whatsoever, having been placed beyond the bounds of the political community (Kogon, 1966).

One danger in explicitly recognizing "political crime" and separating political prisoners from other types of offenders is that they will reinforce each other's opposition to the regime. Consider the case of the well-known sociologist Gino Germani, who was imprisoned for political activity in fascist Italy during the 1930s.

> He learned two specific lessons from the prison experience. First that working-class culture had a coherence and vitality of its own. (His own lower-middle-class background had not exposed him to the true prole-tarian culture before.) For example, there were songs and codes for sending messages through the jail walls that originated in social protest movements a century earlier; all workers knew them and were astonished that Germani did not. Second, he was exposed to both Marxism and the Communist Party. Many radical intellectuals, "some of the best people in Italy" were on the prison island, as were many leaders of the party. [Kahl, 1976]

Of course, mixing political (or politicized) prisoners with garden variety offenders raises the risk of politicizing the entire prisoner population, particularly if certain social definitions (such as ethnicity) link them together.

Political Rights of Citizenship

In *Reynolds* v. *Simms* (1964), one of the great reapportionment cases of the 1960s, Chief Justice Earl Warren wrote, "The right to vote freely for the candidate of one's choice is of the essence of a democratic society, and any restrictions on that right strikes at the heart of representative government." The Chief Justice also pointed out that "history has seen a continuing expansion of the scope of the right to suffrage in this country." Given the centrality of the franchise to the meaning of citizenship, one of the most poignant indications of what conviction of crime means is the disenfranchisement accompanying it.

Indeed, in many states in the United States, an individual convicted of a serious crime *loses the right to vote forever,* unless pardoned by the chief executive.

The drive toward equality that gained momentum throughout the decade of the 1960s led to the passage of the Voting Rights Act and judicial decisions striking down various restrictions on suffrage which prevented minorities from participating in the political process. One might have thought it only a matter of time before the disenfranchisement of prisoners and ex-prisoners would be struck down as well. This proved not to be the case, although the state's interest in disenfranchising felons was not entirely clear (see *Stanford Law Review,* 1973). Even in a Western democracy like Australia, where voting is an obligation (failure to vote is punishable by a fine), individuals serving a sentence for a crime carrying a penalty of one year or more of imprisonment are denied the vote.

Rejecting a prisoner's challenge to the New York law, Judge Henry Friendly of the 2nd U.S. Circuit Court of Appeals put forth the following justification for placing the convict outside the bounds of the political community:

> The early exclusion of felons from franchise by many states could well have rested on Locke's concept . . . that by entering into society every man authorizes the society . . . to make laws for him as the public good of the society shall require. A man who breaks the laws he has authorized his agent to make for his own governance could fairly have been thought to have abandoned the right to participate in further administering the compact. [*Green* v. *Board of Elections,* 1967]

In 1974, the U.S. Supreme Court upheld California's voting law disenfranchising *ex*-felons, thereby putting to rest the legal efforts to extend suffrage to prisoners and ex-prisoners. Writing for the unanimous court, Justice William Rehnquist said:

> Pressed upon us by the respondents, and by amici curiae, are contentions that these notions are outmoded, and that the more modern view is that it is essential to the process of rehabilitating the ex-felon that he be returned to his role in society as a fully participating citizen when he has completed serving his term. . . . But it is not for us to choose one set of values over another. If respondents are correct, and the view which they advocate is indeed the more enlightened and sensible one, presumably the people of the State of California will ultimately come around to that view. And if they do not do so, their failure is some evidence, at least, of the fact that there are two sides to the argument. [*Richardson* v. *Ramirez,* 1974]

Prisoners are not *automatically* disenfranchised in every state in the United States or in all other countries. In those states where disenfranchisement has not been prescribed for all prisoners there has been no opportunity to vote because of the absence of prison polling facilities and absentee ballots. Even with respect to unconvicted pretrial detainees, the refusal to provide absentee ballots has been held not to violate the U.S. Constitution (*McDonald* v. *Board of Election Commissioners of Chicago,* 1969).[11] In West Germany the court has the discretion to deprive the convicted criminal of the right to seek office or to vote if the criminal law specifically provides for this penalty. The laws which do provide for disenfranchisement are those proscribing breaches of the peace, high treason, and endangering the democratic constitutional state. Thus, common criminals are typically permitted to vote by absentee ballot.

In Sweden, also, prisoners are permitted to exercise the franchise. A prisoners' union was formed in Sweden in 1966, and in 1968 its efforts succeeded in changing the law to allow prisoners to vote in general elections. The right of Swedish prisoners to vote and to bargain collectively with the state over wages, hours, and conditions of work marks the furthest extension of the definition of citizenship to prisoners in a Western democracy.

Loss of the right to vote is not the only forfeiture of the political rights of citizenship attached to criminal conviction. The prohibition on holding public office, the ban against service in the armed forces, and exclusion from jury service should also be considered in the same context. The extent to which such political rights are taken away and for how long would be an important issue in carrying out comparative macrosociological research.

Social Rights of Citizenship

In many modern societies the state takes responsibility for assuring the citizen-in-good-standing some minimum standard of living and certain other social and economic benefits and protections. For example, the welfare state provides compensation to those who are unemployed, welfare to those who cannot support themselves, disability payments to those injured on the job. Public education is provided without charge.

At issue for our purposes here is the extent to which these benefits are forfeited once an individual is convicted of crime and committed to prison. Does the social welfare system extend behind the walls? In the United States and England, to take two well-known examples, education is widely available to prisoners. The rules governing the English prison system even provide that illiterates may attend to their schooling instead of working, and almost every prison with which I am familiar in the United States has some sort of educational program. Recent Illinois legislation provides that the state prisons constitute a separate school district on a par with all others in the state. Basic education seems almost to have achieved the status of a right for prisoners in Great Britain and the United States. In addition, social work services, psychological therapy, and job counseling are typical aspects of the American prison regime.

Although the welfare state extends to prisoners, its coverage is only partial. Typically in the United States workman's compensation does not apply to prisoners who are injured in the course of institutional labor. Social security continues to be paid to prisoners, except to those convicted of espionage and similar crimes, who may in the discretion of the court have their social security forfeited forever. In Argentina, *inhabilitación* includes the suspension of state pensions and social security benefits.

One should also consider here the significant deprivations on the right to work which are imposed upon ex-prisoners. In the United States hundreds of occupations are closed to those with a felony record. Where such restrictions on the pursuit of a calling are placed upon ex-prisoners, the society has reinforced the definition of the prisoner as a noncitizen, almost a pariah.

MORAL STATUS OF THE PRISONER IN MASS SOCIETY

Since World War II strong evidence suggests that in the United States, and elsewhere in the West, there has occurred a transition in the prisoner's status. Whereas previously the prisoner had been a pariah, totally separated from the mainstream society, its central institutions and moral community, that status has attenuated as ties have proliferated between outside forces (interest groups, volunteers, courts, media, etc.) and those incarcerated for crime. It would be interesting to explore the question of whether the prisoner is more "acceptable" in American society today.

There is also some indication that a heightened sensitivity to the humanness of the prisoner is occurring in other countries as well. In a survey of correctional practices around the world, John Conrad (1965) found a remarkably "modern" consensus among top prison officials in capitalist and socialist countries alike. The consensus is stated in five postulates: (1) offenders are social deviates; something is wrong with them; (2) punishment exacted by the system is futile; commitment to the prison system is punishment enough; (3) during the period of commitment the correctional agency has an obligation to administer a regime which will equip offenders to "lead a good and useful life on discharge"; (4) because the treatment required by the offender varies from individual to individual in accordance with what is "wrong" with each, the duration and circumstances of the commitment must also vary; (5) all correctional agencies have an obligation to maintain control over committed offenders.

Even if Conrad's observations are still accurate, this is not to say, of course, that actual practice always follows the ideology put out for public consumption. It is an important empirical task to chart the "fit" between law, ideology, and social reality. Still, what seems significant is the strong sense among contemporary prison "professionals" that national and international opinion (embodied in the United Nation's *Standard Minimum Rule for the Treatment of Criminals*) expects a benign and rehabilitative stance toward the prisoner.

Given such developments, it would be most interesting to test Edward Shils's (1962) controversial theory of "mass society" by examining the penal systems of various societies. The key characteristic of "mass society," according to Shils's specialized use of that term, is the heightened sensitivity of the elite to the dignity, moral worth, and humanity of the masses. Whether or not the political and moral aspects of "modernization" have led to a redefinition of the criminal's moral status is a question which might shed light on the growth and elaboration of the welfare state in at least several democratic states. The mass society conception seems less appealing when we look at the moral status of the prisoner in authoritarian (leftist or rightist) societies in which torture, at least of a significant number of "political prisoners," continues (e.g., Laber, 1976). Ideology may be more useful in seeking to explain the differential treatment of prisoners in various industrialized societies. Still, Shils's point is worth pursuing: Does "development," at least under certain circumstances, lead to a greater appreciation of the prisoner's moral worth?

RECOURSE TO COERCIVE SANCTIONS

One key indicator of the prisoner's moral status is the coercive measures which prison officials are permitted to use to maintain order and discipline. At the time that de Beaumont and de Tocqueville toured the American penitentiaries, use of corporal punishment was widespread. In the decades that followed it was utilized on an even greater scale. As was the case with capital punishment, the use of corporal punishment in the United States tapered off in the decades following World War II. For example, in 1968 the last state prison system using the whip to maintain discipline was held to be violating the Eighth Amendment's proscription against cruel and unusual punishment (*Jackson* v. *Bishop,* 1968). Heightened sensitivity to the dignity and moral worth of the prisoner has also led courts to strike down many other practices and conditions. The list includes aversive conditioning, excessive overcrowding, sensory deprivation, use of Thorazine, poor medical care, poor diet, etc. In several cases, not merely prison practices but the prison (or jail) itself has been declared violative of "evolving standards of decency which are the mark of a civilized society."

Recent exposés of conditions in French prisons have led to the establishment of a cabinet level minister in charge of penal facilities in that country. In England, according to Conrad (1965:13), the reintroduction of corporal punishment is "massively blocked by the unwillingness of any public agency, especially the Prison Commission, to administer it. It is as though the correctional administrator, having shed the role of turnkey, finds his new role too attractive to return to the old ways."

None of this is to say that all abuses have disappeared from the prisons. Clearly, this is not the case in American prisons or, for that matter, in schools, courts, hospitals, old age homes, welfare bureaucracies, etc. Nor is it to say that prison conditions will continue to improve unilinearly. It may be that, the drive toward redefining the moral status of the prisoner having temporarily reached its limits, there is now a countertrend which reemphasizes the threat of criminality and the necessity of punishment.

Comparative macrosociological inquiry might profitably focus upon the kinds of coercive sanctions permitted in various societies. Which countries, for example, allow corporal punishment, deprivation of food, electric shock, torture, and killing? To what extent are the prison administrators held accountable for the lives and well-being of their prisoners? Are records kept? Are investigations pursued? Are prison officials and lower echelon personnel ever held liable before the criminal and civil law for abuses in their treatment of prisoners?

CONCLUSION

I began this chapter by noting that prison scholarship is dominated by micro level analyses of the attitudes, values, and roles of prisoners and staff. I hope to have shown that the findings of these many studies could be enriched by paying more attention to the shifting role of the prison in modern society. Both longitudinal and comparative cross-sectional studies might illuminate which trends in the larger society are most responsible for the organization that develops behind the walls.

Beyond shedding light on the operation of the prison, however, the types of macrosociological research on which I have touched should be pursued because they may add much to our basic knowledge of the dynamics of total societies. Imprisonment is the keystone of coercive control in modern society. How the prison and its segments articulate with the larger society will increase our understanding of society's distribution of power, stratification, and system of legal rights and obligations.

NOTES

1. Morris Janowitz (1970) has noted that the term "macrosociology" should be reserved for holistic studies of entire societies. Comparative macrosociology has most often

focused on modernization and the consequences of economic and social trends for political institutions. The lack of macrosociological study of prisons is surprising given the centrality of the institutions of social control in defining social and political norms.

2. David Rothman's recent (1971) historical study of the rise of the American penitentiary in the first three decades of the 19th century constituted an important institutional analysis, albeit not a comparative study, of the prison. Rothman argued that the invention of the penitentiary in the early 19th century was a product of the idealism of the Jacksonian period which led to the belief that the young American nation had almost unlimited capacity to solve its social problems.

3. With characteristic insight, de Beaumont and de Tocqueville (1964:63) made this connection:

> In investigating the organization of the new establishments, we have been struck with the importance which is attached to the individuals who direct them. As soon as the penitentiary system was adopted in the United States, the personnel changed in nature. For jailor of a prison, vulgar people only could be found; the most distinguished persons offered themselves to administer a penitentiary where moral direction exists.

The authors also reflected on the type of individuals who involved themselves in watching over how the prisons were run (p. 80):

> There are in America, as well as in Europe, estimable men whose minds feed upon philosophical reveries, and whose extreme sensibilities feel the want of some illusion. These men, for whom philanthropy has become a matter of necessity, find in the penitentiary a nourishment of this passion. . . . Others, perhaps without so profound a conviction, pursue, nevertheless, the same course; they occupy themselves continually with prisons; it is the subject to which all the labors of their life bear reference. Philanthropy has become for them a kind of profession, and they have caught the monomania of the penitentiary system, which to them seems the remedy for all evils of the society.

4. Erving Goffman (1961:121) has pointed to the significance of the status background of the "total institution's" leadership for legitimizing institutional authority:

> If [the topmost staff] are to move with grace and effectiveness in the wider community, then it may be advantageous for them to be recruited from the same small social grouping as leaders of other social units in the wider society. Further, if staff persons are uniformly recruited from a stratum in the wider society that has a firmly legitimated higher ranking than the stratum from which inmates are uniformly recruited, then the cleavage in the wider society will presumably lend support and stability to the rule of the staff.

5. One of America's most famous prisoners, the late Nathan Leopold (1957), suggested that in the 1930s and 1940s the often noted stratification among prisoners based on their offense was really a stratification system based on social class. The assignment of prisoners to minimum, medium, and maximum security institutions within a single prison system also raises important questions about the impact of social class on punishment within prison (see Steele and Jacobs, 1977).

6. I am indebted to Wasim Bari Salimi for bringing to my attention the Pakistini and Indian laws cited in this chapter.

7. I am indebted to my colleague, Professor Rose K. Goldsen, for calling this practice to my attention.

8. The notion that the criminal should be stripped of his citizenship and made to suffer a "civil death" can be traced to Greek and Roman societies.

9. I am indebted to my colleague Oscar Garibaldi for bringing to my attention and translating the Argentine law.

10. Note the parallel in *A Clockwork Orange* (Burgess, 1962:92):

He just sort of looked right through us poor plennies, saying in a very beautiful real educated goloss: "The Government cannot be concerned any longer with outmoded penological theories. Cram prisoners together and see what happens. You get concentrated criminality, crime in the midst of punishment. *Soon we may be needing all our prison space for political offenders"* (emphasis added).

11. A controversy widely carried in American newspapers and newsmagazines during the spring and summer of 1976 involved a lower court's interpretation of Massachusetts' voting law. The court held that, in the absence of explicit disenfranchising and of any limitation on entitlement to absentee ballots, prisoners were allowed to vote. Inmate Carl Vellaca of the Massachusetts Correctional Institution in Concord ran for a seat on the Board of Selectmen. Despite a vigorous campaign, the prisoner lost. But the controversy has stimulated efforts to close the "loopholes" in the Massachusetts law.

REFERENCES

ADLER, H. (1958). "Ideas toward a sociology of the concentration camp." American Journal of Sociology, 63:513-522.

BARKER, F. (1944). The modern prison system in India. London: Macmillan.

BIDERMAN, A. (1968). "Internment and custody." Vol. 8, pp. 139-148 in D.E. Sills (ed.), International encyclopedia of the social sciences. New York: Macmillan.

BURGESS, A. (1962). A clockwork orange. New York: Norton.

CLEMMER, D. (1958). The prison community. New York: Rinehart.

COHEN, N., and RIVKIN, D. (1971). "Civil disabilities: The forgotten punishment." Federal Probation, 35:19.

CONRAD, J. (1965). Crime and its correction. Berkeley: University of California Press.

CRESSEY, D., and KRASSOWSKI, W. (1958). "Inmate organization and Soviet labor camps." Social Problems, 5(winter):217-229.

De BEAUMONT, G., and de TOCQUEVILLE, A. (1964). On the penitentiary system in the United States and its application in France. Carbondale: Southern Illinois University Press.

European Committee on Crime Problems (1963). The status, selection and training of prison staff. Stasbourg: Council of Europe.

FLYNN, E. (1972). My life as a political prisoner. New York: International Publishers.

GOFFMAN, E. (1961). Asylums. Garden City, N.Y.: Doubleday.

Green v. Board of Elections (1967). 380 F.2d 445 (2nd cir.).

HUGHES, E. (1964). "Good people and dirty work." In H. Becker (ed.). The other side: Perspectives on deviance. London: Free Press of Glencoe.

JACKSON, G. (1970). Soledad brother: The prison letters of George Jackson. New York: Coward, McCann, and Geoghegan.

——— (1972). Blood in my eye. New York: Random House.

Jackson v. Bishop (1968). 404 F.2d 561, (8th cir.).

JACOBS, J. (1976). "Stratification and conflict among prison inmates." Journal of Criminal Law and Criminology, 66:476-482.

——— (1977). Stateville: The penitentiary in mass society. Chicago: University of Chicago Press.

JANOWITZ, M. (1970). "The logic of political conflict." In M. Janowitz, Political conflict: Essays in political sociology. Chicago: Quadrangle Books.

KAHL, J. (1976). Modernization, exploitation and dependency in Latin America. New Brunswick, N.J.: Transaction Books.

KOGON, E. (1966). The theory and practice of hell. New York: Berkley Medallion.

LABER, J. (1976). "Philippines torture." New York Times, October 30, p. 23.

LEOPOLD, N. (1957). Life plus ninety-nine years. Garden City, N.Y.: Doubleday.

MARSHALL, T.H. (1964). "Citizenship and social class." In Class, citizenship and social development. Garden City, N.Y.: Doubleday.

McDonald v. Board of Election Commissioners of Chicago (1969). 394 U.S. 802.

Miller v. Twomey (1973). 479 F.2d 701 (7th cir.).

Reynolds v. Simms (1964). 377 U.S. 533.

Richardson v. Ramirez (1974). 418 U.S. 24.

ROTHMAN, D. (1971). Discovery of the asylum: Social order and disorder in the republic. Boston: Little, Brown.

RUSCHE, G., and KIRCHHEIMER, O. (1939). Punishment and social structure. New York: Russel and Russel.

SCHIEN, E. (1960). Coercive persuasion. New York: Norton.

SHILS, E. (1962). "The theory of mass society." Diogenes, 39.

SOLOMON, R. (1976). "Lessons from the Swedish criminal justice system: A reappraisal." Federal Probation, 40(3):40-48.

SOLZHENITSYN, A. (1973). The Gulag Archipelogo. New York: Harper and Row.

——— (1975). The Gulag Archipelogo II. New York: Harper and Row.

Stanford Law Review (1973). "Note, disenfranchisement of ex-felons: A re-assessment." 25:845.

STEELE, E., and JACOBS, J. (1977). "Untangling minimum security: Concepts, realities and implications for correctional systems." J. of Res. in Crime and Delinquency, 14(1):68-83.

SYKES, G. (1966). Society of captives. New York: Random House.

THOMAS, J. (1972). The English prison officer since 1850. London: Routledge and Kegan Paul.

WARD, D. (1972). "Inmate rights and prison reform in Sweden." Journal of Criminal Law, Criminology and Political Science, 63.

WILLIAMS, J. (1975). Changing prisons. London: Peter Owen.

WRIGHT, E. (1973). The politics of punishment. New York: Harper and Row.

PART II.

THE FUNCTIONS
OF
CORRECTIONS AND PUNISHMENT

Chapter 5

THE CORRECTIONAL EFFECTS OF CORRECTIONS: A SURVEY OF EVALUATIONS

DAVID F. GREENBERG

A professed goal of corrections is to prevent future criminal activity on the part of those who are "corrected." This survey will review evaluations of the existing array of correctional dispositions and programs in order to assess the degree to which this goal is being attained.[1]

The survey is organized as follows:

A. Early diversion

B. Probation intensity

C. Imprisonment

D. Probation with nonresidential programs

E. Programs in conventional institutions

F. Unconventional institutions

G. Parole

H. Programs after release

AUTHOR'S NOTE: *An earlier version of this survey was commissioned by the Committee for the Study of Incarceration. I am grateful to Robert Martinson for helpful assistance in the early stages of the preparation of this survey and to Meredith Gould for assistance with the literature search.*

A. EARLY DIVERSION

Contact with Police

In a national sample of juveniles, the rate of self-reported delinquency was higher among juveniles apprehended by the police than among matched juveniles who had escaped apprehension after a delinquency, but the number of youths compared was small (Gold and Williams, 1969). In a larger study of a Philadelphia male birth cohort, boys who received more serious police dispositions were more likely to be apprehended for later delinquencies than those who received the more lenient disposition (Wolfgang et al., 1972). Neither study can exclude spuriousness due to uncontrolled variables, and the Philadelphia study cannot distinguish higher offense rates from higher apprehension rates.

Postarrest Dispositions

A diversion project may intervene after an arrest but before prosecution or a juvenile court hearing.

A Los Angeles diversion program involved random assignment of juveniles to four dispositions: counsel and release, filing of a petition without detention, referral to a social service agency without purchase of services, and referral with purchase of services. In a follow-up lasting less than one year, rearrest rates were comparable among all groups when prior record was controlled (necessary because the randomization broke down); multiple arrests were more frequent in the petitioned group and least frequent in the group counseled and released. However, self-reports showed no significant differences in delinquency among the four groups (Klein, 1975), indicating that differences in multiple arrests were due to differential labeling.

A similar finding is reported in a program in Champaign and Urbana, Illinois, which, in lieu of juvenile court referrals, assigned randomly selected apprehended youths to college students who were to supervise and help them. The diverted juveniles had significantly fewer police contacts and juvenile court referrals, but no differences from their controls in any of the measures of self-reported delinquency (Davidson et al., n.d.).

In a study of 2,290 youths referred to the probation intake of eight California counties, McEachern (1968) found in a one-year follow-up that the delinquency of youths who were officially made wards of the court declined over the previous 12 months more than did the delinquency of youths who were not officially labeled as wards, but that contact with a probation officer was associated with a higher rate of offenses (surveillance effect?).

In an analysis of Philadelphia male delinquent careers, Thornberry (1971) found that among the noninstitutional dispositions the more severe were associated with lower rates of return to crime, except among youths who were black or of lower socioeconomic status or whose initial offenses were considered especially serious.

In Project Crossroads in Washington, D.C., and in the Manhattan Court Employment Project of the Vera Institute in New York City, prosecution is suspended for up to 90 days for defendants in specified offense categories, while participants receive individual and group counseling and educational and vocational assistance. Dismissal of charges is contingent on favorable staff evaluations of program participation. Initially, Project Crossroads served juveniles and adults, but was restricted almost entirely to adults after being found ineffective for juveniles. Both programs have claimed modest success, citing reductions in rearrest rates of 10-15% (Leiberg, 1971; Rovner-Pieczenik, 1970; Vera Institute, 1972); however, program participants, having had to meet screening criteria not required of controls, have probably been more favorable risks. Those with unfavorable terminations, sometimes precipitated by arrests, have had a higher recidivism rate. In addition, participants have had a lower rearrest rate only while actually in the Crossroads program; after leaving it, their rearrest rates have been the same as those of controls (Mullen et al., 1974:140-142, 145-148). This might reflect either a deterrence effect of program supervision or the success of program administrators in shielding participants from arrest or indictment. Two subsequent reanalyses of the Vera program, though limited by inadequacies of data, have suggested that reduction in recidivism has been small or nonexistent (Zimring, 1974; Mullen et al., 1974:150-151).

Another program, modeled after these two, was set up in Minneapolis. Depending on the criteria used for success, the program had either no substantial effect on rates of rearrest or a small beneficial effect that disappeared within one year after program termination. Comparison with controls was on the basis of matching, and questions have been raised about the comparability of the groups and bias in the reporting of arrests (Mullen et al., 1974:107-114; Zimring, 1974:152-157).

Parallel to the vocationally oriented Project Crossroads, a program was established in Washington, D.C., for defendants whose crimes were believed to stem from psychological rather than economic problems. Subjects tended to be charged with lesser sex offenses, nonviolent property crimes, and drug offenses. The program included individual and group therapy, as well as vocational rehabilitation and family counseling. Program subjects and matched controls were followed for periods ranging from seven to 21 months (for an average of more than a year), with no significant differences in rearrest rates (Mullen, 1974:184-186).

"Unofficial probation" is a status granted to a juvenile by probational or court staff *without* adjudication when guilt is admitted and both the juvenile and the parents consent. In Yolo County, California, candidates for informal probation were randomly divided into a control group to be counseled and released and an unofficial probation group. After six months the two groups were compared in terms of number of referrals to probation, days to referral, and number of petitions filed with the court. All differences favored the informal probation group, but none were statistically significant (Venezia, 1972).

B. PROBATION INTENSITY

Juveniles

An evaluation of small case load probation for juveniles in Los Angeles County involved a random assignment to either intense supervision or normal probation, with the intensely supervised group receiving two and one-half times as many contacts with supervisors as the other group. Male youths under intense supervision were detained slightly less often (4.9% versus 46.7%) and were committed to the California Youth Authority less often (15% versus 25%, a difference which barely fails to achieve significance at the 0.05 level). For females the differences were quite small; rates of redetention were 20% versus 28%, and commitment rates were 8.7% versus 11.8% (Kawaguchi and Siff, 1967).

Several other studies of Los Angeles juvenile probation have been reported. With small matched samples of boys, Feistman (1966) found nonsignificant differences in revocation in favor of boys placed in case loads of 16, as compared with those placed in case loads of 86. In a small matched sample, Adams (1966) found that girls under intensive supervision (15 in a case load) had redetention rates of 34% compared to 38% placed in standard case loads of 50; they also remained out of detention longer and were redetained for shorter periods. For boys, redetention rates in small case loads were 41.2% compared to 44.2% for controls, but length of detention was again lower for boys under more intense supervision.

Adults

Federal probationers in the Northern District of California were randomly assigned to case loads of varying size. At the end of two years, those in the smallest case loads had slightly lower rates of detention for new offenses, but the difference was not significant. They also had a far higher rate of technical violation of regulations than the others, probably a surveillance effect (Robison et al., 1969).

C. IMPRISONMENT

Prison or Jail Versus Probation[2]

A comparison of the one-year recidivism of 2,148 adults placed on probation with the one-year recidivism of 2,561 others jailed by the Superior Court in California's 13 largest counties showed that probationers avoided arrest for a new crime or for a technical violation of probation or parole regulations more often than persons who had been jailed (65.8% versus 48.6%). The difference persisted when controlling individually for county, sex, age, race, prior record, and instant offense and simultaneously for offense and age, offense and race, and offense and prior record (Beattie and Bridges, 1970).

In another study, the two-year failure rate (new offense or technical violation) of adult male Wisconsin probationers was compared with that of matched prisoners released on parole. Both groups consisted largely of property offenders. Among first offenders, probationers succeeded slightly more often than parolees (70% versus 67.1%); among those with one prior felony conviction, the success rates were about the same (58.3% versus 56.1%); and, among repeat offenders, parolees succeeded slightly more often than probationers (48.2% versus 51.3%). For the latter two groups, the differences were not statistically significant (Babst and Mannering, 1965).

In a statistical analysis of juvenile court dispositions in Philadelphia, Thornberry (1971) found *lower* rates of recidivism for those who had been incarcerated than for those who had not.

Length of Sentence Served in Prison

When matching techniques have been used to compare offenders serving sentences of different length, longer sentences have been found to be associated with higher or identical failure rates (Mueller, 1965; Bull, 1967; Jaman and Dickover, 1969). In the "natural experiment" that occurred in Florida, when a large number of prisoners were released before the termination of their sentences following the U.S. Supreme Court's decision in *Gideon* v. *Wainright,* those released early showed significantly lower recidivism rates (13.6% versus 25.4%) than matched individuals who served substantially longer sentences (Eichman, 1966). On the other hand, multivariate regression analysis of parole failure in California, utilizing many more variables than were used in the matching studies, suggest that time served had little or no impact on outcome (Kassebaum et al., 1971:269; Kolodney et al., 1970).

In an *experimental* study, California prisoners granted parole were divided at random into a group released six months early and a group released at the regular time. Comparison of the two groups showed them to be similar with respect to numerous attributes. Recidivism rates, broken down by category of violation, were essentially identical (Berecochea et al., 1973). This finding held true for each category when inmates were classified into currently used typologies of prisoners. Similar results have been obtained in experimental studies of time served by addicts released from Civil Addict Program institutions (Beckett, 1974). The effect of a wider variation in sentence length is not disclosed by these studies.

D. PROBATION WITH NONRESIDENTIAL PROGRAMS

Juveniles

In the Provo (Utah) experiment, 15- to 17-year-old persistent delinquents were randomly assigned to probation or to an experimental, nonresidential program that included "guided group interaction" (a form of intensive group counseling) and a schedule of work or school lasting all day. Comparisons were also made with boys released from a reformatory, but without random assignment. In a follow-up lasting four years, it was found that there were no significant differences in various measures of recidivism between the two randomly selected groups, but there were pronounced differences in favor of the nonincarcerative programs when comparison was made with reformatory releases (Empey and Erickson, 1972). When rates before and after intervention were compared, however, it appeared that all forms of intervention may have reduced recidivism about equally (Fisher and Erickson, 1973).

The Essexfield program was a program for 16- to 18-year-old male delinquents in Newark, New Jersey, similar in nature to the Provo program. A subsequent study compared outcomes associated with ordinary probation, the Essexfield program, residential guided-group interaction (involving several New Jersey programs, including Highfields, which is described below in section F), and placement in the reformatory at Annandale. Among those who completed the programs, recidivism rates at 30 months (as defined by the imposition of a penal sanction by the court) were: probation 15%, Essexfield, 48%, group centers, 41%, and Annandale 55%, with Essexfield having a higher mean number of recidivist offenses per recidivist than the other programs. When boys who failed to complete the programs were included, recidivism rates changed to 32% for probation and 45% for group centers, the other rates remaining the same. When boys were matched on the basis of race, socioeconomic status, and delinquency history to equalize risks, recidivism rates remained lower for probation, but differences among the other three dispositions were not statistically significant (Stephenson and Scarpitti, 1974).

In a similar program for younger delinquents (aged 13½ to 15½) in Louisville,

Kentucky, no significant differences were found when the success rate of the experimental group was compared with that of probationers. Those who completed the program had a higher rate of recidivism than those who did not (Lipton et al., 1975:264).

In the first phase of the California Youth Authority's Community Treatment Project (CTP), male and female delinquents from Sacramento and Stockton between the ages of 13 and 19 spent four to six weeks at a reception center and diagnostic clinic and then at random were assigned to incarceration for several months followed by parole or were sent home on parole to participate in the CTP program, which assigned them to homogeneous case loads not exceeding 12 juveniles on the basis of assessed maturity level and life circumstances. The treatment for each case load was based on the interpersonal maturity scheme widely used for classification in California Youth Authority programs.

Initial reports indicated that, while experimental youths on the whole recidivated less often than controls, some personality types fared better in the experimental program, others fared better in the conventional program, while the remainder did about equally well in either circumstance. These results were then called into question on the grounds that experimentals had actually committed more violations but were handled more leniently by administrators, who thus created an artificial "success" for the program (Lerman, 1968). Reanalysis of the data suggests that experimentals and controls committed offenses at about the same rate, apart from a higher rate of status offenses among experimentals (Lerman, 1975:58-67).

Palmer (1973, 1974a, 1974b) has presented additional evidence, using measures less prone to bias, suggesting that for "neurotic" youths, who make up a large proportion of the California Youth Authority population, the program did reduce recidivism, but that for other groups it was not necessarily advantageous and, in some cases, it was disadvantageous. He thus offered the finding that the overall effect was not favorable to the experimentals (Palmer and Herrera, 1972). These findings are based on only a portion of the data and fail to distinguish the results of the therapeutic program from the results of simply avoiding incarceration of the juveniles or of placing them in short-term detention as a social control device (as specified in the program).

Replication of the CTP study in Los Angeles, San Francisco, and Oakland found so significant differences between treatment and control groups (Pond, 1970, 1974; Lerman, 1975:69-70), and a comparison of youths exposed to the CRP-type program in San Francisco and those given guided-group interaction, a different treatment modality, found no significant differences in a variety of measures of recidivism, with one exception: at 12 months there were substantially fewer arrests for more serious offenses in the CTP-type program. At

18 months, however, the differences, though substantial, were no longer statistically significant (Palmer and Herrera, 1972).

In a comparison of standard probation with nondirective group counseling for young California males, Adams (1966:32-33) found that experimental youths had significantly fewer contacts with police but had small, nonsignificant differences in deprivations of liberty after six months. In another study of small-group counseling based, according to the report, "on principles of social psychology," 19 juvenile felony probationers exposed to the counseling were matched on the basis of age, race, sex, probation officer, and length of time on probation with 19 other felony probationers who did not receive group counseling. For several months the treatment seemed to lead to a reduction in arrests (26.3% of the counseled youth were arrested at least once within five months after treatment began, as compared with 47.7% for controls); however, during the next five months, the controls marginally outperformed the treatment group (Ostrom et al., 1971).

In another enriched probation program, 14- to 18-year-old males received small case load probation supplemented with a variety of social services, including family counseling and educational and vocational assistance. An evaluation found the program marginally superior to conventional probation (Lipton, 1975:65-66).

In Lincoln and Lancaster, Nebraska, high-risk misdemeanant youths (aged 16 to 25) were randomly assigned to routine probation or to volunteer probation counselors. As measured by rearrests for nontraffic offenses, experimental youths had a very substantial reduction in the frequency and severity of recidivism and in the number of offenses per recidivist. A comparison of arrests before and during the program was also highly favorable to the experimental program (Ku, 1974). Postprobation results are not given, so it is unknown whether the reduction persists after program termination.

A similar program in a Michigan court was less successful. Juvenile probationers (aged 12 to 17) were randomly assigned to regular probation or to citizens who provided tutoring or who led group counseling involving the youths and their parents or who served as volunteer probation officers. On the basis of a six-month follow-up, the evaluation concluded that the program did not reduce self-reported delinquency, contacts with police, or penetration into the juvenile justice system. In fact, each of the three programs appeared to increase delinquency temporarily (Berger et al., 1975).

Adults

An experimental program for adult probationers in California involved academic upgrading, vocational assessment, job finding, and job placement, as well as stipends of up to $30 a week for as long as 26 weeks. The program did not function as had been hoped because a scarcity of jobs in the area made job placement difficult. Although the randomization procedure for assigning probationers to conventional probation or to the experiment did not work perfectly, controls and program participants differed on only a few traits, when compared. After six months, 7% of the training group and 10% of the controls had received a new conviction, the difference not being significant at the 0.10 level (Venezia and McConnell, 1972).

A program for repeat offenders in Oakland County, Michigan, provided an array of social services, referral to other agencies, placement in small probation case loads, and group counseling, all to participants selected randomly from a pool of offenders who would otherwise have been sent to prison or placed on ordinary probation. According to the evaluation by the National Council on Crime and Delinquency, "Initial results point to success." However, the success consisted of a failure, for "the failure rate of probationers receiving project supervision was a disappointing 14%, even greater than the 9% failure rate of the control group receiving regular probation supervision. The statistical significance of this result is not supported." The report suggested that the difference may have been a product of more intense surveillance for program participants, but it failed to reconcile this conjecture with a characterization of the staff as "advocates for our clients as opposed to being surveillance and enforcement people" (National Council on Crime and Delinquency, n.d.:9, 14).

In a program conducted by the Northern California Service League, misdemeanants were diverted from jail to mandatory individual counseling sessions and compared with matched jailed misdemeanants. After six months at large, the diverted group had a higher success rate (as defined by no arrests or fewer than three arrests with no convictions) than the control group, but the difference was not large (78.9% versus 69.5%) or statistically significant (Lipton et al., 1975:176, 181).

In Rochester, New York, probationers diagnosed as "job ready" were randomly divided into two groups: a group that received employment counseling from volunteers with expertise in such fields as manpower training and industrial psychology and a group that received no counseling. Evaluations at six, nine, and 12 months found no significant differences in new arrests or convictions (Cronin, 1975).

On the theory that cultural barriers interfered with the development of a helping relationship between probation or parole officers and their clients, part-time paraprofessionals, some of them ex-convicts and all coming from lower class backgrounds, were hired as federal probation officer case aides to assist the regular probation officer in Chicago. Randomly selected experimental probationers and parolees assigned to the aides showed no lower recidivism than controls who received conventional supervision (Beless and Rest, n.d.).

In a study conducted in Spokane, Washington, probationers who, while on probation, were assigned a volunteer citizen on a one-to-one basis were matched on the basis of sex, age, past record (prior arrests versus no priors), and present offense (property, person, or public order) with offenders who were fined or jailed. After a year at large, 31% of the probationers had been rearrested or reconvicted, as compared with 56% of the jailed or fined group (Moynahan, 1975). Month-by-month recidivism rates showed that this difference arose from the first three months after release; subsequent failure rates for the two groups were almost identical. Unfortunately, the report lumped fined and jailed offenders together and then compared experimental probationers with the aggregate, but not with ordinary probationers. Moreover, the comparison was restricted to individuals who successfully completed probation (Moynahan, 1976) and thus was biased in favor of the experimentals.

Two experiments involving drunkenness have been reported. In San Diego, chronic drunkenness offenders were randomly assigned to no treatment, to treatment at an Alcoholic Rehabilitation Clinic, or to attendance at five meetings of Alcoholics Anonymous—members of all three groups receiving a $25 fine and a 30-day suspended sentence conditional on abstention from alcohol for one year. The success rate for the no treatment group was 44%, for the clinic group 32%, and for the Alcoholics Anonymous group 31%, the differences not being statistically significant. These success rates were substantially *lower* than those obtained in the pilot phase of the study, in which all offenders were sent to Alcoholics Anonymous and threatened with an escalated penalty if arrested again (Ditman et al., 1967). This suggests a possible deterrent effect.

The comparative effectiveness of ordinary probation, therapeutic probation (entailing counseling, inpatient treatment at a mental hospital for at least a week, or outpatient treatment at the county jail), and fines for persons found guilty of drunken driving for the first time was studied in the Denver County Court by making assignment to alternative dispositions on a rotating basis for more than a year. The driving history for each driver was obtained for a year afterwards and for two years before conviction. None of the sanctions was superior to any other in reducing rates of repetition (Ross and Blumenthal, 1974).

E. PROGRAMS IN CONVENTIONAL INSTITUTIONS

Academic Education

Most of the studies of in-prison academic educational programs have utilized either no controls at all or controls for a limited number of offender variables through matching procedures. Some report a reduction in recidivism associated with education, others an increase; but in all cases the differences have been extremely small, generally no more than a few percentage points (Leopold, 1941; Glaser, 1964; Schnur, 1948; Saden, 1962).

At the Pennsylvania State Correctional Institution at Camp Hill, a matching procedure was used to establish a population from which random assignments to a college education program in the humanities were made. At the end of 33 months, approximately 30% of those released from each group had been returned to prison (Lewis, 1973).

Vocational Programs

An evaluation of vocational training in a men's penitentiary in the state of Washington (covering such skill areas as office machine repair, auto mechanics, barbering, body and fender work, machinist work, carpentry, drafting, dry cleaning, electronics, and shoemaking) used a matching procedure to compare program participants and nonparticipants and found no significant differences in rates of parole violation in a follow-up lasting roughly three years; 43.1% of trained prisoners and 39.2% of untrained prisoners violated parole (Lipton et al., 1975:198).

In a study of the postrelease performance of men who had received training and basic education at the Draper Correctional Center in Alabama, where "behavior modification" methods are used, released prisoners who did or did not have such training had the same number of violations at the end of three years (Jenkins et al., 1974).

In a follow-up lasting from six months to a year, male California prisoners who received training in bakery or body and fender work were compared with those who received no training. When success rates were compared with those expected on the basis of the prisoners' base expectancy scores (scores on a prediction equation derived from earlier follow-ups using multiple regression), it was found that "trained parolees had significantly more difficulty than would have been predicted . . . while a comparable group of *post hoc* matched untrained parolees had just about as much difficulty as might have been expected" (California Department of Corrections, 1963:39). In a more recent study, California prisoners received vocational training in auto mechanics, auto body and fender repair, mill and cabinet work, masonry, shoe repair, sheet metal work, culinary arts, meat cutting, baking, dry cleaning, welding, machine shop work, landscaping, refrigeration and air-conditioning work, electronics, general shop work, silk screening, sewing machine repair, offset printing, and office machine repair. The parole outcome of these trainees at six and 12 months was no different fom what would have been expected on the basis of base expectancy scores (Dickover et al., 1971).

Also in California, women prisoners who received training in ceramics, cosmetology, vocational sewing, laundry work, vocational housekeeping, and vocational nursing (preparation to be a nurse's aide) were compared with women released during the same year who did not receive training but whose institutional work assignments were related to areas where training was offered. The two groups had essentially the same average base expectancy score, prior criminal record, and past drug history—and the same rate of return to prison within one year after release (Spencer and Berecochea, 1971).

On the basis of such evaluations, a publication of the California Department of Corrections concluded:

> Profitting from the experience of history, the Department of Corrections does not claim that vocational training has any particular capability of reducing recidivism. [Dickover et al., 1971]

An IBM training program for young male offenders (aged 16 to 21) at the Rikers Island jail in New York City claimed success, because 52% of the offenders who received remedial education and training in the use of data-processing equipment remained out of jail for at least a year after release, compared to 34% of the untrained group. It was later found that this difference disappeared when program dropouts were included in the evaluation and that the randomization procedure had broken down during the program, so that the training group received better risks during the latter part of the study (Lipton et al., 1975:206).

Women in a Milwaukee jail who participated in a training program lasting on the average one month and offering vocational training and academic education (including grooming, child care, reading, writing, spelling, business filing, vocational guidance, and group counseling) were compared with untrained women, and no differences in outcome were found after the women had been seven months at large (Ketterling, 1972).

In a randomized experimental design, a combination of vocational counseling and work experience for 15- to 16-year-old males in a New York youth institution was compared with no counseling and work experience. At six months, 7.4% of the experimentals and 12.0% of the controls had been returned to a correctional institution; at 12 months, the corresponding figures were 10.9% and 14.3%, the difference not being significant. The study was plagued with problems of implementation, which may have reduced the impact of the program (Lipton et al., 1975:184-186, 206-207).

Work Release

In a study of work release at the Santa Clara jail in California, 100 participants were matched with 100 nonparticipants on the basis of marital status, alcohol and drug use, attitudes, and personality characteristics. After 18 months, arrest rates were twice as high for nonparticipating inmates as for those who participated, and two and one-half times as many were committed to the state prison (Rudoff and Esselstyn, 1973; Rudoff, 1974). The report omits absolute rearrest and reconviction rates for these groups.

In Washington, D.C., 120 misdemeanant and felon work-release participants were matched with nonparticipants on the basis of offense type, age at first arrest, number of previous convictions as an adult, and number of prior commitments as an adult. Failure was defined as a new conviction resulting in incarceration for a month or more, parole revocation for a new arrest or technical violation, or incarceration pending the final disposition of an arrest or revocation proceeding. After eight months at risk, work-release participants had an 18.4% failure rate, compared to 30.2% for the nonparticipants. When in-program failures were included with work-release program completers, participants had a substantially *higher* failure rate than controls, though such an inclusion may have been unfair to the work-release program, since some of the in-program failures were minor in character (Adams, 1975).

In a comparison of crudely matched work-release and non-work-release participants in North Carolina, differences in rearrest and reconviction rates were small, unfavorable to work release, and not statistically significant. When the lengths of new sentences were compared for the two groups, the mean sentence length was significantly shorter for the work-release participants, a finding that the evaluator interpreted as indicating a tendency toward involvement in less serious offenses. A before-after comparison showed that participants decreased their average length of sentence, whereas nonparticipants increased their mean sentence length. These differences persisted when multiple regression was used to control statistically for a number of offender attributes (Witte, 1975).

Work-release participants at the Massachusetts Correctional Institution at Concord were compared with (1) individuals who would have been eligible but who had been released several years earlier and (2) nonmatched inmates released at roughly the same time whose applications for work release had been rejected. The three groups were similar with respect to a number of background variables, but differed significantly on others. As measured by rates of return to custody for 30 days or more after a year at risk, all three groups had virtually identical rates of recidivism. When the first of the two comparison groups was used to construct a base expectancy score for participants, it was found that the expected rate of recidivism was 7% higher than the rate observed, the difference not being significant (LeClair, 1973).

In a study of a work-release program in the San Mateo jail which excluded narcotics, sex, and violence offenders, 110 work furlough inmates were compared with 94 controls released two years earlier. In a follow-up lasting four years, it was found that 23% of the work furlough inmates had no arrests and 43% had no convictions, as compared with 13% and 23% for controls. The differences tended to decline over time. Since furlough participants had more favorable social backgrounds and were not at risk during the same period, the results were not conclusive (Jeffrey and Woolpert, 1975).

In an evaluation of the California work-release program for jail and prison inmates, Bass (1974) found that 29% of the participants escaped or were returned to the institution for a new offense or violation of the program's rules during the program. Of those released to parole from work release, 7% had been returned to prison within six months compared with 8% of the nonparticipants. The parole success rate for participants at six months was 89% compared to 88% for participants, a negligible difference. Moreover, actuarial considerations suggested that work-release participants should have been a better risk. Since the worst risks in the participant group were probably among the 29% who were not released to parole, the program may have increased recidivism.

An experimental study of work release in Florida involved a random assignment of eligibles to a work-release group or a control group, with a comparison showing the two groups to be similar with respect to many background variables. In a three-year follow-up there were no statistically significant differences on a large number of measures of recidivism (Waldo and Chiricos, 1975).

Individual Interview Therapy

Individual interview therapy conducted by clinical psychologists was evaluated for older institutionalized delinquent boys in California in the PICO program. At intake, boys were classified as "amenable" or "nonamenable" to treatment. ("Amenability to treatment was ascertained through pooled clinical judgments. . . . Although the most salient ingredient of amenability appeared to be the quality of anxiety, the typical amenable ward might be more fully described as 'bright, verbal and anxious.' In addition to these primary characteristics, the judgment of amenability was also influenced by evidence of 'awareness of problems,' 'insight,' 'desire to change,' and 'acceptance of treatment.' "). Each group was randomly subdivided into a treatment group and a control group, creating four samples of boys: treated amenable (TA), treated nonamenable (TN), control amenable (CA), and control nonamenable (CN). [3] The follow-up period was 33 months for each subject. Among the amenables, unfavorable or poor discharges were given to 30% of the treated and 36% of the control youths; among the nonamenables, to 44% of the controls and 49% of the treated. Thus, among those considered amenables, the treatment group seemed to do better, while among the nonamenables, the treatment group did worse (Adams, 1970). However, neither difference is statistically significant. At the end of the evaluation period, the TA group had spent considerably less time in custody than the other groups. All indicators of success were measures of official actions such as commitment to prison or suspension of parole. The relationship between these actions and violation rates is uncertain (Adams, 1961).

Short-term individual interview therapy has also been evaluated in California youth institutions. At the Preston School of Industry, both amenable and nonamenable older adolescent males (average age 17.4) were randomly assigned to classical interview therapy twice a week for an average of less than nine months. Fifteen months after release, 58.5% of the treated and 47.7% of the untreated youths had been removed from parole by revocation or bad discharge, the difference not being statistically significant. In addition, there were no significant differences in seriousness of violation, and the outcome in relation to treatment was unrelated to amenability. In the Nelles School for Boys, a younger population (median age 14.8) was randomly divided into an untreated group and a treatment group that received "reality-oriented" therapy, including extensive informal contact between youths and therapists in recreational activity. At the end of a 15-month follow-up, 59.7% of the treated and 73.8% of the untreated boys had received a parole revocation or bad discharge from parole, a difference that was not significant. Again, amenability was unrelated to outcome (Guttman, 1963). Seckel (1974b) contended that the Preston differences became significant at the 0.05 level and that the Nelles results became significant at the 0.09 level after corrections for differences in group risk were made using an analysis of variance, but he did not comment on why such corrections were needed. A later study of the Preston program, also reported by Seckel, found no significant differences between treatment and control groups.

The effect of individual interview therapy on institutionalized teenaged delinquent girls in California was evaluated in a design employing post hoc matching for background variables. No significant differences in rates of parole suspension were found for those who received individual psychotherapy, individual psychotherapy supplemented by group therapy, or no therapy (Lipton et al., 1975:214-215).

Several experiments involving adults have also been reported. At Chino and San Quentin in California, men receiving individual psychotherapy and intensive group therapy had the same success rates as controls who participated in the regular institutional program (California Department of Corrections, 1958).

At Walpole, a men's prison in Massachusetts, a four-year follow-up was done for inmates who received at least 25 weeks of individual psychotherapy. The recidivism of the therapy group was compared with an expected rate derived from base expectancy scores. Since the expected rate was 68% but the observed rate was 53%, the program was rated highly successful (Carney and Bottome, 1967). The base expectancy score formula employed in this study was quite crude, using only 6ur predictor variables: number of prior arrests, age, education, and number of juvenile incarcerations.[4] Consequently, risk may have been inadequately controlled. Moreover, restriction of the comparison to those who completed 25 weeks of therapy suggests the possibility of bias originating in the exclusion of dropouts.

Group Counseling (Pragmatic Problem-Solving Emphasis) and Group Therapy (Insight)

In an evaluation of group therapy for inmates diagnosed as mentally ill or defective, epileptic, drug addictive, or mentally abnormal (including psychotic cases and sex offenders), the rates of return to prison of 257 inmates who had been released from the California Medical Facility at Vacaville during the years 1958-1962 and who had spent at least a year in group therapy with the same therapist were compared with the return rates of 257 other prisoners with the same base expectancy score who had been released during the same years from other California prisons and who had no group therapy experience. At one year, 74% of the experimental group remained on parole as compared with 67% of the controls. At two years, the rates were, respectively, 55% and 51% and, at three years, 46% and 44% (Jew et al., 1972). None of these differences is significant, and all are substantively small (the authors claimed the first difference to be significant, but they are mistaken).

In a later study of group therapy at the California Medical Facility, 736 male group-therapy patient/prisoners released between 1965 and 1968 were compared with a control group of other prisoners, who were matched with the California Medical Facility prisoners on the basis of base expectancy score, offense, and prior prison record and who had not been exposed to group therapy. After six months at large, 68% of the treated prisoners had encountered no problem or difficulty, compared to 63% of the untreated group. This difference was not significant. At one year, the comparable figures were 51% and 44%; at two years, 36% and 30%. The last two differences are significant but small. There was a significant difference in returns to prison at six months at the 0.01 level, but the difference quickly narrowed and was not significant at one and two years. If those classified as having "major problems" are grouped with those returned to prison as failures, a difference in failure rates of 6% in favor of the treated group at the end of two years is significant. The study reports positive effects with older homicide and sex offenders who had few prior prison commitments, and it reports negative effects for young robbery, drug, and assaultive offenders with lengthy prison records (Jew et al., 1975).

Although prisoners were matched with controls in this study, additional screening took place, since only prisoners who exhibited motivation to change and were considered amenable were admitted to the program. There was no comparison with an untreated group diagnosed as experiencing the personality disorders or other psychological attributes of the patient group. Prisoners so diagnosed could well have been better risks than the base expectancy score indicates. The measure of failure in this study was an administrative action, a possible source of bias. Finally, the authors made computational errors in significance testing. Contrary to their claim, homicide offenders did not show a statistically significant reduction in recidivism; the only significant reduction was for sex offenders. Moreover, no account was taken of the fact that when multiple comparisons are made, the probability of obtaining a significant result by chance is much higher than the significance level indicates. One significant difference out of nine is not strong evidence for treatment effectiveness for anyone.

In another study of group counseling in California, inmates were randomly divided into a control group and a group assigned to an "intensive living-group treatment" program. At the end of one year, 79% of the treated group and 71% of the control group had a "favorable adjustment," a difference which did not quite achieve statistical significance in a two-tailed test, but did in a one-tailed test (Robison and Kevorkian, 1967). By the end of the second year, the difference had essentially disappeared (California Department of Corrections, 1971:19, citing J.O. Robison and R. Bass), and a later reanalysis found evidence of initial differences between treatment and control groups that made the initial randomization appear suspect (Robison, 1976).

In a large-scale experimental assessment of group counseling for men imprisoned at a medium security institution in California, nearly a thousand prisoners were randomly divided into a control group and three experimental groups, each of which received a different form of group counseling. In a follow-up lasting three years, group counseling was found to have had no effect on recidivism for the prisoners as a whole or for any distinguishable subgroup of prisoners (Kassebaum et al., 1971).

At the Paso Robles School for Boys in California, an institution holding a population whose median age was 16.7, boys were randomly divided into four living units of 50 boys each. In one, meetings of the entire unit were held four times a week; in another, there were weekly sessions of smaller groups; in a third, both types of meetings were held; and in the fourth, there were no group sessions. All boys received the standard institutional program of academic and vocational training, work, recreation, and individual counseling and casework. In evaluations conducted 15 and 30 months after release to parole, there were no significant differences among the groups in percentage of parole revocations or bad discharges (Seckel, 1965, 1974:13-15).

A similar experiment conducted at the Youth Training School in California with boys whose median age was 19 involved small group counseling weekly for the randomly selected treatment groups, but not for controls. There were no statistically significant differences between treatment and control groups in the percentage of violators. According to the evaluator, "Since completion of the ... group counseling studies, regular and small group counseling has, as a matter of policy, been made an integral part of the living unit programs at all Youth Authority reception centers, institutions and camps" (Seckel, 1965, 1974:18).

In another study of group therapy, 41 pairs of institutionalized boys of average age 16, matched on the basis of age, IQ, race, socioeconomic background, type of offense, number of previous offenses, total time incarcerated during life, and nature of institutional adjustment were assigned at random to a control group or to a program of therapy consisting of 40 group sessions and 20 individual therapy sessions. A year after release, the therapy group had 28 boys remaining in the community, the control group 16, a difference that is significant at the 0.01 level; the therapy group also had fewer offenses per returnee (1.94 versus 3.07), a difference significant only at the 0.1 level. Therapy failures included one armed robbery and another armed robbery-murder. Information about the seriousness of offenses committed by controls was not reported (Persons, 1967).

Favorable results have also been reported in a study of 70 institutionalized adolescent girls in Kentucky, who were randomly assigned to either a group receiving mandatory group therapy (two sessions a week for 3 months with therapists chosen for qualities of empathy and nonpossessive warmth) or an untreated control group. During the three years prior to therapy, the therapy and control groups spent, respectively, 82% and 78% of the time out of institutions; in the year after release these figures become 54.4% and 40.0% respectively, a highly significant difference (Truax et al., 1966). It should be noted that the measure of success was an official reaction; neither offense rates nor offense seriousness was measured independently. Moreover, a comparison of the time spent in institutions before and after therapy suggests that institutionalization itself might have had harmful effects which therapy was not entirely able to overcome.

A form of group therapy that included prisoners' "significant others" was evaluated by randomly dividing young adult California honor camp inmates who had significant others into two groups. In one group, each boy received approximately eight hours of group therapy with his significant other (usually a mother, wife, or girlfriend) over a three-month period, while boys in the other group did not. The evaluation, based on a follow-up in which time at risk ranged from five to 17 months, reported a difference in arrest rates in favor of the treatment group that was significant at the 0.005 level, but there was no significant difference in reincarceration rates (Haworth, n.d.). Robison, however, has observed that the randomization procedure was abandoned during the experiment, with the treatment group receiving better risks. He reported that the difference in arrest rates was actually significant at the 0.05 level (barely) and that the difference was entirely due to marijuana arrests. Arrest rates for drug sales and for crimes against persons or property were identical for the two groups (Robison, 1973).

Contact with Outsiders

The six-month parole success rate for California male prisoners who participated in an experimental program of conjugal visiting and home furloughs was 80%, a percentage which was higher than the 60% success rate expected from the base expectancy score and which could not be explained on the basis of background differences between participants and nonparticipants (California Department of Corrections, 1971:43). It seems possible that differences in strength of family ties, not included in the base expectancy formula, could have contributed to the difference in outcomes.

The Fellowship Program of the Massachusetts Correctional Institution at Norfolk brings local churchmen into the institution to enter into "meaningful dialogues" with inmate members of the program. Some participants remain in contact with their clergy "out-mates" and receive assistance from them after release from prison. Using the base expectancy score to compare expected with observed recidivism at 31 months after release, the evaluators concluded that the program reduced recidivism from 47.0% to 37.8%, with the improvement greater than average for black inmates, older inmates, and inmates convicted of crimes against the person (Panogopoulos and Gardner, 1969). The limitations of the Massachusetts base expectancy score had already been noted. Of relevance here is the fact that the score, based on objective attributes, cannot take into account differences in motivation or conventionality of values, which might lead some prisoners but not others to participate in a program involving visiting clergy.

In a volunteer sponsor program at the Washington State Reformatory, inmates were selected on the basis of similar release dates and their lack of social contact with anyone outside and were divided into two groups, the inmates in one group being given one-to-one contact with outside volunteer sponsors and the inmates of the other group being excluded from the program. Although the matching procedure was crude, a comparison of the groups found no significant differences between them for 10 different attributes related to recidivism (Lawyer, 1972).

"Behavior Modification" Methods

At the Nevada Youth Training Center, delinquent male youths whose average age was 14 were assigned (on the basis of available bed space) to either a control cottage or a cottage housing between 18 and 26 wards in which a "token" economy was employed to reward desired social behavior and educational advancement. Tokens could be used to purchase institutional privileges and were weighted in parole decisions. Although the treatment did result in a modest gain in educational achievement, it did not change the recidivism rate (Sloane and Ralph, 1973).

In Northern California a treatment program based on a token economy and parole-contingent point system was compared with a program organized around treatment contracts and transactional analysis (applied in twice-weekly small-group therapy sessions and in the rest of the routine); 15- to 17-year-old delinquent boys were randomly assigned to two California Youth Authority institutions, each of which had one type of program but not the other. After a one-year exposure to risk, 32% of each group had been removed from parole. There was, however, evidence of moderate interaction between treatment modality and interpersonal maturity level. Recidivism rates for subjects released from the same institutions before the experiment began had been 42-44% (Jesness, 1974:26).

The program at the Draper Correctional Center in Alabama, described in the earlier section on vocational training, also employed "behavior modification" techniques (Jenkins et al., 1974).

F. UNCONVENTIONAL INSTITUTIONS

The institutional programs described thus far have all been implemented in conventional prisons and reformatories. In recent years, attempts have been made to eliminate the purportedly criminogenic features of these traditional institutions by establishing low-custody, small population institutions in which a milieu favorable to rehabilitation could be established more successfully.

The earliest of these, located on the former Lindbergh estate in Highfields, New Jersey, entailed short-term confinement to a low-security residence. The boys worked during the day and participated in leisure-time recreation in the nearby town and in guided group interaction. For some period after release, recidivism among Highfields boys was lower than among boys committed for a much longer period to the state reformatory. This reduction was larger for blacks than for whites (Weeks, 1958). No attempt was made to determine whether the significant variable was the length of detention or the difference in treatment, or whether both were important. The groups themselves were not entirely comparable and were not at risk during the same period. Revocation for Highfields boys was handled by the probation agency; for reformatory boys, it was handled by the parole agency; thus different standards might have been employed in the revocation process. More Highfields boys entered the armed services (the Korean War was fought at an opportune moment for them), and more were discharged early from supervision, reducing their period at risk. Most of the reformatory boys were returned to custody for technical violations; few for new offenses. There was no comparison with ordinary probation. There was also some weak evidence that differences in outcome began to disappear after several years (McCorkle et al., 1958).

A replication of the Highfields study using a more rigorous research design was attempted in Jefferson County, Kentucky, but the attempt was unsuccessful. In the initial design, delinquents whose offenses were judged to be of moderate seriousness were to be assigned at random to probation or to Southfields, a "therapeutic" residential institution, while serious cases were to be divided randomly between Southfields and Kentucky Village, the state reformatory. The judges who agreed to this were shortly thereafter voted out of office, and their successors refused to agree to a random assignment. As a result, the three dispositions did not receive equally risky cases. One year after program termination, success rates among the groups were: probation 77%, Southfields graduates 70%, Kentucky Village graduates 53%, and Southfields nongraduates (those who were dropped from the program before completing it) 46%. Definitive conclusions about the effects of the different dispositions could not be drawn, but, when qualitative assessment of differences in risk were taken into account, it appeared unlikely that Southfields had been superior to ordinary probation in reducing recidivism (Miller, 1970).

In another test of a "therapeutic milieu," delinquent boys were sent to a residential community treatment center in Los Angeles, where the program included guided group interaction at the neighborhood high school. Their recidivism rate was about the same as that of control delinquents sent to a standard residential correctional institution for male juveniles (Empey and Lubeck, 1972).

Short-term residential confinement in a reception center-clinic with a heavy therapeutic emphasis was tested in two experiments involving random assignment of older delinquent boys (minimum age 16 in the first experiment, ages 15 to 18 in the second) to the ordinary California Youth Authority institutional program or to the experimental programs. Both experimental programs utilized individual and group counseling (practical problem-solving discussion), academic education, work experience, and frequent meetings of the living group. One program lasted five months; the other, which also held group meetings with boys' parents, lasted three months. In neither case was there a statistically significant difference in parole outcome between the conventional and experimental programs. In both studies, there seemed to be some evidence that the experimental programs had been somewhat helpful to older youths (Seckel, 1969, 1974a; Knight, 1969).

To see whether the Community Treatment Project (described in Section D above) could be extended effectively to boys who were being sent to conventional reformatories and whether its effectiveness would improve with those boys who were not being influenced favorably by placement in the nonresidential CTP program, the project began to experiment with a therapeutically oriented *residential* setting in Sacramento. Eligibles were first classified according to whether it was believed that their treatment needs would best be served in a residential or a nonresidential placement; then random assignments to the residential and nonresidential program were made from each group. Evaluation after 18 months suggested that those diagnosed as requiring the residential setting were more likely to recidivate when placed in the community program than when placed in a residential setting, 94% of the former group and 58% of the latter group have been apprehended for at least one offense during the evaluation period, a statistically significant difference. For each month at risk, the "incorrectly" placed group (those in the community) had an offense rate more than twice as high as the "correctly" placed group (residential disposition). Of the boys thought *not* to require residential placement, those given such a placement had a monthly offense rate slightly higher than those in the community program, but the difference was not significant (Palmer, 1974b).

In another phase of the California Treatment Project study, delinquents in Stockton and Sacramento placed in privately operated group foster homes housing a maximum of six youths at one time were compared with CTP experimental youths in the same cities who were not placed in group homes. Assignment to the group homes was not random, but base expectancy scores suggested that the group home youths may have been slightly worse risks. After 15 months, the group home youths had a substantially lower recidivism rate; at 24 months they had a somewhat lower rate, the difference being smaller than at 15 months (Palmer, 1972). Given the extremely small size of the population studied, the finding should be treated with caution.

In California, delinquent boys 16 years or older were assigned at random to regular Youth Authority institutions or to minimum security forestry camps, where they did conservation work. After 15 months on parole, boys released from the camps had a slightly but not significantly higher rate of recidivism. Previous research had established that the recidivism rates of camp graduates were lower than anticipated on the basis of base expectancy scores, suggesting that the camp experience reduced recidivism. The later result suggests that the earlier difference may have been due to selection for the camps on the basis of factors not included in the base expectancy formula but linked with parole success (Moloff, 1967). Because the programs at the two camps differed in many ways, a comparison of recidivism rates for the two camps was also undertaken, and no significant differences were found (Seckel, 1974c:41-42).

At Fricot Ranch, a California youth facility for 8- to 14-year-old boys, the hypothesis that smaller living units would increase staff-ward interaction and thus reduce recidivism was tested in an experiment that randomly assigned boys to 20- or 50-bed living units. The smaller units were characterized by greater contact between staff and youths, greater informality, and more emotional support from staff. After a year on parole, 36.8% of the boys in the 20-bed unit and 52.2% of the boys in the 50-bed unit had been suspended from parole and returned to an institution, mostly for serious multiple offenses, the difference being statistically significant. Boys in three of the eight interpersonal maturity levels did better in the small lodge; for the other types, there were no significant differences. After two years at large, differences in outcome between the units began to decline. After three years, violation rates for the small and large units were, respectively, 73% and 83%; at five years, 82% and 90%. Despite the randomization procedure, there were sharp differences between the units with respect to race, broken homes, and socioeconomic status, all placing the boys in small units at an advantage. It is possible, therefore, that the difference in rates either originated in a statistical fluctuation that gave better risks to the small units or originated in a breakdown of the randomization procedure (Lerman, 1968).

The effect of sending delinquent boys to camp has also been studied. Homeward Bound is a voluntary residential program of severe physical challenge for adjudicated delinquent boys aged 16 or over. The program includes community service, hiking, running, learning wilderness survival skills, practicing ecology, learning seamanship, studying ropes and knots, rock-climbing, and going on a 10-day mobile trek and on a 3-day solo expedition in the woods. The selection of campers was on a rotating basis, with noncampers committed to a training school for six to nine months; the two groups were similar in background attributes. Recidivism (not defined in the published report) was 20.9% for camp boys, as compared with 42.7% for controls during the period at risk. Camp boys who did recidivate did so after a longer period than controls

(Willman and Chun, 1973). An evaluation of Outward Bound, a similar program, found very similar results in a one-year follow-up (Kelly and Baer, 1971), but a later study with a longer follow-up found that differences narrowed and were not significant at five years (Nold and Wilpers, 1975).

All the previous studies in this section involved boys. In Los Angeles, several experimental and quasi-experimental studies of short-term detention of juvenile girls in a "therapeutic" milieu found, in follow-ups lasting five to six months, that treatment girls had redetention rates somewhat lower (differences of 9-17%, not significant) than girls placed in conventional juvenile detention centers (Adams, 1966).

In Washington, D.C., young adult offenders aged 17-23 were assigned at random to Lorton Reformatory or to a halfway house in a predominantly black section of the city. House residents progressed in stages from residential confinement to nonresidential parole, then total release. The program in the house involved work or school attendance, with "treatment" being nontherapeutic in orientation and restricted to interaction with other house residents. By comparison, Lorton inmates participated in therapeutic group sessions conducted by a trained psychologist and were then released to a halfway house before discharge from supervision. Both groups had similar rearrest rates (Koshel, 1973:55-59).

After arrival at a reception center, adult male offenders from San Diego were assigned at random to Crofton House (a halfway house in San Diego) or to a regular honor camp, in each case for a period averaging between three and four months. The halfway house program included guided group interaction, and residents also held jobs in the community. In a follow-up lasting three months, halfway house residents had a slightly higher recidivism rate, but the difference was not significant (Lipton et al., 1975:269, 280).

In another study, adult offenders initially sentenced to jail for at least four months were randomly assigned to the jail or to a community rehabilitation center, where they participated in a therapy program and held a job. Recidivism rates for the two groups were similar (Lamb and Goertzel, 1974).

G. PAROLE

Intensity of Supervision: Juveniles

In Massachusetts, 14- and 15-year-old male parolees were placed in standard case loads of 75 boys for a six-month period or in small case loads of 25 boys for intensive supervision by specially trained parole officers and for group counseling. Assignment was not random, but boys in the two groups were found to be closely matched with respect to 12 attribute variables. At six months there were no significant differences in proportions adjudicated for a new offense, commitments to an institution, length of incarceration for those institutionalized, or mean seriousness of offense (Schwitzgebel and Baer, 1967).

Delinquent boys and girls released from Minnesota juvenile institutions were assigned at random to conventional supervision or to an experimental case load with no supervision, contact between parole agent and parolee occurring only when initiated by the parolee. For neither boys nor girls did experimental status have any significant effect on length of time to first arrest or apprehension for those who were arrested or apprehended. More control boys than experimentals had parole revoked within 10 months (38% compared to 21%); for girls, the comparable figures were 45% and 34%. When the parolee's status was experimental, parole revocation was more likely to have been for a serious offense; 16.6% of the experimental boys and 19% of the control boys had parole revoked for a serious offense, a very small difference. The comparable figures were 10% and 3% for girls, but the number involved was very small. The main effect of more intense supervision thus seems to have been to increase a boy's chances of parole revocation for a low seriousness offense (Hudson, 1973).

In California, Alameda County juvenile parolees were randomly assigned to intense supervision (36-boy case loads) or standard supervision (72-boy case loads). The intensely supervised youths in the first cohort (who were paroled during the first six months of the experiment) had parole revoked slightly less often than those in the normal case load, but the difference was significant only at six months, not at 12 or 18 months, and was later traced to differential treatment in the revocation process. Experimentals had been detected in as many offenses of the same average severity as controls but were treated more leniently when caught. In the second cohort (those paroled during the second six months of the program), revocation rates were slightly higher among experimentals than controls, but the difference was not significant (Johnson, 1962; Davis, 1974:49-52; Lipton et al., 1975:104-115, 164-167).

Intensity of Supervision: Adults

Over a period of years, the California parole agency conducted a series of experiments to determine the effect of varying intensity of parole supervision on the recidivism of adult males. In the first study—SIPU I—parolees released on schedule and those paroled 90 days early were assigned either to normal 90-man case loads or to 15-man case loads for intensive supervision lasting three months, followed by transfer to 90-man case loads. During the first phase of the study, parolees in intensely supervised case loads had lower rates of rearrest for major offenses than those in normal case loads (13.1% versus 18.8%) and lower rates of return to prison (6.7% versus 10.1%). Though small, these rates were statistically significant but were later traced to placement of better risks in the small case loads. In the second phase of the study, risks were more evenly distributed, and the effect disappeared.

In SIPU II, the size of the experimental case load was increased to 30, and the period of intensive supervision was extended from three months to six. At 6.5 and 12.5 months there were no significant differences in recidivism between experimentals and controls (Adams, 1967; Lipton et al., 1975:116-119).

In SIPU III, a comparison of men in 35-man case loads with those in 72-man case loads, when the period of intense supervision was further extended to more than a year, found that after a year at risk, those in small case loads had a higher rate of no arrests and a lower rate of reimprisonment; the differences were 4-5% and significant. When those with no arrest and only minor arrests were aggregated, there were significant differences between experimentals and controls. The same pattern held at two years. By region, treatment effects appeared to be modest in the North (5-7% differences) and absent in the South. There was some evidence suggesting that small case loads were more effective with modest risks but had little effect for very good or very bad risks (Adams, 1967; Lipton et al., 1975:120-129); however, there was also evidence that differences in this phase may have stemmed from differential decision making that originated in the agency's desire to demonstrate the effectiveness of small case loads (Robison and Smith, 1971).

In SIPU IV, assignments were made to 15-man, 30-man, and 70-man case loads. Although there were small and significant differences in the proportions of each group experiencing no arrest or minor arrests, there were no significant differences in terms of major arrests, technical revocations of parole, or returns to prison with a new commitment. There was again evidence that medium-sized case loads were more effective in reducing recidivism for some risk levels than for others, but the differences were not statistically significant and did not entirely agree with SIPU III as to which risk levels were the ones helped (Adams, 1967; Havel, 1965; Lipton et al., 1975:129-136).

Following the SIPU experiments, the Parole Unit Program was established. Case loads were set at approximately 35, but with variation on the basis of the seriousness of the parolee's offenses and other factors, the purpose of the variation being to make allowance for some cases requiring more supervision time than others. After a year at risk, 65.8% of the parolees in the work unit had a favorable parole outcome classification, compared to 62.6% in conventional parole. This difference of 3.2% was traced to differences in level of risk. When the base expectancy score was controlled, the difference in favor of the work unit disappeared, and conventional parole was found to lead to significantly lower rates of technical violations (Robison and Takagi, 1968; Robison and Smith, 1971).

Further experimentation with parole case loads in California explored the consequences of drastically reduced supervision. Here it was found that good-risk parolees assigned to minimal supervision (one face-to-face contact every three months unless the parolee requested help or showed signs of criminal involvement) had the same failure rates in every category of parole failure as parolees at the same risk level assigned to conventional supervision (California Department of Corrections, 1963:73).

Other studies showed that prisoners released on ordinary parole did not seem to perform better after release than prisoners released without any supervision at all (California Department of Corrections, n.d.:121-125; Mueller, 1965) and that early discharge from parole was associated with somewhat lower rates of known criminal involvement (Jaman et al., 1974).

As part of its study of parole case load size, narcotics offenders released from the California Department of Corrections were assigned to 30-man or 70-man case loads with what Adams (1967) has called "inconclusive results." In a later study, experimental 15-man and 45-man case loads were compared with the standard 70-man case loads. Adams reports that "the experimentals as a whole performed significantly better than the controls, but no difference was apparent between the 15-man and 45-man case loads."

An additional study, summarized by Norman Holt (1974), looked at the recidivism over a 12-month period of Los Angeles parole violators who had violated parole but who were nevertheless continued on parole. Their rates of rearrest were virtually the same as those of parolees freshly released from prison, and their rate of return to prison was only slightly higher. Their rate of return to prison was substantially *lower* than the rate for technical violators who were briefly returned to prison and then released.

H. PROGRAMS AFTER RELEASE

Vocational Programs

A mixed group made up of released federal prisoners on parole or discharged from supervision and federal probationers was randomly divided into a control group and a group eligible for assistance from the Division of Vocational Rehabilitation. Because it was recognized that the population to be helped would have multiple needs and that arbitrary restrictions might interfere with the effectiveness of the program, division counselors were empowered to do anything they wished to rehabilitate their clients without regard to budgetary restrictions. The strongest emphasis was on vocational training, but counselors were able to purchase other services, engage in counseling, or dole out cash allowances. As measured by arrests, convictions, incarcerations, technical violations of parole regulations, employment rates and income, the controls did slightly better than those receiving assistance, but differences were small and not statistically significant (Fulton, 1969).

In Minnesota, a randomly selected group of parolees received vocational counseling, group counseling, financial assistance, occupational role playing, job placement, and educational or vocational training, while controls received none of these services. During the first year on parole, failure rates for the training group were moderately lower than for the controls (34.4% versus 45.1%), but the difference was not statistically significant and disappeared when the program ended (Ericson and Moberg, 1968).

Another study of vocational programs for parolees was conducted in New York City. Eligibility was restricted to 17- to 23-year-olds with at least a year remaining under New York State parole supervision. The program involved comprehensive psychological testing, educational-vocational and supportive counseling, vocational training, and job placement services and was evaluated by comparing program participants with other parolees matched for race, alcoholism, narcotics addiction, month of release to parole, age, number of previous arrests, crime of conviction, and duration of remaining supervision at the time of release. A follow-up ranging from two to 10 months after release from prison (very short) found that 15% of the project members had new arrests or technical violations of parole, compared to 23% for the control group; they had 6% returns to prison for a new crime or technical violation of regulations, compared to 12% for the comparison group. Neither difference was significant at the 0.10 level (Witt, n.d.).

In an experimental study of the effect of job placement and financial assistance for male prisoners released from Maryland state prisons and returning to live in the Baltimore area, eligibles were randomly divided into four groups: a control group, a group that received an allowance of $60 a week for subsistence, a group that received job placement services, and a group that received both the allowance and placement services. Low risks (first offenders, men over 45, those with large savings, and those who had no record of property crime) and high risks (heroin users and chronic alcoholics) were excluded, since it was felt that the program would be unlikely to alter the recidivism of either group to any great degree. Though job placement was successful in finding jobs for a number of the men, it did not reduce unemployment. Recidivism rates, as measured by the proportion of each group arrested, the length of time to rearrest, the number of men with multiple arrests, and the seriousness of offense, were quite similar for all four groups (Lenihan, 1973).

Another study of financial assistance to parolees was conducted in the San Francisco area. A random sample of male parolees was made eligible for direct financial assistance from parole agents of up to $80 a week for as long as 12 weeks. The recidivism of this sample was then compared with that of ineligible controls. Although a comparison of background variables of eligibles and ineligibles was moderately favorable to the ineligibles, at six months 79.9% of eligibles and 71.2% of controls were classified as successes. This difference was not statistically significant. For some categories of inmates, differences in recidivism were favorable to the eligibles; for others, unfavorable (Reinarman, 1973).

Group and Individual Counseling

In Pennsylvania, parolees classified as "nonaggressive predatory offenders" (burglary, larceny, forgery) were randomly divided into a control group which received ordinary parole supervision and a treatment group. Treatment consisted of placement in a small case load for intensive supervision on parole, individual and group psychiatric therapy, nonpsychiatric group sessions, individual counseling, and vulnerability to placement in a residential center when the parolee was thought to be in danger of returning to criminal activity or had violated a parole regulation. Here the center was to be used in lieu of return to prison. Although the treatment group had more returns to prison, more new offenses, and more technical violations than the control group, the differences were not significant. The evaluators found significant background differences between the treatment and control groups, to the disadvantage of the former, and have suggested that this difference may have contributed to the negative findings; but quantitative estimates of the effect of these differences was not presented (Maiser, 1969).

Halfway Houses and Foster Homes

Several halfway house programs for released prisoners have been evaluated. In Gary, Indiana, a halfway house for 18- to 25-year-old males released from Pendleton Reformatory provided residents with jobs in Inland Steel's Gary plant and other job placements for those not qualifying at Inland. Counseling was available from the house staff. Residence in the house was voluntary, without any effect on parole status. At the end of one year, the failure rate for house residents was 21%, compared to 16% for nonresident parolees. Those in the house were subject to more intense surveillance (higher risk of apprehension but possibly more effective deterrence) and may have been worse risks, since those who had an option to live with their families tended to do so (Vasoli and Fahey, 1970).

Juvenile parolees placed in a halfway house in Portland, Oregon, where they received vocational training and group counseling for several months after release had a higher rate of return to confinement at six months than parolees who received vocational training but did not reside in a halfway house—43% versus 31%, the difference not being significant (Lipton et al., 1975:270-280; Keller and Alper, 1970).

Boys released from Wisconsin training schools who returned to their own homes were compared with those placed in boarding homes or group homes. Although those who returned to their own homes were considered the best risks, they had a considerably higher rate of reincarceration within six months after release (Monson and Cowden, 1968). A similar finding was reported from Ohio (Keller and Alper, 1970:154).

Federal "prerelease guidance centers"—in essence, halfway houses for federal parolees—have received several evaluations. Because of the inadequacy of control procedures, results have not been clear-cut: the centers may or may not have had a small impact on recidivism. There was some evidence that, while the centers may have reduced the recidivism of young, multiple-offender car thieves, they may also have increased the recidivism of prisoners in other categories (Keller and Alper, 1970:155-156).

Two Los Angeles halfway houses for male narcotics addicts have also been evaluated. In one case, prison inmates were randomly assigned to either normal parole or residence in the half way house for an indefinite period as a condition of parole; in the halfway house they were charged $3 a night whether or not they were working (in some cases prison release funds were confiscated), and they were subjected to intense surveillance and offered group counseling. The house was located in a high drug-use, high crime area. The other halfway house was used to relieve overcrowding in the civil commitment facility to which addicts were being committed. Those released when the house was filled formed a control group. In neither case did the halfway house have a measurable effect on recidivism (Geis, 1966; Berecochea and Sing, 1971).

According to Adams (1967), men released from a prerelease center for addicts in California performed significantly worse on parole than men released directly from prison.

DISCUSSION

This survey indicates that many correctional dispositions are failing to reduce recidivism, and it thus confirms the general thrust of the Lipton, Martinson, and Wilks survey, which ended in 1967 (Lipton et al., 1975; Martinson, 1974). Much of what is now done in the name of "corrections" may serve other functions, but the prevention of return to crime is not one of them. Here and there a few favorable results alleviate the monotony, but most of these results are modest and are obtained through evaluations seriously lacking in rigor. The blanket assertion that "nothing works" is an exaggeration, but not by very much.

For someone who has believed that programs of the kind described here should work, the largely negative evaluations call for explanation. This was not undertaken here; it was not part of the commission that led to the undertaking of this survey, and such an explanation might be difficult, since many evaluations provide only sketchy descriptions of the programs themselves. However, the uniformity of results suggests that explanations probably do not lie in the details of particular programs.

I never thought it likely that most of these programs would succeed in preventing much return to crime. Where the theoretical assumptions of programs are made explicit, they tend to border on the preposterous. More often they are never made explicit, and we should be little surprised if hit-or-miss efforts fail.

The diversity of programs showing an initially favorable effect which disappears after subjects have been released for some time suggests to me that the limited effects that programs do have may be achieved, not through the conventionally imagined therapeutic effects of the programs, but by increasing legitimate aspirations and commitment to the avoidance of illegal behavior, probably as a result of social attention and, in some instances, possibly through special deterrence. That this effect slowly extinguishes when offenders return to their old social worlds is exactly what we should expect; it shows the limitations of an individual approach to the elimination of criminality.

NOTES

1. The survey is limited to studies conducted in the United States and extends to the end of 1975. Studies were included if they involved a sufficient number of subjects to warrant meaningful conclusions, involved programs in which entry originated in contact with the criminal justice system (thus excluding community delinquency prevention programs), used a control group to establish a baseline for comparison, and measured success in terms of reduction in recidivism. Limitations of space required the exclusion of methadone programs.

There is no central listing of all evaluations of correctional programs. My search included journals which regularly publish papers in this area, as well as the relevant abstracting journals for the years covered. Many unpublished studies have also been included. If the original unpublished study was no longer available, but a description of it is to be found in a published work, I have cited the published source, to aid the reader who wants more detail than is given here. When my text refers to the "significance" of a finding, it should be understood that this is statistical significance, and, unless otherwise indicated, the level will be 0.05 in a two-tailed test.

2. Section D, which reports studies involving probation plus nonresidential programs, is also relevant to this comparison, since some of the studies summarized there use prisoners as controls.

3. Altogether, 1,600 boys participated in the experiment, but results have been reported only for the first 400, and inquiries concerning outcomes for the remaining 1,200 have not been acknowledged.

4. By comparison, the California base expectancy score utilizes 12 variables, yet explains less than 20% of the variation in parole outcome at one year after release and only 5.7% of the variation at three years after release.

REFERENCES

ADAMS, S. (1961). "Interaction between individual interview therapy and treatment amenability in older youth authority wards: Inquiries concerning kinds of treatments for kinds of delinquents" (California Board of Corrections). Pp. 548-561 in N. Johnston, L. Savitz, and M.E. Wolfgang (eds.), The sociology of punishment and correction (2nd ed.). New York: John Wiley.

——— (1966). "Development of a program research service in probation: Final report" (Research report no. 27). Los Angeles: Los Angeles County Probation Department.

——— (1967). "Some findings from correctional caseload research." Federal Probation, 31(December):48.

——— (1975). Evaluative research in corrections: A practical guide. Washington, D.C.: U.S. Government Printing Office.

BABST, D.V., and MANNERING, J.W. (1965). "Probation versus imprisonment for similar types of offenders—A comparison by subsequent violations." Journal of Research in Crime and Delinquency, 2:61.

BASS, R.A. (1974). An analysis of the California Department of Corrections work furlough program in fiscal year 1969-1970. San Francisco: California Department of Corrections, Bay Area Research Unit, Research Division.

BEATTIE, R.H., and BRIDGES, C.K. (1970). Superior Court probation and/or jail sample. Sacramento: Bureau of Criminal Statistics, California Department of Justice.

BECKETT, G.E. (1974). "California Civil Addict Program release outcome trends: 1966 through 1972 release cohorts" (Civil Addict Program research unit report no. 116, November). Sacramento: Civil Addict Program.

BELESS, D.W., and REST, E.R. (n.d.). "Probation Officer Case Aide Project: Final report, Phase I." Chicago: University of Chicago Law School.

BERECOCHEA, J.E., JAMAN, D., and JONES, W. (1973). "Time served in prison and parole outcome: An experimental study" (Research report no. 49). Sacramento: California Department of Corrections, Research Division.

BERECOCHEA, J.E., and SING, G.E. (1971). "The effectiveness of a halfway house for civilly committed narcotics addicts" (Report no. 42). Sacramento: California Department of Corrections.

BERGER, R.J., CROWLEY, J.E., GOLD, M., GRAY, J., and ARNOLD, M.S. (1975). Experiment in a juvenile court—A study of a program of volunteers working with juvenile probationers. Ann Arbor, Mich.: Institute for Social Research.

BULL, J.L. (1967). "Long jail terms and parole outcome" (Research report no. 28). Sacramento: California Department of Corrections, Research Division.

California Department of Corrections (1958). Intensive treatment program: Second annual report. Sacramento: Author.

California Department of Corrections, Research Division (1963). Annual research review, 1962. Sacramento: Author.

――― (1971). Annual research review, 1970. Sacramento: Author.

――― (n.d.). California prisoners, 1968: Summary statistics of felon prisoners and parolees. Sacramento: Author.

CARNEY, F.J., and BOTTOME, E.D. (1967). "An evaluation of a mental health program in a maximum security correctional institution." Unpublished paper, Massachusetts Department of Corrections.

CRONIN, R.C. (1975). A report on the experience of the Probation Employment and Guidance Program: September 1973-May 1975. Rochester, N.Y.: University of Rochester, Graduate School of Management.

DAVIDSON, W.S., RAPPAPORT, J., SEIDMAN, E., BERCK, P.L., and HERRING, J. (n.d.). "The diversion of adolescents in legal jeopardy: An experimental examination." Unpublished paper.

DAVIS, C. (1974). "The Parole Research Project." Pp. 49-53 in K.S. Griffiths and G.S. Ferdun (eds.), A review of accumulated research in the California Youth Authority. Sacramento: California Youth Authority.

DICKOVER, R.M., MAYNARD, V.E., and PAINTER, J.E. (1971). "A study of vocational training in the California Department of Corrections Research Division" (Research report no. 40). Sacramento: California Department of Corrections.

DITMAN, K., CRAWFORD, G., FORGY, E., MOSKOWITZ, H., and MacANDREW, C. (1967). "A controlled experiment on the use of court probation for drunk arrests." American Journal of Psychiatry, 124:160-163.

EICHMAN, C. (1966). "Impact of the Gideon decision upon crime and sentencing in Florida: A study of recidivism and socio-cultural change" (Research monograph 2). Tallahassee: Florida Division of Corrections, Research and Statistics Section.

EMPEY, L.T., and ERICKSON, M.L. (1972). The Provo experiment. Lexington, Mass.: Lexington Books.

EMPEY, L.T., and LUBECK, S. (1972). The Silverlake experiment: Testing delinquency theory and community intervention. Chicago: Aldine.

ERICSON, R.C., and MOBERG, D.O. (1968). "The rehabilitation of parolees." Minneapolis: Minneapolis Rehabilitation Center.

FEISTMAN, E.G. (1966). "Comparative analysis of the Willowbrook-Harber Intensive Services Program" (Research report no. 28). Los Angeles: Los Angeles County Probation Department, Research Office.

FISHER, G.A., and ERICKSON, M.L. (1973). "On assessing the effects of official reactions to juvenile delinquency." Journal of Research in Crime and Delinquency, 10(July): 177-194.

FULTON, W.S. (1969). "A future for correctional rehabilitation? Federal Offenders Rehabilitation Program: Final report." Olympia: Washington Coordinating Council for Occupational Education, Division of Vocational Rehabilitation.

GEIS, G. (1966). The East Los Angeles Halfway House for Narcotics Addicts. Los Angeles: Institute for Crime and Delinquency.

GLASER, D. (1964). The effectiveness of a prison and parole system. Indianapolis: Bobbs-Merrill.

GOLD, M., and WILLIAMS, J.R. (1969). "National study of the aftermath of apprehension." Prospectus, 3:3.

GUTTMAN, E.S. (1963). "Effects of short-term psychiatric treatment on boys in two California Youth Authority institutions" (Research report no. 36). Sacramento: California Youth Authority.

HAVEL, J. (1965). "Special intensive parole unit, phase four, parole outcome study" (Research report no. 13). Sacramento: California Department of Corrections.

HAWORTH, G. (n.d.). "The impact of significant others on the reduction of recidivism." Unpublished paper.

HOLT, N. (1974). "Rational risk-taking: Some alternatives to traditional correctional programs." Paper presented to the American Correctional Association Conference on the Parole-Corrections Project, San Antonio, Texas.

HUDSON, C.H. (1973). An experimental study of the differential effects of parole supervision for a group of adolescent boys and girls. Washington, D.C.: Law Enforcement Assistance Administration.

JAMAN, D.R., BENNETT, L.A., and BERECOCHEA, J.E. (1974). "Early discharge from parole: Policy, practice and outcome" (Research report no. 51). Sacramento: California Department of Corrections.

JAMAN, D.R., and DICKOVER, M. (1969). "A study of parole outcome as a function of time served" (Research report no. 35). Sacramento: California Department of Corrections, Research Division.

JEFFREY, R., and WOOLPERT, S. (1974). "Work furlough as an alternative to incarceration: An assessment of its effects on recidivism and social cost." Journal of Criminal Law and Criminology, 65:405-415.

JENKINS, W.O., WITHERSPOON, A.D., DEVINE, M.D., De VALERA, E.K., MULLER, J.B., BARTON, M.C., and McKEE, J.M. (1974). "The post-prison analysis of criminal behavior and longitudinal follow-up evaluation of institutional treatment." Montgomery, Ala.: Rehabilitation and Research Foundation.

JESNESS, C.F. (1965). "The Fricot Ranch study." Sacramento: California Youth Authority.

--- (1974). "The Youth Center Research Project preliminary findings." Pp. 26-32 in K.S. Griffiths and G.S. Ferdun (eds.), A review of accumulated research in the California Youth Authority. Sacramento: California Youth Authority.

JEW, C.C., CLANON, T.L., and MATTOCKS, A.L. (1972). "The effectiveness of group psychotherapy in a correctional institution." American Journal of Psychiatry, 129:602-605.

JEW, C.C., KIM, L.I.C., and MATTOCKS, A.L. (1975). "Effectiveness of group psychotherapy with character disordered prisoners" (Research report no. 56). Sacramento: California Department of Corrections, Research Division.

JOHNSON, B. (1962). "Parole performance of the first year's releases, Parole Research Project: Evaluation of reduced caseloads" (Research report no. 27). Sacramento: California Youth Authority.

KASSEBAUM, G., WARD, D.A., and WILNER, D.M. (1971). Prison treatment and parole survival. New York: John Wiley.

KAWAGUCHI, R.M., and SIFF, L.M. (1967). "An analysis of intensive probation services, Phase II" (Research report no. 29). Los Angeles: Los Angeles County Probation Department.

KELLER, O.J., Jr., and ALPER, B.S. (1970). Halfway houses: Community-centered correction and treatment. Lexington, Mass.: Lexington Books.

KELLY, F.J., and BAER, D.J. (1971). "Physical challenge as a treatment for delinquency." Crime and Delinquency, 17(October):437-445.

KETTERLING, M. (1972). "Rehabilitation of women in the Milwaukee County Jail: An exploration experiment." Unpublished Ph.D. dissertation, University of Michigan.

KLEIN, M.W. (1975). "Alternative dispositions for juvenile offenders: An assessment of the Los Angeles County Sheriff's Department's Juvenile Referral and Resource Development Program." Unpublished paper.

KNIGHT, D. (1969). "The Marshall Program: Assessment of a short-term treatment program, Part I: Parole outcome and background characteristics" (Reserach report no. 56). Sacramento: California Youth Authority.

KOLODNEY, S., PATTERSON, P., DAETZ, D., and MARX, R.L. (1970). A study of the characteristics and recidivism experience of California prisoners. San Jose, Calif.: Public Systems, Inc.

KOSHEL, J. (1973). Deinstitutionalization–Delinquent children. Washington, D.C.: Urban Institute.

KU, R. (1974). The Volunteer Probation Counselor Program, Lincoln, Nebraska. Washington, D.C.: National Institute of Law Enforcement and Criminal Justice.

LAMB, H.R., and GOERTZEL, V. (1974). "Ellsworth House: A community alternative to jail." American Journal of Psychiatry, 131:64-68.

LAWYER, A.G. (1972). "The effects of social attention on recidivism." Journal of Volunteers with Delinquents, 1:2.

LeCLAIR, D.P. (1973). "An evaluation of the impact of the MCI Concord Day Work Program." Unpublished paper, Massachusetts Department of Corrections.

LEIBERG, L. (1971). Project Crossroads: A final report to the Manpower Administration. Washington, D.C.: National Committee for Children and Youth.

LENIHAN, K.J. (1973). "Money, jobs and crime: An experimental study of financial aid and job placement for ex-prisoners." Unpublished paper, Bureau of Social Science Research, Washington, D.C.

LEOPOLD, N. (1941). Education in prison and success on parole (Statesville Correspondence School monograph series no. 1). Joliet, Ill.: Statesville Penitentiary Correspondence School.

LERMAN, P. (1968). "Evaluative studies of institutions for delinquents: Implications for research and social policy." Social Work, 13:55.

––– (1975). Community treatment and social control: A critical analysis of juvenile correctional policy. Chicago: University of Chicago Press.

LEWIS, M.V. (1973). Prison education and rehabilitation: Illusion or reality? University Park: Pennsylvania State University, Institute for Research on Human Resources.

LIPTON, D., MARTINSON, R., and WILKS, J. (1975). The effectiveness of correctional treatment: A survey of treatment evaluation studies. New York: Praeger.

MAISER, T. (1969). Resocialization of the paroled non-aggressive predatory offender. Washington, D.C.: U.S. Department of Justice.

MARTINSON, R. (1974). "What works? Questions and answers about prison reform." Public Interest, 10(spring):22-54.

McCORKLE, L.W., ELIAS, A., and BIXBY, F.L. (1958). The Highfields story: An experimental treatment project for youthful offenders. New York: Henry Holt.

McEACHERN, A.W. (1968). "The juvenile probation system." American Behavioral Scientist, 11:1.

MILLER, L.C. (1970). "Southfields: Evaluation of a short-term inpatient treatment center for delinquents." Crime and Delinquency, 16:350.

MOLOFF, M.J. (1967). "Forestry camp study: Comparison of recidivism rates of camp-eligible boys randomly assigned to camp and institutional programs" (Research report no. 53). Sacramento: California Youth Authority.

MONSON, L., and COWDEN, J.C. (1968). "How effective is aftercare?" Crime and Delinquency, 14:360-366.

MOORE, R.N. (n.d.). "Evaluative research of a community-based crime prevention program." Unpublished paper.

MOYNAHAN, M.J. (1975). "Volunteer probation counselors in Spokane County, Washington." Spokane: District Court Probation Office.

——— (1976). Personal communication.

MUELLER, P.F.C. (1965). "Advanced releases to parole" (Research report no. 20). Sacramento: California Department of Corrections, Research Division.

MULLEN, J. (1974). Pre-trial services: An evaluation of policy related research. Cambridge, Mass.: Abt Associates.

MULLEN, J., CARLSON, K., EARLE, R., BLEW, C., and LI, L. (1974). Pre-trial services: An evaluation of policy related research. Cambridge, Mass.: Abt Associates.

National Council on Crime and Delinquency (n.d.). Instead of prison: A report on the Community Treatment Project for Repeat Offenders, Oakland County, Michigan. Hackensack, N.J.: Author.

NOLD, J., and WILPERS, M. (1975). "Wilderness training as an alternative to incarceration." Pp. 155-169 in C.R. Dodge (ed.), A nation without prisons: Alternative to incarceration. Lexington, Mass.: Lexington Books.

OSTROM, R.M., STEELE, C.M., ROSENBLOOD, L.K., and MIRELS, H.L. (1971). "Modification of delinquent behavior." Journal of Applied Social Psychology, 1:118.

PALMER, T.B. (1972). "Differential placement of delinquents in group homes: Final report, the Group Home Project." Sacramento: California Youth Authority.

——— (1973). "Response to 'Social control and community treatment of juvenile delinquents: Issues in correctional policy' by Dr. Paul Lerman." Unpublished paper.

——— (1974a). "Observations and specific analyses in response to Dr. Lerman's 'A methodological note on the CTP analysis.' " Unpublished paper.

——— (1974b). "The Youth Authority's Community Treatment Project." Federal Probation, 38:3.

PALMER, T.B., and HERRERA, A.H. (1972). "Community Treatment Project post-discharge analysis: An updating of the 1969 analysis for Sacramento and Stockton males." Unpublished paper.

PANAGOPOULOS, L., and GARDNER, J.C. (1969). "An evaluation of the effect of the fellowship program at M.C.I., Norfolk, on Recidivism." Unpublished paper, Massachusetts Department of Corrections.

PERSONS, R. (1967). "Relationship between psychotherapy with institutionalized boys and subsequent community adjustment." Journal of Consulting Psychology, 31:137.

POND, E.M. (1970). "The Los Angeles Community Delinquency Control Project: An experiment in the rehabilitation of delinquents in an urban community" (Research report no. 60). Sacramento: California Youth Authority.

——— (1974). "The Los Angeles Community Delinquency Control Project study." Pp. 49-51 in K.S. Griffiths and G.S. Ferduns (eds.), A review of accumulated research in the California Youth Authority. Sacramento: California Youth Authority.

REINARMAN, C. (1973). Direct financial assistance to parolees project. San Francisco: Scientific Analysis Corporation.

ROBISON, J.O. (1973). "Correctional research." Federal Probation, 27(September):59-60.

——— (1976). Personal communication.

ROBISON, J.O., and KEVORKIAN, M. (1967). "Intensive treatment project, Phase II, Parole outcome: Interim report" (Research report no. 27). Sacramento: California Department of Corrections.

ROBISON, J.O., and SMITH, G. (1971). "The effectiveness of correctional programs." Crime and Delinquency, 17(January):67-80.

ROBISON, J., and TAKAGI, P. (1968). "Case decisions in a state parole system" (Research report no. 31). Sacramento: California Department of Corrections, Research Division.

ROBISON, J.O., WILKINS, L.T., CARTER, R.M., and WAHL, A. (1969). "The San Francisco Project: A study of federal probation and parole: Final report." Unpublished paper, San Francisco Project.

ROSS, H.L., and BLUMENTHAL, M. (1974). "Sanctions for the drinking driver: An experimental study." Journal of Legal Studies, 3:53-61.

ROVNER-PIECZENIK, R. (1970). Project Crossroads as pre-trial intervention: A program evaluation. Washington, D.C.: National Committee for Children and Youth.

RUDOFF, A. (1974). "Jail inmates at work: Technical supplement." Sacramento: California Department of Rehabilitation, Division of Vocational Rehabilitation.

RUDOFF, A., and ESSELSTYN, T.C. (1973). "Evaluating work furlough: A followup." Federal Probation, 27(June):48-53.

SADEN, S.J. (1962). "Correctional research at Jackson prison." Journal of Correctional Education, 15:22.

SCHWITZGEBEL, R.K., and BAER, D.J. (1967). "Intensive supervision by parole officers as a factor in recidivism reduction of male delinquents." Journal of Psychology, 67:75.

SCHNUR, A. (1948). "The educational treatment of prisoners and recidivism." American Journal of Sociology, 54:142.

SECKEL, J.P. (1965). "Experiments in group counseling at two youth institutions" (Research report no. 46). Sacramento: California Youth Authority.

––– (1969). "The Fremont Experiment: Assessment of residential treatment at a Youth Authority reception center" (Research report no. 50). Sacramento: California Youth Authority.

––– (1974a). "Short-term treatment studies." Pp. 7-12 in K.S. Griffiths and G.S. Ferdun (eds.), A review of accumulated research in the California Youth Authority. Sacramento: California Youth Authority.

––– (1974b). "Individual and group counseling." In K.S. Griffiths and G.S. Ferdun (eds.), A review of accumulated research in the California Youth Authority. Sacramento: California Youth Authority.

––– (1974c). "Forestry camp studies." Pp. 40-45 in K.S. Griffiths and G.S. Ferdun (eds.), A review of accumulated research in the California Youth Authority. Sacramento: California Youth Authority.

SLOANE, H.N., and RALPH, J.L. (1973). "A behavior modification program in Nevada." International Journal of Offender Therapy and Comparative Criminology, 17:190-296.

SPENCER, C., and BERECOCHEA, J. (1971). "Vocational training at the California Institute for Women: An evaluation" (Research report no. 41). Sacramento: California Department of Corrections, Research Division.

STEPHENSON, R.M., and SCARPITTI, F.R. (1974). Group interaction as therapy: The use of the small group in corrections. Westport, Conn.: Greenwood.

THORNBERRY, T.P. (1971). "Punishment and crime: The effect of legal dispositions on subsequent criminal behavior." Unpublished Ph.D. dissertation, University of Pennsylvania.

TRUAX, C.B., WARGO, D.G., and SILVER, L.D. (1966). "Effects of group psychotherapy with high adequate empathy and nonpossessive warmth upon female institutionalized delinquents." Journal of Abnormal Psychology, 71:267.

VASOLI, R., and FAHEY, F. (1970). "Halfway houses for reformatory releases." Crime and Delinquency, 16:292.

VENEZIA, P.S. (1972). "Unofficial probation: An evaluation of its effectiveness." Journal of Research in Crime and Delinquency, 9(July):149.

VENEZIA, P.S., and McCONNELL, W.A. (1972). "The effect of vocational upgrading upon probationer recidivism: A one-year evaluation of the Singer/Graflex Monroe County Pilot Probation Project." Davis, Calif.: National Council on Crime and Delinquency.

Vera Institute (1972). The Manhattan Court Employment Project of the Vera Institute. New York: Author.

WALDO, G.P., and CHIRICOS, T.G. (1975). "Evaluating social policy: An empirical assessment of work release." Paper presented at the annual meeting of the American Sociological Association.

WEEKS, H.A. (1958). Youthful offenders at Highfields. Ann Arbor: University of Michigan Press.

WILLMAN, H.C., Jr., and CHUN, R.Y.F. (1973). "Homeward Bound, an alternative to the institutionalization of adjudicated juvenile offenders." Federal Probation, 38(September):52-58.

WITT, L.R. (n.d.). "Final report on Project Develop." U.S. Department of Labor, Manpower Administration, and State of New York Division of Parole.

WITTE, A.D. (1975). Work release in North Carolina: An evaluation of its post-release effects. Chapel Hill, N.C.: Institute for Research in Social Science.

WOLFGANG, M.E., FIGLIO, R.M., and SELLIN, T. (1972). Delinquency in a birth cohort. Chicago: University of Chicago Press.

ZIMRING, F.E. (1974). "Measuring the impact of pre-trial diversion from the criminal justice system." University of Chicago Law Review, 41(winter):224-241.

Chapter 6

PRISON DRUGS, PSYCHIATRY, AND THE STATE

RICHARD SPEIGLMAN

Understanding state propaganda which suggests that prisoners are mentally ill requires a study of the technology, ideology, and politics of prison psychiatry. Central factors in such a study are commitments on the part of United States capitalism to protect its economic structure, the repression which is required to continue this process, and simultaneous attempts to acquire a veil of legitimacy for the capitalist system. The latter involves processes of mystification which rely on medicine, technical innovations, and the manipulation of false consciousness among masses of citizens. Because of the failure of a major

AUTHOR'S NOTE: *This essay is an outline of the analysis in my dissertation from the now extinct School of Criminology at Berkeley, California. For greater detail on these topics, I refer the reader to Speiglman (1976). That research evolved from the political movements of the 1960s and 1970s in the United States and the work of my comrades at the School of Criminology, in particular those working in the Union of Radical Criminologists (for the union's perspective, see the journal* Crime and Social Justice*). Part of the ideology that we shared was that "crime" must be seen as a more profound concept than that commonly accepted under the state or legal definition of crime. That is, it is more important to deal with crimes of racism, sexism, exploitation, and imperialism than many of the state-defined crimes to which the criminal justice system attends. In this essay, however, I revert to the state definition of crime, because my subject is a state agency which most assuredly does not consider a more expansive definition. Thus, I advise the reader that my use of the term "crime" is unfortunately an archaic one, but one that nevertheless continues to require our critical attention in examining the practice of state agencies.*

criminal justice institution—the prison—to control and rehabilitate prisoners in a period of economic crisis, prison repression today is characterized by the appearance of technologies of coercion including psychosurgery, brainwashing, aversive conditioning, and, most pervasive, the use of psychoactive drugs—major tranquilizers especially.

This essay considers prison psychiatric repression in the light of recent national trends.[1] Particular attention is on the California prison system, long considered the model for progressive corrections.

Psychoactive drug use in United States prisons reflects the interests of the capitalist state. Although perhaps introduced as a humanitarian reform, therefore, drug use need not benefit prisoners. In practice, this and other technologies instead produce profit for industry and a repressive societal mechanism operating under a veil of legitimacy. These psychiatric technologies are reforms which serve to strengthen existing institutions without altering the underlying exploitative character of U.S. capitalism. In the case of prisons, the "criminal" surplus population may be "successfully" treated through drugs and released to the streets. This drugged parole keeps ex-prisoners out of the mainstream of the economy and serves dual functions for the capitalist state: retaining legitimation while absorbing some of the pressure of unemployment. Amidst political and economic crises the state relies on tranquilizers, correctional psychiatrists, and a medical facade to repress the threat to the ruling class which surplus labor brings. This is part of the tendency generally within the criminal justice system to pacify, mystify, and legitimate.

PRISONS AND CRISIS

Prisons reflect the larger society. At the same time that economic and political problems assailed the ruling class generally by the late 1960s, the state

My use of male pronouns in reference to prisoners and their psychiatrists in the Seguin Unit reflects the fact that my study was done in a men's prison. Hence, my continual use of masculine pronouns indicates the limitation of my research. At the same time, my impression is that women prisoners—at least in California—are repressed similarly to, if not more forcefully than, men. This subject requires more attention. (In addition, the psychiatrists in the Seguin Unit were men, although I did meet several women practicing psychiatry in other parts of the prison system in California.)

My work, specifically, came out of a dissertation collective of Berkeley radical criminologists. Annika Snare, June Kress, Lynn Cooper, Mary Marzotto, Marty Williams, and Tom Nagy read, criticized, and helped my work with creative and committed energy. This particular essay reflects the added advice of Richard Quinney, Ellen Bernstein, Bob Martin, and David F. Greenberg. I thank them all.

faced serious problems within the prisons. Budget difficulties and problems of institutional overcrowding encircled state officials. Racism in the larger community also pervaded the prisons, at times discrediting correctional officials. Prisoners, many of them conscious of their exploitation as poor people as well as of the racism practiced against them, began to strike back. Inadequate, overcrowded prisons suffering from disrepair, in combination with a heightened political consciousness in the society's economically marginal groups, produced prison rebellions, assaults, and bad publicity by the late 1960s. The public was aware that prisons were not doing their self-defined work of rehabilitation and also that there was substantial racism, unrest, and violence pervading the institutions.

In the early 1970s, the United States ruling class found itself in the following difficult situation with regard to prisons. There was a need for strong control over dissident groups generally in the country. The prison movement was increasingly political and particularly strong, inside and out. The state was under threat from prisoners' organizational cohesiveness, support, and activity. Further, there was a legitimacy crisis. The crisis in legitimacy was directly related to the public's increased awareness of and concern about economic inequality, the war in Vietnam, crime in the streets, Watergate, and depressive living conditions. The state, agent of the ruling class, faced an additional crisis in its treatment of prisoners.

Liberal legislative investigations and reports, news articles, and public meetings criticized the less-than-smooth operation of the prison system. Added critique and activity from the radical left further undermined the credibility of prison systems and the criminal justice system generally.

The resultant requirement was that the state quietly but decisively divest the prisons of some less-threatening criminals through probation-subsidy programs and institute new technical control over the remaining prisoners. Because the state itself was suffering from a fiscal crisis, costs had to be limited (O'Connor, 1973).[2] The state will try a variety of approaches, turning to the most secure, least expensive kind of lockup possible.

Historical conditions made possible the contemporary psychotechnical alternative. There was a strong ideological basis for relying on the treatment-rehabilitation model. A new twist to the old formula produced psychotechnical physical control. It met the requirements of low cost but high appearance of legitimacy. The approach augmented the state's image through the appearance of humanity, liberality, and effectiveness.

At the lower custody extremes of the punishment hierarchy, officials have substantial control over prisoners through carrot-stick inducements. Privileges are valuable and subject to being rescinded. At the top, the situation is different.

Threats of harsher punishment carry less weight. Most of the prisoners at this level have rejected the inducements which abound in minimum conditions. George Jackson, for example, repeatedly stressed that the prison had virtually no more control over him when he was locked up. The result is that the prison must look to more extensive use of immediate physical control over these prisoners. The "Adjustment Center," or isolation, is one such tool.

Direct control is of increasing importance when prisoners have rejected honor programs, as many did by 1970. The California prison administrators' practice, as outline in the following official statement, was to utilize segregated housing (California Department of Corrections, 1974:21):

> The most recent action taken by the administration of the correctional system is the increase in security control for those few inmates requiring this kind of program. This group, estimated as less than ten percent, will not be allowed to mix with other inmates and lead insurrections, produce knives, or assault others.

Direct physical control in this manner is both expensive—expense is encountered at the simplest levels, such as bringing food to the prisoners since they are not allowed to leave their cells to attend the dining hall—and a threat to the credibility of corrections.

A different approach, one with a long history, relies on the notion that prisoners are sick and require psychological or physiological treatment. Over the years, prison officials have explored various techniques which might prove useful in supplanting direct physical control over prisoners. With the contradictions presented by the political economy and the prisoners' movement, officials continue to expend resources in this area.

Within the larger context of state needs for legitimacy and control, the state and its prison officials balance economic resources in the light of the level of technology available for repression within the prisons. At times, strong state needs to repress political movements coincide with the availability of economic resources to implement a wide range of technical innovations. In other cases the state may see the need for repression as secondary to fiscal requirements. On the prison level the result in such an event would be long-term lockup in the least expensive but politically acceptable manner.

In this decade, prison systems have developed and experimented with a variety of techniques. Behavior modification, psychosurgery, and even sophisticated lockups like the California Medical Facility's Maximum Psychiatric Diagnostic Unit or the federal START program proved unproductive in terms of fiscal and legitimation requirements. Drugs, however, continue to dominate the current field because of their professional and benign appearance.

A few years ago the use of tranquilizers was almost rare in state prisons.

Today, large segments of prisoners within various prisons—those considered management problems—are kept continuously drugged. At any one time, now, fully one-quarter of the prisoners at the California Medical Facility and California's Men's Colony are on heavy doses of major tranquilizers. In addition, there are hundreds of convicts in those prisons taking other drugs. Other prisons throughout the country also prescribe massive amounts of drugs for many prisoners. When sensory deprivation or murder is necessary but illegitimate, the state drugs.

DRUGS, MENTAL HEALTH, AND ECONOMY

An understanding of contemporary changes in state prisons takes us not only to an historical account of correctional facilities but also to an analysis of the social role of mental hospitals. In reviewing mental health ideology, institutional arrangements, and technical developments, one sees the basis for corresponding developments in prisons. A crisis of legitimacy and economy in the prisons similar to that in state hospitals a few years earlier led to the utilization of similar technological forms in the prison system.

The mental hospital has undergone a major transformation in the 20-odd years since 1955. Overcrowded, brutal, and scandalous institutions have changed into modern-looking hospitals. These changes have remained at the microscopic level, epitomized and led by the introduction of new drugs into the psychiatric technology repertoire. Resultant effects on institutions have been deceptive, falsely described as revolutionary changes. The putative revolution, however, has merely been a shift of the political-economic and social role of the old state and county hospitals, most often to community mental health facilities. The community mental health movement has closed many hospitals.[3] The old, large institutions which remain no longer appall the public. Instead, walls newly painted pastel colors, modernized facilities, and personnel dressed in professional whites meet the observer's eye to instill confidence. These superficial changes within the mental hospitals, in addition to the move into community facilities, followed the development and introduction of the major tranquilizing medications in the 1950s. The most important of these newly synthesized drugs was chlorpromazine, much better known through its monopoly trade name for many years, Thorazine.

Chlorpromazine was at first perceived as taking pressure off an overworked hospital staff. Later, it became clear that the drug was a boon to the state more generally. Swazey (1972:347) has explained that enthusiasm for Thorazine was originally limited to the hospitals:

The possibility of effectively treating mental disorders with a safe, simple chemical agent—one that could be administered readily and relatively inexpensively to large numbers of patients—was a special desideratum for psychiatrists working in the overcrowded and inadequately staffed public mental hospitals of the 1950s.

Later, devotion to the drugs spread to the legislative chamber as well.

A great amount of faith was put in the new drug by the state as larger perspectives were drawn. Researcher Crane (1973:125) has explained this in the context of the state's necessity to retain legitimacy and fiscal strength. Reliance on drugs was largely due to administrators' unsuccessful efforts to improve the image of their psychiatric institutions, the "chronic shortage of trained personnel and spiraling costs of medical care." The result, he says, was faith in psychopharmacological agents. Now, the situation is such that drug therapy is considered indispensable. In part, this is due to an early perception that the drugs save the state millions of dollars; in part, because of the added legitimacy that the state gains. In 1963, a U.S. Senate Committee on Appropriations report detailed that the country had saved about $2 billion in reduced number of patient-beds because of the drugs. By the 1970s, Swazey (1972) reported, the National Institute of Mental Health was estimating that the cost of schizophrenia amounted to $14 billion annually. The slightest cut in expenses could be considerable to big business mental health.

The use and reliance on drugs continues in spite of and in the face of potential dangers to patients from long-term exposure to chemical agents. Unforeseeable dangers are ignored, as are permanent neurological disorders which have become commonplace among patients treated with the phenothiazines and other drugs (Crane, 1973). In spite of the uncertainty about their long-term effects, the drugs are used because of the numbers of "mentally ill persons" and limited treatment facilities.

On a local scale, and more recently, a similar explanation for the use of drugs came from a San Francisco Social Services Department caseworker who said of the mentally retarded in that city (Ross, 1974:6):

> Of course they're drugged. . . . Half the welfare community is walking around tranquilized. . . . They'd get talkative when visitors come. They'd demand more services and want to go out instead of sitting on an old couch all day if they weren't on drugs.

To do more would require vast sums of money for staff, institutions, and other services.

Drugs are at the center of treatment programs because the state finds them effective. Drugs are less expensive than full services. They disguise or camouflage social and political problems and provide legitimacy to the state. They are an inconspicuous form of repression and inhumanity. Some writers (Crane, 1973:125) are appalled at the personal costs arising from the drugs themselves: patients on drugs who are unproductive, ex-patients perhaps "as dependent and alienated as those confined to an institution." Swazey (1972, quoting Mosher and Feinsilver, 1971:1) has provided figures which suggest that, partially because of drugs, only 15% to 40% of those schizophrenics living in the community achieve self-support through work or successful functioning as housewives.[4] Neither author, however, recognizes that the masses of unemployed who do not seek work reduce strain from the capitalist economy. Many subsist at poverty welfare levels. Others are dependent on their families for support. In either case, even with state-supplied medication, these people are a cheaper state expense when on drugs than when in institutions.

With its medication, the drug industry bestowed a heritage of pastel institutions, progressive medicine, and enlightenment. These drugs became a creation mystifying thousands of persons termed psychotic and millions of family members and friends. Most importantly, Thorazine permitted an era of invisible repression to overtake state hospitals and the modern institutions which have followed. The drug brought a standard treatment form which officials were shortly to add to the prison systems of the country as well.

DRUGS AND TECHNOLOGY

A full comprehension of the prison roles which drugs and doctors play must look beyond technological advance and fiscal and legitimacy requirements. Any complete picture of the psychiatric and drug phenomena in prisons must take into consideration the role of the drug industry.

Since the sulfa and antibiotic wonder drugs became available for broad use in the late 1930s and the mid-1940s, more people have recovered from major illnesses, in a quicker and smoother period, in spite of many serious drug-induced reactions. The certainty of health which these and other later drugs promise millions of people is characteristically lacking in one particular class of drugs, the tranquilizers. With those drugs the physicians and health industry profit in the form of eased treatment, monetary reward, and a sense of accomplishment, while the patients gain little uncompromised health. The "cure" rate for tranquilizers has lagged far behind other modern drugs. As a result, one must question the massive resources poured into advertising, marketing, and promoting the use of tranquilizers and other psychoactive drugs.

In the prison system, the capitalist drug industry influences administrative, fiscal, therapeutic, and political decisions through drug policies. One can see the health interests of the convicts subordinated to these other considerations in treatment programs as well as in experimentation on new drugs. Questions arise about the wisdom of long-term, widespread use of drugs in an ever-expanding sphere of prisoner-patients and parolees. Unexamined are questions of the impact that systematic drug dependence has on both prisoners and institutions, a kind of social addiction, and questions of possible political and biological fallout from chronic use. Instead, the drug industry's promises of easier work for staff, better management of prisoners, a mythical and mystical cure for criminals and crime, and repression of the political consciousness of prisoners all join to bring tons of drugs into U.S. prisons.[5]

As Bernstein and Lennard (1973:21) have suggested, drugs are "particularly functional for maintaining an uneasy and strained social system. . . . The use of drugs thus diminishes the pressure to seek other and more fundamental solutions." The result is that both individuals and institutions are convinced that "there is a pill for every ill, and that there is—in fact, there *must* be—a chemical answer to every physical, emotional, and sociological discomfort of mankind" (Silverman and Lee, 1974:22).

In the early years of California's modern prison history, difficult prisoners were treated to brutalities and isolated cells and, in places like the California Medical Facility (CMF) at Terminal Island, to electric shock. Slowly, small amounts of drugs were used. At CMF's later home in Vacaville, by the mid-1960s, the drug era had taken hold. In the area for prisoners allegedly mentally ill, Seguin Unit, the institution provided medical treatment and television as the predominant therapy. Medicine and the Unit psychiatrist became the crucial foci of the ward. Throughout the Unit, prisoners visit and ask to see the doctor constantly, not only because he is the ultimate power but also because a visit provides something to do: freedom from a cell, talk, or treatment of an injury. Because of detrimental living conditions and with more medical attention available than most people on the outside receive, many men locked up become conscientious about their health. Others become preoccupied by it. Pills, the most developed technology within medicine, are critical objects of attention, behavior, and policy.

More significantly, the drugs have become part of a complex "treatment" pattern at CMF and elsewhere because they can control the anger and madness generated by prisons and bypass the necessity for humane crime-control programs. The words of CMF workers portray the importance of this approach to institutional problems. A medical technical assistant who had been with CMF since shortly after the Vacaville facility opened drew the following historical picture:

Thorazine and Stelazine were new, and they were realizing more benefit and what they could do. If a man is acting up, you know you got to give him something. Use a PRN [*pro re nata,* drug to be administered "as needed"], where we can hit him if an extra dose is needed. Then the doctor can decide. We've always had them for emergencies.

Another medical technical assistant described the conditions in Vacaville's early S-Wing, a part of Seguin Unit: "When they [the major tranquilizers] came out, they were a godsend for down there. They were orangutans," he punctuated. This attitude of faith in medication and the drug industry is quite general. At a statewide meeting of the California Correctional Psychiatrists' Association in April 1971, the physicians applauded the drugs for providing "significant assistance in the control of psychotic thinking, overwhelming anxiety, depression, and serious acting-out behavior." This professional, assuring language finds translation in concrete descriptions.

A CMF psychiatrist elaborated on the importance of drugs by describing that when prisoners get "out of control" they are put in a more secure place and given a "more intensive medication or some type of psychopharmaceutical treatment to bring them down." In short, one psychologist put it, "You medicate a lot of the psychiatric symptoms."

Dr. Robert Kuehnert, recalling the first use of tranquilizers at CMF, Terminal Island, described the effect as follows: "It came as a quiet, blessed relief." More graphically, Dr. David Schmidt from San Quentin said that tranquilizers "relieve anxiety, tension, hold down riots, knifing, blackmail, and gambling." When asked during a CMF Special Treatment Board meeting whether a particular man was on Thorazine because he was schizophrenic, Dr. Alvin Groupe responded, "No, to calm him down." In a similar situation, a note in a Seguin Unit resident's file said, "The medication can be used to slow down his disruptive and aggressive behavior, but there is little chance of it altering his thought disturbance to a significant extent." Clearly, the drugs serve purposes other than the health of the recipients. Administrators note the importance of having the prison as an easy place in which to work. Former CMF Superintendent Dr. Marion King's comment on tranquilizers was: "It made it a better place to live in, and things were quieter, and there wasn't as much trouble. We needed less staff." Drugs make the staff happier, hold down institutional costs, and permit the prisons to operate. As a result, after over 20 years on the market, drugs now pervade and delimit the daily activity in large parts of California prisons. They absolve the institutional officials from responsibility for structural changes otherwise necessitated by the bankrupt criminal justice system.

Because the use of drugs has a wide impact on prisoners and their prison existence in California and the rest of the country, it is important to take a closer look at the dynamics of drug use. There is a dangerous game played out between convict and psychiatric staff. To be released from the indeterminate sentence (a type of sentencing prevalent in California until 1977), the prisoner had to have positive reports written about him to the Adult Authority, California's parole board.[6] Such psychiatric reports would find the convict rehabilitated in the value-laden terms of the middle-class, usually white doctor. To gain acceptance from the professional mental health staffer, the poor, often Third World, prisoner had to articulate an alien philosophy, often until he actually believed it. The prison was—and still is—thereby exchanged for walls built up within: a new ideology, a false, nonmaterialist consciousness.

In practice and in the words of several psychiatrists, this mind control or class warfare is clear. Dr. David Owens described to Jessica Mitford how the prison treatment had to include assaults on the prisoners' values. "Your treatment is not done when you have the guy stopped hallucinating and seeing delusions —you are really just starting then because you have to start treating character disorders and try to change the value system and make some kind of law-abiding citizen out of him" (Mitford, 1976). An Adult Authority and parole release report on a CMF prisoner formerly at Soledad said that the prisoner's denial of responsibility for his imprisonment deterred attempts to alter his behavior and his value system. Finally, during rounds in the Seguin Unit one day, a prisoner asked the psychiatrist I was with for a reduction in dosage. Before responding, the doctor asked the prisoner whether he was keeping his "old ideas." The convict responded, "I'm dropping those."

Drugs and their psychiatrist-pushers are part of the larger program to establish false consciousness in politically unacceptable prisoners. As adjusters, Howard Levy (1970:9) wrote, prison psychiatrists "do meet with a certain measure of success. And this is the evil, for to be 'adjusted' to one's own imminent destruction is to promote the cause of one's self-victimization; it invites the victim's mind suicide." Since values reflect class background and position, the mind suicide of many prisoners adds up to class warfare.

CHEMICAL PACIFICATION

One result of drug use for increasing numbers of prisoners is that much of their energy finds a focus on the drugs and their use, thereby undermining potentially threatening ideas and acts against the system which utilizes the drugs. Drugs, then, depoliticize in two ways. Physically, they combat potential conditions for opposition against the prison or capitalist system. In addition, they convert prisoners into docile people concerned with the dose, time, form, and type of the next administration. As a result, drugs are not forced upon all prisoners. Rather, many convicts see that medications play important roles in their lives.

For example, some prisoners believe that medication suggests a medical explanation for their criminal behavior, thereby increasing their chances for parole. As explained to me by several prisoners, their illegal behavior takes on the appearance of medical causation, logically permitting recovery and hence their release from responsibility for the criminal act. As a result, officials can see after "recovery" that there is no expectation of future criminal activity. Hence parole follows, the logic goes. Some prisoners simply desire a high or chemical escape for as much of their prison time as possible. Still others hoard their drugs and use them in place of money or cigarettes for black market trading.

To whatever variety of uses prisoners put the drugs, the medications are available—and must be seen—as the result of administrative policy. Drugs are adopted as the major solution to the fiscal and political crisis in a sophisticated classification and tracking program within the prison system. They lead to effective control of many prisoners and organizations and a new power structure within the system. The psychiatrists play double-agent roles, allegedly serving both prisoners and authorities.

PSYCHIATRY AND THE STATE

Prison psychiatry plays an increasingly large role in contemporary state strategies for repression and legitimation. Psychiatrists can explain and repress prison dissonance simultaneously. Titles offering legitimacy and degrees permitting the administration of drugs soothe both prisoners and the public and mystify the politics of punishment. Prison doctors serve the administration through such functions as authoring parole reports, providing intelligence on their patients, and cooling out and indoctrinating prisoners and interested citizens with individualistic understandings of imprisonment.

This development was not the product of an enterprising doctor but a strategy of the state. The technologies and professional roles must always be kept in historical context. Psychiatrists and their Thorazine for mid-century prisoners—like Ritalin for school children, Valium for oppressed housewives, and welfare for the poor—are specific tools at particular times.

Today drugs have begun to supplement and replace iron bars. Whether administered inside a prison or on the streets through community mental health clinics, drugs provide the mechanism for sifting large numbers out of the productive system. After a period in which rehabilitation was thought (or publicized as) possible through group therapy, the inherence of criminal status now is often described as biological and permanent. Drug therapy, then, is seen as a permanent requirement for most prisoners begun on drugs. Group therapy continues as well because of its control quality, and treatment philosophies pervade the rhetoric of prisons.[7]

The treatment model provides comfort to liberals, letting them believe that progress is under way. It also consoles the state (and the warden) with the knowledge that there is a powerful—and socially acceptable—mechanism for repression.

The state relies on depoliticization through the medicalization and individualization of prisoners' conditions. The system—prison and entire capitalist economy—is defended, protected, and rationalized when the correctional psychiatrists insist that they are humane service workers.

Psychiatrists in particular obscure people's understanding of their experience and prevent their recognition of the social bases and collective nature of their oppression. The editors of *Health/PAC Bulletin* (1970; see also Center for Research on Criminal Justice, 1975) wrote, "Psychiatry and psychology have become the pseudo-scientific underpinning for a repressive ideology which promotes alienation, from oneself, from others, and from reality."

The prison doctors themselves require particular attention as they, like the drug industry, form a critical link between some otherwise unimportant chemicals and a use of those drugs in the bodies of prisoners in a political context. Psychiatrists contribute legitimacy to the state repressive apparatus through their status as medical doctors. Their language, education, dress, and work setting combine to signify that psychiatry utilizes medicine to treat persons diagnosed as mentally ill and by implication that what we term "mental illness" is a physical affliction similar, say, to pneumonia. Appeals to this medical model of mental illness and criminality, a high degree of professionalism, and specialized technology combine to form a mystifying and repressive ideology and practice.

The result is that, in psychiatry as well as other areas, medicine becomes a major institution of "social control" in place of law and religion (Zola, 1972). Thus we should not be surprised if in a time of capitalism's fiscal and ideological crisis we read in the press (*San Francisco Chronicle,* 1975) that "ten per cent of the U.S. population or more than 20 million people suffer from some form of mental or emotional illness." Since there is "new hope for mental cases" because doctors have "learned that much mental illness is basically biological in nature" and successfully treated through chemicals, it therefore comes as no shock to learn that criminals in particular are mentally disordered.

Mental illness, then, is political and ideological as practically defined and treated. Pushing the concept even further, one finds good indication that what we consider mental illness is even politically caused. Phyllis Chesler's *Women and*

Madness (1972) argued convincingly that many women are delivered to or seek psychiatric treatment and hospital refuge as a result of their powerlessness in a sexist society. Although operating under a facade of treatment and reform, mental hospitals are no less repressive than prisons, Chesler and others would argue. Rather, psychiatrists are a more refined method for obtaining submission.[8]

As a result, psychiatrists gain central roles as institutional rule keepers. Their administration of drugs is a direct contribution to institutional physical and political control. The use of drugs represses three ways: through direct use, through threat of use, and through effects on prisoners' ideologies. Drugs are an efficient form for isolating difficult prisoners.

The extent to which drugging becomes a large part of the psychiatrist's job becomes clear from reading the minutes of a 1973 psychotropic drug meeting at the California Medical Facility:

> Because of the staff shortages and the fact that one psychiatrist is covering all of S-Wing right now, the patients receive very little of the psychiatrist's time and heavier reliance is placed on the use of medication.

Another aspect of this role expansion reflects the degree to which officials rely on psychiatrists for purposes of legitimation or direct repression.

Providing additional support to prison and parole officials, the psychiatrists devote a great deal of time to administrative matters. The energy spent on parole considerations has become so great that many members of the departmental staff in California voice distress about the topic. Things seem to have gotten worse—at least until very lately. As early as 1967, the minutes of the Chief Psychiatrists' Conference (California Department of Corrections, 1967) reflected this concern with parole:

> It is the general experience of the Departmental psychiatrists that a great portion of their time is devoted to writing reports and that some of this is not sufficiently valuable or productive that it should absorb time which might be spent in treatment.

Correctional psychiatrists educate and serve California's parole board, the Adult Authority, providing rationales for their decisions and delivering medicinal protection in cases which might otherwise endanger the state's legitimacy. Part of this work involves a cycle from massive report writing and direct involvement with the Adult Authority to less voluminous activity.

Although employed by the Department of Corrections, not the Adult Authority, the psychiatrists often feel that they work for the parole board and in fact devote a great deal of energy to activities that make sense only in light of decisions about parole. The Adult Authority's concern is with safety, to inhibit repeated criminal behavior on the part of prisoners released from prison. There is another type of safety that is implicit but not spelled out. The Adult Authority, like the rest of the criminal justice apparatus, has as its primary responsibility the perpetuation of the capitalist system. This includes a strategy to support the legitimacy of the system; that is, the safety of the system (and the Adult Authority is included here) is most important. Accordingly, the Adult Authority relies on its tools like psychiatrists to protect the political and economic system from attacks. From the Adult Authority's point of view, it is politic to have threatening convicts on parole only if their repeated criminality and criticism of the capitalist system can be muted.

How does the legitimacy end of the Adult Authority-psychiatrist function operate? There are several dimensions to the process. Legitimacy accrues through medical-psychiatric rationales for decisions. More particularly, tenuous state legitimacy is retained in those cases of incorrect decisions (that is, when a parolee commits another serious crime) if medical-psychiatric explanations can protect the Adult Authority. Also, to whatever degree possible, the Adult Authority utilizes psychiatric reports as predictors of future behavior.

In an earlier era, the Adult Authority was said to have looked at Rorschach test results in an attempt to predict future behavior and hence parole risks. On this use, then-Department of Corrections psychiatrist Harvey Powelson commented:

> To use them to predict behavior is about as valid as using a crystal ball. My sense of the situation was that the Adult Authority used the tests for rationalizations for what they'd already decided based on their own intuition. [Mitford, 1973:102]

The use of psychiatric categories and reports for political defense and legitimation is best explained in the words of a prisoner no longer in the Seguin Unit but still on psychoactive drugs in his postpsychotic category "C" status. "Probably I'll remain a 'C' until I leave," he said. "That way it doesn't make them look stupid if I fuck up [on parole] because I'm a Cat. 'C.' What else would you expect?" Further, the Adult Authority protects itself and the state by seeing to it that many prisoners are released on parole only with the stipulated prescription of tranquilizer medication.

Whether they are conscious of it or not, much of the psychiatrists' work can be understood as custodial repression. Goffman (1961:371-372) foresaw this dynamic operating when he described the psychiatrists' dilemma as follows:

> Where the psychiatrist cannot, or does not want to, leave the state mental hospital, some other paths appear to have been established for him. He may redefine his role from that of a server to that of a wise governor, embrace the custodial aspects of the institution, and devote himself to enlightened administration.

The result is a patchwork of service to prisoner-patients and to the state.

A newsletter put together by San Francisco Bay Area prison activists (Red Family, 1971:7) summarized the situation in the following brief comment:

> In short, the realities of this "rehabilitative ideal" of the "humane prison" are that (1) it disguises social control as therapy, (2) it strips a prisoner of rights, (3) it demands that a prisoner shape up to an authoritarian model out of touch with fundamental political, economic, and emotional realities. Or, as one convict said, "We are caught between the 19th Century punitive guard and the 1984 headshrinker."

The confusion of service and punitive roles becomes a concrete ambiguity.

The state of California considers its prison psychiatrists to be in a doctor-client relationship with the state itself. Accordingly, the prison psychiatrist may relate to prisoners as both clients and subjects, but, officially, prisoners are the latter, subjects. The California attorney general (1960) determined that the state is the client of the practicing prison psychiatrist and that the psychiatrist provides data on prisoners (the subjects). It was his attempt to transcend this legalistic reality which led to the firing of California prison psychiatrist Frank Rundle. Instructed to turn over the psychiatric records of a staff member's alleged prisoner assailant, Rundle refused, citing doctor-client privilege. The Department of Corrections administration decided otherwise and fired Rundle on the spot for insubordination. Author Min Yee (1973:184) wrote the following about the psychiatrist's double-agent status:

> Asked about the Rundle firing, a high-ranking CDC official told me, "Well, the dumb bastard wasn't doing his job. Those files are our files. He was supposed to get to know the inmates and tell us which ones were dangerous. He just didn't know what he was there for."

As Goffman (1961:353) would put it, in the system that Rundle challenged we see the server become the governor. In Daniels' (1972:147) words, the physician-psychiatrist takes responsibility *for* the patient, not *to* the patient.

From this analysis it is easier to comprehend the activities of prison psychiatrists. Administrative concerns by far outweigh direct therapy hours, and punitive treatment takes precedence over service to the prisoner. Through any number of routes—accepting the definition of the state as client, leaving final responsibility to "custodial" decision makers, and other ways—the psychiatrist submerges service to prisoner-patients below custodial activity structured by the state.

One result of this practice is that medical or psychiatric definitions isolate prisoners' understanding of their situations, making organizing efforts unlikely to succeed. While forms of psychiatric technology such as therapy groups lead to the breakdown of solidarity through the creation of informers, drug treatment puts the prisoner inside individual chemical walls. The effect is similar: isolation. The result is that prisoners turn to their psychiatrists for help—adjustment in medication regimens. This takes place outside prisons as well. At whatever level, inside prison or not, medicalization and individualization go together, jointly undermining consciousness of class, class collective conditions, and organized resistance.

This process takes place not at the direction of independent professionals, but, rather, psychiatrists, like technocratic functionaries generally, operate under the pervasive control of capital. That is, as the Schwendingers (1974:154) have said, technocrats themselves are instruments of class domination. Magali Sarfatti Larson (1972:29) came to a similar conclusion. In her analysis of the technological-professional process she noted:

> The presence and role of the technocrats allow the dominant ideology to develop along the lines of technical rationality and of scientific management of nature and society. The function of this ideology is to legitimize the profoundly anti-democratic character of the power structure. De-politicization of the masses is the ideological recourse of a system of domination which uses technocratic rationality and the fiction of scientific government to equate progress with the effects of its rule.

Professionals and technologies operating within the liberal medical model ideology provide hegemonic and violent repressive means for state use.

This is not a recent discovery. Frantz Fanon (1965) noted that the colonizing doctor evidenced his position through certain attitudes and, more importantly, through particular active practice. For example, Fanon cited the role of the doctor who produced a certificate of natural death for an Algerian who had succumbed to torture or execution. "On the strictly technical level, the European doctor actively collaborates with the colonial forces in their most frightful and most degrading practices" (1965:137). An example given was the administration of truth serum.

A close reading of technicians and technology in the prisons indicates that these innovations are only superficially humanitarian reforms. Rather, they are political agents to repress prisoners and nonprisoners and to retain as much legitimacy as possible for the criminal justice system and the state. Drug use in particular comes out of corporate liberal theories about treatment and repression. The use of drugs originates from material conditions of capitalism, including efforts of the drug industry to maximize profits. Drugs produce repression and legitimation for the state.

Drugs and other forms of prison therapy not only repress prisoners themselves. In addition, the medical facade legitimates the capitalist system, thereby repressing all its falsely conscious citizens. U.S. District Judge David Bazelon (1972:151-152), at a meeting of correctional psychologists, discussed the camouflage of important issues about crime:

A second method of camouflaging the real issues—and the one that should concern us here—is to divert the public's attention by calling on experts to provide a pill that will magically make all of our problems disappear. Instead of facing up to the true dimensions of the problem and admitting that violent crime is an inevitable by-product of our society's social and economic structure, we prefer to blame the problem on a criminal class—a group of sick persons who must be treated by doctors and cured. Why should we even consider fundamental social changes or massive income redistribution if the entire problem can be solved by having scientists teach the criminal class—like a group of laboratory rats—to march successfully through the maze of our society?

Bazelon is correct in pointing out that one reason for the camouflage is that it is considerably less expensive to hire psychologists than to alter the economic structure. It is important to add, though, that the psychologists themselves are not solely responsible. A capitalist class dominates rule making and policies and supports positions for psychologists and other prison functionaries.

In 1967 the President's Commission on Law Enforcement and Administration of Justice observed that, in an era of reliance upon scientific and technical assistance, the criminal justice system officials "have almost no communication with the scientific and technical community" (p. 245). Clinical workers, partly because of this criticism, try to justify their work and institutions to the public through greater reliance on technology. In turn, the state also benefits from good public relations because technological advances demonstrate to the public that progress is under way, at the same time that the focus of attention remains fixed on individualistic causes, not political or economic sources of crime. New, improved methods of psychiatric repression play a large part in demonstrating that crime *is* an individual problem and that the state institutions are dealing with those causes. The corollary, further, is that systemic conditions of sexism, racism, and class exploitation require no change or attention.

Were it not convenient to indicate that a great many prisoners are somehow mentally ill, the state might have a difficult time escaping the charge that society and the criminal justice system are repressive, racist, and based on a class system. Instead, the disproportionately large number of Third World and poor people in prison is portrayed as the product of poor mental health, whatever the cause of that.

Economic life under advanced capitalism in the United States has meant massive unemployment, underemployment, and exploitative wages for workers.

A large reserve army of workers has served to keep many employed laborers insecure and accepting of a class system that includes poverty even for those working. Movements to escape this status under a classist, racist, and sexist system have met with massive repression from the state in a variety of forms.

Prisons are one part of that repressive apparatus that constrains those in the reserve army of unemployed. Prisons, or their threat, aid in keeping millions of unemployed or exploited workers in the reserve army or living a life of despair. The ruling class does not tolerate "subversives" who will not accept their place in the system.

To function within the U.S. political economy, prisons, like the entirety of the criminal justice system, must retain public legitimacy. In a period of increased consciousness both among the general public and among prisoners, this legitimacy began to slip. Finding it more difficult to defend the practice of mass torture used to manage the state's prisoners, officials turned to new techniques for repression, those which would find a better press. It was unimportant that these treatments would have no effect in "rehabilitating" the prisoner. In fact, because "rehabilitation" would require the prisoners' ultimate release to the community—and the workplace—it would be counterproductive to strive toward this end. Instead, the prisons have come to rely increasingly on an ideology and technology that removes growing numbers from the full-time workplace.

In prisons we see two state functions simultaneously. The number of imprisoned people reduces the pressure of a surplus population and simultaneously threatens substantial numbers of other citizens to keep them repressed (that is, for example, respecting private property) while underemployed or further exploited.[9] At the same time, though, the number of imprisoned may itself threaten the legitimacy of the state and, in addition, stretch its budget to a critical point if the prisons incorporate humane conditions. Adding more resources to the prisons—hence vying for additional legitimacy—either undermines the very capitalist surplus that the state tries to support or further weakens the state through additional tax burdens on the poor.

What is most apparent from this perspective is that drugs—and other forms of psychiatric technology—play a medicinal role for the entire economy. They repress and contribute to false consciousness inside prisons and outside them. In a context of political and economic crisis, we find the state relying on tranquilizers and the psychiatric profession, from behind a facade of medical imagery, to provide repression of surplus labor threats to the ruling class. At the same time, the state relies on the medical model to retain legitimacy for its capitalist system.

Chemical pacification is one technique in an arsenal of devices to maintain prisoners' submission under a veil of public legitimacy. Playing a key role in the contemporary prison, medication provides a relatively easy job for doctors and officials, lends legitimacy to the state criminal justice apparatus, and produces profits for the drug industry. For the prisoner, though, drugs can contribute to indefinite imprisonment, be part of an assault, or turn political protest to a management problem.

The medical solution prevails, in part, because it is pragmatic and convenient, and in the short run it seems to be effective. The pressure from administrators for a quiet institution, the technical problems presented by large numbers of prisoners, and the cynicism of an overworked and unappreciated staff—all these lead to pragmatic and routine solutions.

Dangerous drugs are part of a prison program that involves questionable health care overall. Prisoners, like poor people generally, are unable to get decent medical care when they want it, and bad health care is practiced against them when they do not want it. More than anything else, drugs relieve officials of responsibility for treatment as pressure upon them from demanding prisoners is chemically undermined. Similarly, the officials can announce that something is being done for the prisoners. That the something amounts to an excuse for doing very little is not made known.

Drugs are one technique now available for the state to utilize in the repression of politically conscious, dangerous, or simply difficult prisoners and simultaneously in the legitimation of the capitalist system. Historically, criminals were banished from society. Then, they were put to hard labor and in solitary confinement for reflection and punishment. Today, with fiscal pressures as well as political contradictions threatening the state, prison walls are increasingly a disservice. Accordingly, through drugs, repressive forms of behavior modification, and such programs as electrostimulation of the brain, invisible walls are built inside the individual.

It is not a one-sided process, however, and prisoners and others have developed techniques for fighting back. A central concern of the state in utilizing psychiatric weaponry has been the attainment of legitimacy along with efficacy. Accordingly, one route open to the resisting prisoner is to discredit the legitimacy of the prison or the state. Throwing off the state's mystification and challenging its legitimacy is not an easy task for prisoners. They are vulnerable to direct retaliation and long-term punishment for any resistance. Nevertheless, this is one way many prisoners have engaged in struggle to counter repressive prison instruments. Nonprisoners can help, and have helped, and are generally open to less direct retaliation.

NOTES

1. Repression is a specific state function to perpetuate the capitalist system. According to Wolfe (1973:6), "Repression is a process by which those in power try to keep themselves in power by consciously attempting to destroy or render harmless organizations and ideologies that threaten their power." The repressive process can utilize any of a wide variety of techniques. Crime control is a major device in the repressive strategy, one of a number of reproductive mechanisms which ensure the continuation of existing relationships.

Explicit use of the state's police power is one form of repression. Others might include less overt forms of force, like grand juries, the educational system, and advertisements. In addition, the use of certain drugs is a direct form of repression, both inside prisons and outside them. The state utilizes one form of repression rather than another depending on the immediacy of the threat perceived and the efficacy of the repressive technique.

2. The capitalist system is subject to a massive conflict. Whether one calls the critical tendency "disaccumulation," as did Carson (1972), or a problem in absorbing the surplus, as did Baran and Sweezy (1966), the situation is the same.

> Quite simply, the economic system faced a perpetual problem of having more and more potential workers to absorb. Therefore, it became important to develop and elaborate techniques of limitation and control on the labor force itself. [Carson, 1972:22]

The problem for the state is that in operating for the interests of the ruling class it must simultaneously (O'Connor, 1973:6) "try to fulfill two basic and often contradictory functions—*accumulation* and *legitimation*." That is, the state must aid the accumulation of surplus, yet portray the accompanying underemployment and unemployment as legitimate. The latter task is exceedingly difficult at times. The rationalization of its status to a surplus population is uncertain and relies on continued obfuscation of the exploitation inherent in capitalism. To perform this legitimation task, then, is increasingly a problem, and increasingly advanced capitalism must rely on undisguised repression to limit emerging class and revolutionary consciousness (Carson, 1972).

The state superstructure in capitalist society reflects and influences the economic base of production. In recent years, the United States economy has been one of recurring instability and social, political, and economic crises. Out of the unemployment and "stagflation" of the recent period have come increased demands on the system from workers, Third World people, women, students, gays, and other groups of militant activists. (See San Francisco Bay Area Kapitalistate Collective, 1975.) Capitalists were, however, determined to absorb or co-opt protests and make the system work. Resultant operations in the criminal justice system reflect that basic political-economic reality.

3. This "movement" grew out of legislative support for the decentralization of mental health treatment facilities. Objections to usually uncritical views of the progressive facade of this trend are voiced by such groups as the Network Against Psychiatric Assault (San Francisco), the Mental Patients Liberation Front (Boston and elsewhere), and the State and Mind (formerly Rough Times) collective.

4. I utilize this information although I object to the sexist implication that in our current society functioning as a housewife should generally be seen as a "success." I also object to the notion that there are not, or should not be, househusbands as well.

5. In important ways prison tranquilizers are like drugs from other places and eras. In 1917, William D. Haywood (Renshaw, 1967:185-186) told of lumber bosses distributing cocaine and heroin in southern lumber camps, especially among black workers. The bosses "knew that when they [the workers] became addicted to the drugs that they were sure to return to their jobs. It was the strongest method of holding them—stronger than the chains of chattel slavery or the ships of the turpentine bosses." There is almost universal agreement that any drug that one can get on the streets is available inside prisons. This availability is in addition to the prison-supplied drugs and must be seen as a product of administrative policy (see Brewer, 1974). Hard drugs to pacify workers are similar to tranquilizers and other drugs used to keep prisoners imprisoned and ghetto residents quiet.

6. The California legislature relegated the state's indeterminate sentence to a place in history as of mid-1977. What this will mean in practice is not yet clear, although it seems that officials will have somewhat more difficulty utilizing their discretion in holding up parole dates. As a result, it is likely that use of other direct physical agents—like drugs—may replace the power of indeterminate release dates as repressive forces.

7. Individual therapy has long been seen as too expensive for prison use, and group therapy has been discredited for a decade now.

8. One must beware of authors like Kittrie (1971:4) who say that "The therapeutic state proclaims more humane attitudes and promises greater skills for the control of antisocial conduct," for Kittrie goes on to say that we must rationalize therapy, protecting the liberty and individuality of our society, "to benefit from the fruits of a new age." He ignores the reality of class, thereby implicitly throwing his support to the ruling class.

9. Current figures are difficult to find, but in 1972, when unemployment in the United States registered almost five million people, prisons and jails pulled some one-third of a million people out of the work force. Additional numbers were in juvenile facilities. The conclusion that one comes to is that correctional facilities hold a significant quantity of people in terms of the labor force.

REFERENCES

BARAN, P.A., and SWEEZY, P.M. (1966). Monopoly capital. New York: Monthly Review.

BAZELON, D.L. (1972). "Psychologists in corrections—Are they doing good for the offender or well for themselves?" In S.L. Brodsky (ed.), Psychologists in the criminal justice system. Marysville, Ohio: American Association of Correctional Psychologists.

BERNSTEIN, A., and LENNARD, H.L. (1973). "The American way of drugging." Society, 11(May/June).

BREWER, M. (1974). "Drugs and death in San Quentin." San Francisco Bay Guardian, (October 5-8):10-11.

California Attorney General (1960). Opinions (vol. 43, no. 7, October 22). Sacramento: Author.

California Correctional Psychiatrists Association (1971). "Summary of topics discussed at meetings, April 3, 1971, in San Francisco and July 17 and 18, 1971, Carmel, California. Sacramento: Author.

California Department of Corrections (1967). "Minutes." Annual Conference of Chief Psychiatrists, November 2-3.

——— (1974). Crime and violence on the streets and in the prisons. Sacramento: California Department of Corrections.

California Medical Facility (1973). "Minutes." Psychotropic Drug Meeting, May 20.

CARSON, R.B. (1972). "Youthful labor surplus in disaccumulationist capitalism." Socialist Revolution, 2(May-June).

Center for Research on Criminal Justice (1975). The iron fist and the velvet glove. Berkeley, Calif.: Center for Research on Criminal Justice.

CHESLER, P.H. (1972). Women and madness. Garden City, N.Y.: Doubleday.

CLANON, T.L. (1970). Memo to business manager Wensel, CMF, entitled "Budget for tranquilizers," April 6.

CRANE, G.E. (1973). "Clinical psychopharmacology in its 20th year." Science, 181(July 13).

DANIELS, A.K. (1972). "Military psychiatry: The emergence of a subspeciality." In E. Friedson and J. Lorber (eds.), Medical men and their work. Chicago: Aldine.

FAIRBANKS, R. (1970). "Time in prison held no factor in rehabilitation." Los Angeles Times, March 3, p. 3.

FANON, F. (1965). A dying colonialism. New York: Grove Press.

FRIEDRICH, O. (1975). "Going crazy." Harpers (June).

FUSFIELD, D.R. (1968). "The basic economics of the urban racial crisis." Conference Papers of the Union for Radical Political Economics, December.

GOFFMAN, E. (1961). Asylums. Garden City, N.Y.: Anchor.

Health/PAC Bulletin (1970). "Editorial: The medical means of repression." May.

JACKSON, G. (1970). Soledad brother. New York: Bantam.

KITTRIE, N.N. (1971). The right to be different: Deviance and enforced therapy. Baltimore: Johns Hopkins University Press.

LARSON, M.S. (1972). "Notes on technocracy: Some problems of theory, ideology, and power." Berkeley Journal of Sociology, 17.

LEVY, H. (1970). "Prison psychiatrists: The new custodians." Health/PAC Bulletin (May).

MITFORD, J. (1973). Kind and usual punishment. New York: Knopf.

––– (1976). Personal communication.

MOSHER, L.R., and FEINSILVER, D. (1971). Special report: Schizophrenia. Chevy Chase, Md.: Center for Studies of Schizophrenia, National Institute of Mental Health.

O'CONNOR, J. (1973). The fiscal crisis of the state. New York: St. Martin's.

President's Commission on Law Enforcement and Administration of Justice (1967). The challenge of crime in a free society. Washington, D.C.: U.S. Government Printing Office.

Red Family, People's Press, and Friends (1971). War behind walls (September). San Francisco.

RENSHAW, P. (1967). The Wobblies. New York: Anchor.

ROSS, B. (1974). "Chaos in the board and care homes—San Francisco's mentally retarded: Tranquilized and forgotten." Bay Guardian, 8(August 3-16).

San Francisco Bay Area Kapitalistate Collective (1975). "Watergate, or the eighteenth brumaire of Richard Nixon." Unpublished manuscript (February).

San Francisco Chronicle (1975). "New hope for mental cases." August 4.

SCHWENDINGER, H., and SCHWENDINGER, J.R. (1974). The sociologists of the chair. New York: Basic Books.

SILVERMAN, M., and LEE, P.R. (1974). Pills, profits, and politics. Berkeley: University of California Press.

SPEIGLMAN, R.C. (1976). "Building the walls inside: Medicine, corrections, and the state apparatus for repression." Unpublished D.Crim. dissertation, University of California, Berkeley.

SWAZEY, J.P. (1972). "Chlorpromazine: Innovation and revolution in the drug treatment of mental disease states." Unpublished manuscript, Committee on Brain Sciences.

U.S. Senate, Committee on Appropriations (1963). Report (Departments of Labor, and Health, Education, and Welfare, and Related Agencies Appropriations Bill, 1964).

WOLFE, A. (1973). The seamy side of democracy. New York: McKay.

YEE, M.S. (1973). The melancholy history of Soledad Prison. New York: Harper's Magazine Press.

ZOLA, I.K. (1972). "Medicine as an institution of social control." Sociological Review, 20(November).

Chapter 7

PUNISHMENT AND DETERRENCE:
BAD CHECKS IN NEBRASKA—
A STUDY IN COMPLEX THREATS

FRANKLIN E. ZIMRING

Criminal penalties exist for many purposes: to physically isolate offending populations, to assist in the rehabilitation of offenders, to express society's retributive feelings toward offenders, and to deter potential offenders from the commission of criminal acts. The proper role to be accorded each of these functions in the determination of individual punishment levels for particular crimes is an issue of continuing concern. Traditionally, those concerned with enhancing the deterrent effect of criminal sanctions have argued for increases in the levels of criminal punishment threatened and administered.

Such arguments are based upon the assumption that the threat of severe punishment is a more effective deterrent than the threat of lesser punishment. To the extent that this assumption holds true, it raises the possibility that penalties for particular criminal acts might exceed those necessary, just, or

AUTHOR'S NOTE: *This paper reports one of three "soundings in deterrence" undertaken by the Center for Studies in Criminal Justice between 1965 and 1967. These studies were conducted on the plausible (though currently unfashionable) assumption that construction of general deterrence theory and research methods should be facilitated by a series of modest empirical observations of specific threatened behaviors. The text was prepared in 1967, and it is rendered here with only minor amendments. The list of references has been updated to include four later products of the deterrence project and a number of other recent contributions to deterrence theory and research.*

desirable in light of the criminal law's other functions. Indeed, it has been argued that undue emphasis on the deterrent aspect of punishment may conflict with and impede the law's retributive purposes.[1] Thus investigations of marginal deterrence, comparing the reaction pattern of a threatened population to more severe versus less severe punishment threats, have high priority in the study of deterrence.

One can attempt to study the marginal deterrent effect of different levels of threatened punishment in three ways: (1) by comparing the crime rates in areas with more severe penalties with the crime rates in areas with less severe penalties, (2) by analyzing data from jurisdictions before and after they have changed particular penalties, and (3) by analyzing the effect of more severe threats attached to certain legally distinguished forms of a criminal behavior whose other forms are threatened at a lesser level. The reliability of purely comparative studies depends on finding areas that have different punishment policies toward a particular act but which are so similar in every other way that the differences observed in their crime rates can be attributable to the differences in punishment policy.[2] Given the many factors which might condition an area's crime rate, comparative studies cannot be considered the most attractive means for basic research in marginal deterrence.

Retrospective study, in jurisdictions that have modified their punishment policy concerning particular offenses, is also problematic. "Before and after" comparisons shed light on deterrence only if the other factors that influence crime rates over time hold constant or can be separately measured. A key danger associated with this assumption is that the social conditions which caused changes in the level of the punishment that is threatened for particular forms of criminal behavior may be expected to cause other changes in social conditions which may also affect movements in the crime rate (see Lempert, 1966).

But where the criminal law draws fine distinctions between two closely similar behaviors and threatens one of the two forms, it might be possible to probe the marginal effect of the larger threat by analyzing the distribution of criminal behavior in close proximity to the border between the two criminal threats. In Nebraska, writing insufficient-funds checks up to and including the amount of $35 is a misdemeanor, punishable by a fine up to $100 and up to 90 days in jail. Writing insufficient-funds checks of any amount exceeding $35 is a felony, punishable by up to seven years in prison. Although the law in the books is strict, it is not being uniformly enforced. During the early 1950s, "only 2.2 percent of the bad checks returned by the bankers came to the legal officials" in Nebraska (Beutel, 1957:287). Five facets of bad check law and practice in Nebraska make this a model problem for research in marginal deterrence.

(1) The Differentially Threatened Crimes
Seem to Be a Continuum of the Same Behavior

There is never any unity of incentive, method, or range of offender options within any single category of criminal behavior, let alone between any two categories of crime. For example, it may well be much easier to pass a small check than a large one, and a good proportion of the people in any given jurisdiction who are capable of passing $5 bad checks might not be able to pass $100 bad checks. However, it is difficult to understand why, in the absence of a legal distinction, writing a $34 bad check is greatly different from writing one for $36. This essential similarity of behaviors, evident near the boundary of the two offenses, makes it possible to assume that any gross differences in the rate of criminal behavior on one side of that boundary might be attributed to the difference in legal significance.

(2) The Nature of the Offense

To the extent that bad check writing[3] is considered criminal, it fits the traditional category of a "crime of gains," the kind of offense where many commentators have expected potential offenders to be sensitive to variations in the severity of threatened consequences. It is also a crime which requires more literacy, more legitimate appearance, and a greater contact with social institutions (banks and shops) than many other forms of criminal behavior (Lemert, 1953:295-307; Beutel, 1957:329-345). To the extent that the writing of insufficient-funds checks is intentional, proponents of the dichotomy between crimes of gains and crimes of passion would expect in this area strong indication of the potential for decreasing deviant behavior by increasing the severity of criminal threats.

(3) The Visibility of Bad Checks[4]

Accurate reporting is a major problem in investigating the frequency of criminal behavior. Statistics concerning most forms of criminal conduct, which are based upon reports to the police of the occurrence of the crime, form a small and highly selective sample of the true number and range of crimes committed in the reporting jurisdiction. Because bad checks are written on banks, and the payee will normally attempt to collect on the check, the number of bad checks processed through banks is an accurate estimate of bad check frequencies. This makes it possible to state precisely the rates of both felony and misdemeanor bad check writing.

(4) The Dollar Scale of Bad Checks

Bad check writing at the lower extreme of the misdemeanor classification (e.g., $5) is probably greatly dissimilar from bad check writing at the higher extremes of the felony classification, for reasons other than the Nebraska legal distinction. Because each bad check is for a specific amount, it is possible to construct the distribution of checks for each amount in a given sample, then break down the distribution of bad check writing to control for the general tendency of checks to be lower in amount, and to make special use of the easily isolated clusters of checks in dollar amounts close to the border of the criminal classification. Without data dividing the checks into a number of dollar intervals, it would be impossible to separate the general effects attributable to the size of the check from the specific influence of the legal distinction as influences on bad check writing behavior.

(5) The Greatly Divergent Maximum Penalties

The maximum penalty that can be imposed for passing an insufficient-funds check of $35 or less is a $100 fine and 90 days in jail. The maximum for passing an insufficient-funds check in excess of $35 is seven years in the state penitentiary. Without doubt, extremely low rates of penal enforcement associated with the complex of bad check regulations, as well as a proper exercise of prosecutorial and judicial discretion, substantially reduce the difference in punishment levels for the two offenses in practice. However, it would still be hard to imagine two more similar criminal behaviors than writing $34 and $36 bad checks, threatened more differently than in the Nebraska scheme. The impact of practice on the administration of that basic threat is one of the variables discussed later.

DESIGN

The research design evolved from the control opportunities previously outlined. We thought to study the effects of the extra threat directed at checks over $35 by (1) securing a large and representative sample of insufficient-funds checks written on Nebraska bank accounts and (2) compiling a distribution of these checks by amount, so that the effects of the more severe penal threat could be isolated from the manifold factors which normally result in more bad checks being written for small rather than large sums.

Sample

We secured the cooperation of a large commercial and private deposit bank in Lincoln, Nebraska. The bank supplied us with a record of the amount of each check which it refused to honor during a summer month in 1967. This sample did not cover all of the insufficient-funds checks written upon that bank during that month because the bank, as a general practice, honors a limited number of checks written on accounts which do not have sufficient funds to cover the check, if the checks have been written by customers of long standing with good credit ratings and if the bank is persuaded that the checks are a result of remediable mistakes. This preliminary screening of a total population of bad checks by a high bank official somewhat reduces the possibility of inaccurate personal bookkeeping as an explanation of checks that remain in the Nebraska sample.

There were 1,707 insufficient-funds checks reported by our correspondent bank during the month studied. This total warrants two comments. First, the great number of these checks, most of which were written for amounts between $1 and $100, seemed a sufficient sample for an investigation of the effect of the felony threat on the number of bad checks written for sums in excess of $35. Second, the fact that one bank in one city reported such a high total powerfully confirms Beutel's earlier conclusion (1957) that insufficient-funds check writing is widespread behavior in Nebraska.

Compiling the Distribution

It was initially predicted that a far greater number of checks would be written for smaller amounts (e.g., $5, $10) than for larger amounts (e.g., $35, $45), whether or not the larger sums were within the Nebraska felony classification. It is not necessary to review the many reasons why the social factors that condition the amounts of bad checks make it probable that more such checks will be written for small than large amounts. We sought to control this factor by grouping the bad checks into dollar intervals, so that all checks written for amounts between $0.01 and $1.00 would be grouped into the first interval, all checks written for between $1.01 and $2.00 in the second interval, and so on. A line indicating the declining number of checks written for ascending amounts would then give us, we predicted, a basis for identifying the normal effects of factors, other than the felony threat, which condition the number of checks written for particular sums. Thus, if the drop in the number of checks written in amounts just over the felony line were no greater than a characteristic drop-off of a number of checks by amount in an earlier section in the distribution, it would seem reasonable to conclude that the felony threat had no effect on the amount for which a bad check was written in Nebraska. If, on the other hand, the drop-off noted between the number of checks in the lower ranges of the felony area were greater than that which characterized earlier decreases in the number of bad checks written at each ascending dollar figure, then a marginal deterrent effect could be attributed to the more severe threat covering checks in excess of $35.

We anticipated that two or more distinct subdistributions might emerge from a graphic treatment of the bad check data. It is part of the psychology of check writers to prefer checks for even dollar amounts, when such checks are written for cash rather than goods. Thus, checks for multiples of $5 would be more common in any hypothetical distribution of insufficient-funds checks than those for odd amounts (e.g., $16.34). By compiling our distribution of checks on $1 rather than $5 intervals, we were able to segregate the $5 multiple checks written for cash, or for goods and cash, from the pattern of checks written largely to obtain goods or services.

Our method was straightforward; the results appear clear-cut.

DATA AND FINDINGS

Table 1 presents a distribution of the bad check sample by dollar intervals up to $100. It reveals a steady but uneven decline in the frequency of checks written at ascending dollar levels. Grouped in ascending $5 intervals (Figure 1), the data reveal a steady and fairly even decline in the frequency of bad checks, with two elements of discontinuity: (1) totals for intervals which include amounts evenly divisible by $10 (e.g., $10, $20, $30) tend to be larger than intervals which include dollar amounts ending in five as their round-numbered check amount, and (2) the figures for intervals including $50 and $100 checks are discontinuously large.

Table 1 indicates that the tendency for intervals ending in numbers divisible by 10 to contain more checks is concentrated in the last dollar of each group. Therefore it seems that bad check writers exhibited a strong preference for checks of dollar numbers divisible by five and an even stronger preference for even dollar checks in numbers divisible by 10. The data, as we had anticipated, broke into three subdistributions: a distribution by ascending amount of the number of bad checks written for dollar sums ending in zero ($10, $20, etc.), another of the number of bad checks for dollar amounts ending in five ($5, $15, $25, etc.), and a residual distribution of insufficient-funds checks for amounts divisible by neither 10 nor five (Figures 2 and 3).

Figure 4 represents the distribution by dollar amount of checks from $30 to $40. It shows 44 checks of the sample group written for amounts within the $5 interval below the felony line, and 38 checks written for amounts from one cent to $5 above the minimum felony amount. This itself strongly suggests that no significant deterrent effect can be attributed to the $35 line prescribed by the statute. When we review the number of checks that were $5 above the line with

Table 1. DISTRIBUTION OF BAD CHECKS BY AMOUNT, LINCOLN, NEBRASKA

Amount of Check	Number of Checks	Amount of Check	Number of Checks	Amount of Check	Number of Checks
.01- 1.00	13	35.01-36.00	6	70.01-71.00	3
1.01- 2.00	50	36.01-37.00	2	71.01-72.00	2
2.01- 3.00	88	37.01-38.00	5	72.01-73.00	1
3.01- 4.00	44	38.01-39.00	5	73.01-74.00	4
4.01- 5.00	207	39.01-40.00	20	74.01-75.00	8
5.01- 6.00	52	40.01-41.00	3	75.01-76.00	1
6.01- 7.00	42	41.01-42.00	2	76.01-77.00	3
7.01- 8.00	51	42.01-43.00	6	77.01-78.00	6
8.01- 9.00	24	43.01-44.00	4	78.01-79.00	3
9.01-10.00	211	44.01-45.00	7	79.01-80.00	4
10.01-11.00	24	45.01-46.00	7	80.01-81.00	1
11.01-12.00	35	46.01-47.00	3	81.01-82.00	3
12.01-13.00	18	47.01-48.00	5	82.01-83.00	2
13.01-14.00	34	48.01-49.00	2	83.01-84.00	2
14.01-15.00	85	49.01-50.00	28	84.01-85.00	7
15.01-16.00	24	50.01-51.00	4	85.01-86.00	3
16.01-17.00	10	51.01-52.00	6	86.01-87.00	0
17.01-18.00	11	52.01-53.00	2	87.01-88.00	2
18.01-19.00	13	53.01-54.00	1	88.01-89.00	0
19.01-20.00	74	54.01-55.00	5	89.01-90.00	2
20.01-21.00	15	55.01-56.00	4	90.01-91.00	0
21.01-22.00	10	56.01-57.00	3	91.01-92.00	2
22.01-23.00	20	57.01-58.00	7	92.01-93.00	3
23.01-24.00	7	58.01-59.00	3	93.01-94.00	0
24.01-25.00	47	59.01-60.00	5	94.01-95.00	1
25.01-26.00	11	60.01-61.00	5	95.01-96.00	1
26.01-27.00	14	61.01-62.00	2	96.01-97.00	3
27.01-28.00	3	62.01-63.00	1	97.01-98.00	1
28.01-29.00	11	63.01-64.00	2	98.01-99.00	0
29.01-30.00	45	64.01-65.00	5	99.01-100.00	12
30.01-31.00	5	65.01-66.00	2	100.91-	117
31.01-32.00	7	66.01-67.00	4		
32.01-33.00	9	67.01-68.00	4	Total	1,707[a]
33.01-34.00	4	68.01-69.00	0	Bank sheet	
34.01-35.00	19	69.01-70.00	3	total	1,716

a. The bank sheet total of the Nebraska bank report indicated 1,716 checks. The figure of 1,707 represented all those coded for the present study.

reference to the low central tendencies of the sample as a whole, the conclusion that the $35 line itself does not exert a deterrent effect seems secure. For example, Table 1 indicates that 84 checks were written in amounts between $25 and $30—almost twice as many checks as were written in the $5 interval from $30.01 to $35.00. The $5.00 increase in dollar amount produces a drop-off ratio

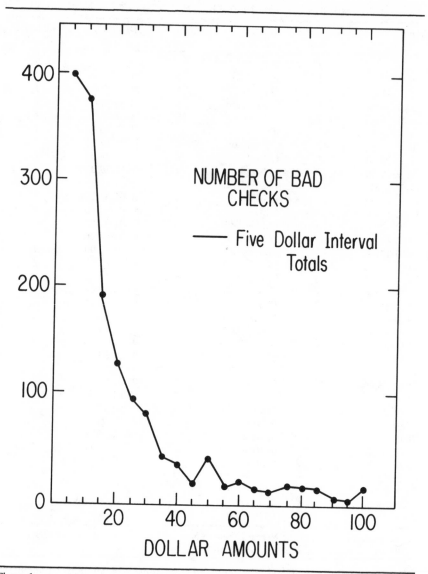

Figure 1.

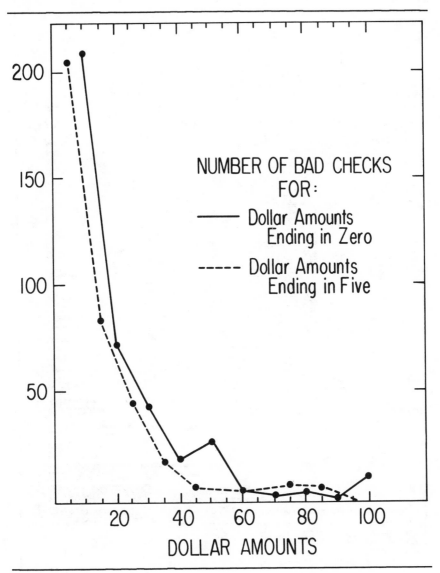

Figure 2.

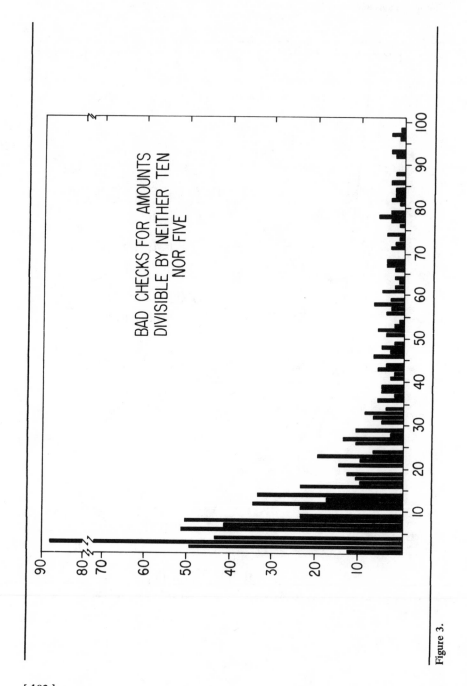

Figure 3.

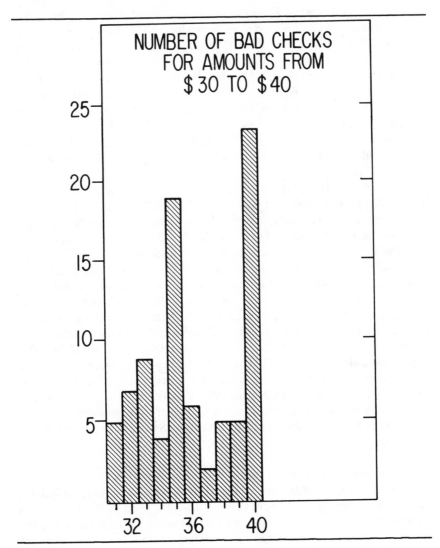

Figure 4.

of about two to one. It is difficult to argue that the next interval can produce a drop-off ratio of only nine to eight and still contain any measurable effect attributable to the more severe threat.

The preference of check writers for $10 divisible amounts rather than $5 divisible amounts invites a separate analysis of the frequency of bad checks written in amounts divisible by 10 and five and the frequency of bad checks written for "odd-numbered" amounts. When "round number" checks are eliminated, the ratios just discussed are somewhat altered. There were 39 checks in the $25.01 to $29.00 interval, 25 in the $30.01 to $34.00 interval, and 19 in the $35.01 to $39.00 interval. With this deletion, the drop-off ratio between the two misdemeanor intervals is 1.56, while the drop-off ratio between the last misdemeanor and first felony ratio is only 1.32. Thus an analysis of the "odd-numbered" checks gives evidence of no deterrent effect attributable to the $35 misdemeanor-felony distinction.

Analysis of the frequency of checks in round-numbered intervals is somewhat more difficult. The decrease between $25 and $35 is 2.47; the decrease between $35 and $45 is 2.71.

The decline on the $10 divisible line is from 74 checks at $20 to 45 checks at $30, to 20 checks at $40, and back up to 28 checks at the $50 level. In the intervals closest to the felony line, the drop-off ratio between $20 and $30 is 1.64, and the ratio between $30 and $40 is 2.25. The increase in ratio, together with the large number of checks at the $50 level, might suggest an effect attributable to the legal distinction. A proponent of this view would find in the increased $30 to $40 drop-off evidence that checks for amounts close to the felony line drop off more sharply than others. The large number of checks written at the $50 level would be used as an indication that the tendency of the number of checks for a given amount to decrease as the amount increases is not as substantial as anticipated. The increase in checks for $50 would therefore suggest that individuals who, in the absence of a regulation, would be expected to write $40 checks, are writing checks for lesser amounts. A better view, however, would recognize that 50 and 100 are particularly round numbers, and that a discontinuously large number of checks written for these dollar amounts is to be expected in the absence of any regulation. Setting aside the $50 checks, the number of checks at any given round-numbered amount over the $35 border decreases steadily.

We have been considering checks for round-numbered dollar amounts near the felony line, but consideration of the entire distribution of checks for dollar sums ending in zero (Figure 2) gives further basis for rejecting deterrence as an explanation of the larger than expected drop-off in the $30 to $40 interval. The drop-off ratio from $10 to $20 (2.85) is slightly greater than that noted between $30 and $40 (2.25). In the total context, then, the drop-off from $30 to $40 no longer seems unexpectedly sharp, as it did when compared only with the drop-off from $20 to $30.

Taken as a whole and analyzed as a series of subdistributions, the data support the proposition that the $35 line itself has no measurable influence on the frequency distribution of bad checks by amount in the Nebraska sample.

This is the basic conclusion available from present data. Such a conclusion is far from stating either (a) that the more severe threat attached to the larger check figure has no deterrent effect or (b) that the more severe threat for larger checks has no deterrent potential. A finding that the $35 line does not influence the distribution of checks on either side of that line is not a complete rebuttal of the deterrence hypothesis, because it can be argued that the more severe regulation has a pervasive effect on bad check writing behavior, but that the effect is more general than our hypothesis supposed. The proponent of such an argument would urge, first, that the existence of the felony threat has led citizens in Nebraska to regard the entire area of insufficient-funds checks as of greater moral importance than they would have ordinarily thought and, second, that the threat produces the general impression that larger bad checks are a more serious offense than smaller bad checks. Such an argument would consider the entire distribution, characterized by a sharp decline in the number of checks by each amount level, as evidence of an "overkill" effect, the tendency of a regulation to have behavioral effects more general than its literal terms.

The data from the present study, as well as previous research into Nebraska bad check behavior, suggest some basis for rejecting the "overkill" argument. First, the previous studies have indicated (Beutel, 1957:355) that the rate of bad check writing in Nebraska is no smaller than in other areas used for comparison. Second, the Nebraska bad check data in the present study indicate a steady decline in the number of checks by ascending amount notable from the very first interval of each subdistribution. The overkill argument would have to assert that the law has its primary deterrent effect in reducing the number of checks by ascending amounts under $20 because this is where the greatest numerical drop-off occurs. The deterrent force of the regulation on the ratio of $3 checks to $8 checks, although a long way from the significant legal threshold, would have to be greater than on the ratio of $31 checks to $36 checks. While it is quite possible for many kinds of regulation to have such a general effect, it seems likely that any regulation with pervasive general effect would also demonstrate some marginal general deterrent effect in accord with the actual legal distinction. No such literal effect can be noted in the data. It is difficult to argue that a regulation which fails to affect behavior in relevant intervals can have such a pervasive effect in irrelevant intervals.

A modest use of comparative data might help resolve whether the $35 distinction in Nebraska law has pervasively altered the distribution of insufficient-funds checks at all dollar intervals from that to be expected in the absence of the regulation. A commercial bank in Champaign, Illinois, provided a tape of comparable insufficient-funds checks covering the month of November 1967 and is reported in Table 2.

Table 2. DISTRIBUTION OF BAD CHECKS BY AMOUNT, CHAMPAIGN, ILLINOIS

Amount of Check	Number of Checks	Amount of Check	Number of Checks	Amount of Check	Number of Checks
.01- 1.00	13	35.01-36.00	10	70.01-71.00	3
1.01- 2.00	65	36.01-37.00	13	71.01-72.00	2
2.01- 3.00	68	37.01-38.00	11	72.01-73.00	2
3.01- 4.00	68	38.01-39.00	4	73.01-74.00	1
4.01- 5.00	190	39.01-40.00	23	74.01-75.00	12
5.01- 6.00	54	40.01-41.00	2	75.01-76.00	3
6.01- 7.00	52	41.01-42.00	5	76.01-77.00	5
7.01- 8.00	50	42.01-43.00	4	77.01-78.00	4
8.01- 9.00	33	43.01-44.00	7	78.01-79.00	2
9.01-10.00	228	44.01-45.00	8	79.01-80.00	2
10.01-11.00	33	45.01-46.00	8	80.01-81.00	1
11.01-12.00	37	46.01-47.00	7	81.01-82.00	3
12.01-13.00	34	47.01-48.00	3	82.01-83.00	0
13.01-14.00	28	48.01-49.00	4	83.01-84.00	3
14.01-15.00	80	49.01-50.00	27	84.01-85.00	3
15.01-16.00	28	50.01-51.00	4	85.01-86.00	4
16.01-17.00	16	51.01-52.00	5	86.01-87.00	1
17.01-18.00	36	52.01-53.00	2	87.01-88.00	3
18.01-19.00	14	53.01-54.00	2	88.01-89.00	2
19.01-20.00	81	54.01-55.00	2	89.01-90.00	4
20.01-21.00	20	55.01-56.00	3	90.01-91.00	2
21.01-22.00	13	56.01-57.00	5	91.01-92.00	5
22.01-23.00	10	57.01-58.00	3	92.01-93.00	1
23.01-24.00	11	58.01-59.00	4	93.01-94.00	1
24.01-25.00	59	59.01-60.00	6	94.01-95.00	2
25.01-26.00	9	60.01-61.00	2	95.01-96.00	0
26.01-27.00	18	61.01-62.00	2	96.01-97.00	3
27.01-28.00	13	62.01-63.00	4	97.01-98.00	4
28.01-29.00	8	63.01-64.00	6	98.01-99.00	2
29.01-30.00	33	64.01-65.00	4	99.01-100.00	18
30.01-31.00	8	65.01-66.00	3	100.01-	298
31.01-32.00	16	66.01-67.00	1		
32.01-33.00	5	67.01-68.00	7	Total	2,063
33.01-34.00	9	68.01-69.00	2	Bank sheet	
34.01-35.00	16	69.01-70.00	8	total	2,069

As Table 2 indicates, the distribution from this bank is generally similar to that noted in the Nebraska sample. The similar check pattern cannot be taken as a conclusive demonstration that the Nebraska law fails to alter the distribution of bad checks by amount, but the similarity is evidence that Nebraska's $35 distinction has not profoundly affected the distribution of bad checks by frequency amounts in irrelevant intervals. While the cities are similar, the social context of check writing and check writers in the two samples may differ. The Nebraska regulation may, in fact, be one indication that insufficient-funds checks over $35 are felt to be a more pressing social problem in Nebraska than in Illinois. However, finding a state without the Nebraska regulation, where the frequency distribution of bad checks shows the same tendency to drop off at dollar intervals far lower than those affected by the Nebraska regulation, suggests that the general tendency to drop off is not attributable to the statute.[5]

In any investigation of marginal deterrence, it is probable that conditions which may vary from threat to threat have a far stronger influence on the reaction patterns of the threatened population than any general characteristics attributable to all threats. Threats may produce different responses in accordance with variations in the behavior threatened, the sanction threatened, the perceived credibility of the threat, the character of the threatened audience, the extent of public knowledge of the terms of the particular threat, and many other factors. Findings such as those discussed above are no indication of the absence of deterrent potential and do not suggest that more severe threats for larger insufficient-funds checks could not effectively alter behavior under some changed conditions. Two aspects of the present Nebraska regulation are the probable causes of the no-deterrent findings above: (1) public ignorance of the specific terms of the bad check law and (2) a suspected credibility gap growing out of the minimal enforcement of bad check regulation.

Writing insufficient-funds checks is not generally regarded as a morally serious deviation (Beutel, 1957:298). In the absence of specific knowledge of the regulatory provisions of the Nebraska statute, a high rate of insufficient-funds checks can be expected. Because the statute regulates marginal behavior and has been enforced in ways not likely to bring the average citizen in contact with the law, Nebraska's unique bad check provisions are probably not widely known. And of course, if the provisions of the threat are not known, one cannot expect from the regulation any effects that could properly be called deterrent.

Additionally, the Nebraska criminal regulation of insufficient-funds checks is not, and has never been, consistently enforced. Fewer than 2% of all insufficient-funds checks written in Nebraska find their ways into the hands of public officials charged with the enforcement of the bad check law (Beutel, 1957:358, Table 68). For the most part, even these checks are given to enforcement officials only to facilitate the collection of the check, and no prosecution for violation of the law ensues. And when prosecutions under the bad check regulation do take place, the usual charge is a misdemeanor, whether or not the $35 limit is exceeded. For this reason, only 33 persons were admitted to the Nebraska State Penitentiary on the basis of insufficient-funds checks during the decade ending in 1953 (Beutel, 1957:319, Table 43). It is also quite probable that any felony prosecutions are so selective that only an unrepresentative sample of the bad check writers in the state of Nebraska is exposed to felony punishment for this behavior.

Any of the conditions discussed above could completely explain the lack of a marginal deterrent effect observable from the present data. It may seem to have been unwise, in light of the probable existence of these conditions in Nebraska, to make this sounding in deterrence, since it can be persuasively argued that such conditions minimize the possibility of a deterrent effect within a regulatory system. But information lags and credibility gaps of varying degrees are found throughout the system of criminal controls, concentrated particularly in areas where advocates have proposed increases in the levels of criminal punishment threatened and administered in the hope of producing marginal deterrent effects.

We know little about the degree of public knowledge of most criminal penalties. Preliminary indications are that public knowledge of specific penalties is quite low, and there is reason to believe that potential offenders are not well informed prior to apprehension and conviction. The study of marginal deterrence in limited information situations is thus of general importance.

And criminal laws in the United States are not consistently enforced. In many cases, we have no way of estimating the limited degree of enforcement of a particular regulation, because we have no way of knowing the true rate of a particular criminal violation. Particularly in the area of "victimless crime," it has been suggested that enforcement ratios are so low as to make Nebraska's felony bad check regulation seem a reign of terror. In addition, since the threat of a more severe sanction may induce greater leniency on the part of police, prosecutors, judges, and juries, there may be some inverse relationship between the degree of punishment threatened for a criminal act and the degree of its enforcement, particularly where the act prohibited is not regarded as seriously wrong by the general population.

Escalating the severity of sanctions has been considered a substitute for a high rate of enforcement. If lack of consistent enforcement is to be expected where marginal behavior is governed by serious threats, Nebraska's bad check law represents one set of conditions where the impact of legal threats should be subjected to critical empirical scrutiny.

NOTES

1. Andenaes (1974) cites the Norwegian jurist Lundstedt as saying, "Punishment has a natural tendency to demoralize the convicted person, and it frequently shunts him over to a class of social outcasts."

2. For a survey illustrating that punishment policy variables are not randomly distributed across various types of social and political systems, see Rusche and Kirchheimer (1939).

3. Normally, the term "bad checks" refers to insufficient-funds checks, no account checks, and forged checks. In the present text, the use of the term "bad checks" refers only to the insufficient-funds variety.

4. This use of the term "visibility" differs from that employed by Lemert (1953), where naive check forgery is said to have "low visibility" because, in the behavior of passing a bad check, there is little to suggest that a crime is being committed—as contrasted with such crimes as robbery, assault, and rape.

5. The only interesting difference between the two distributions is the relatively greater frequency of checks over $100 in the Illinois sample—14% versus 7% in Nebraska. How much of this difference can be attributed to the Nebraska bank honoring the checks of its most credit-worthy customers (see infra) is not known. Further, the precise breakdown in checks over $100 was not kept once Tables 1 and 2 were completed. Whether the difference is attributable to the greater selection in the Nebraska sample, to differences between the cities or banks, or to a "delayed reaction" deterrent impact over $100 cannot be determined from these data.

REFERENCES

ANDENAES, J. (1952). "General prevention—Illusion or reality?" Journal of Criminal Law, Criminology and Police Science, 43:176-198.

––– (1974). Punishment and deterrence. Ann Arbor: University of Michigan Press.

BEUTEL, F.K. (1957). Experimental jurisprudence. Lincoln: University of Nebraska Press.

LEMERT, E.M. (1953). "An isolation and closure theory of naive check forgery." Journal of Criminal Law, Criminology and Police Science, 44:296-307.

LEMPERT, R. (1966). "Strategies of research design in the legal impact study." Law and Society Review, 1:111-132.

MABBAT, J.D. (1939). "Punishment." Mind, 48:152-167.

RUSCHE, G., and KIRCHHEIMER, O. (1939). Punishment and social structure. New York: Columbia University Press.

TITTLE, C.R., and LOGAN, C.H. (1973). "Sanctions and deviance: Evidence and remaining questions." Law and Society Review, 7:371-392.

ZIMRING, F. (1971). Perspectives on deterrence. Washington, D.C.: U.S. Government Printing Office.

––– (1972). "Of doctors, deterrence and the dark figure of crime: A note on abortion in Hawaii." University of Chicago Law Review, 39:699-714.

ZIMRING, F., and HAWKINS, G. (1968). "Deterrence and marginal groups." Journal of Research in Crime and Delinquency, 5:100-114.

––– (1973). Deterrence: The legal threat in crime control. Chicago: University of Chicago Press.

PART III.

PROCESS:
CRIMINALIZATION AND DECRIMINALIZATION

Chapter 8

THE STATE DEPARTMENT AS MORAL ENTREPRENEUR: RACISM AND IMPERIALISM AS FACTORS IN THE PASSAGE OF THE HARRISON NARCOTIC LAW

SCOTTY EMBREE

The federal narcotics legislation of 1914 represents an instance of government intervention into the affairs of medicine, industry, and laymen alike. The major piece of legislation, the Harrison Narcotics Act, constituted the first time that the federal government established control over the domestic distribution and use of drugs, specifically narcotics. It was also the first piece of legislation to draw distinctions between drug use for medical purposes and drug use for unsanctioned purposes. This body of criminal legislation, with its enabling regulations, forged definite, legitimate channels through which the specified narcotic drugs should pass from the point of importation to consumption.

Historically, this act marked the first time that the federal government sought to regulate *intra*state commerce. Structurally, the passage of this act was part of a process which extended federal power at the expense of states, and it reflected

AUTHOR'S NOTE: *This paper is drawn from my Ph.D. dissertation (Embree, 1973). The writing was supported by a National Institute of Health fellowship. I would like to thank Eliot Freidson, Richard Quinney, and Edwin Schur for their advice and encouragement throughout the project.*

I am also indebted to David F. Greenberg, Howard S. Becker, Adele Clark, Paul Salisbury, and Harvey Catchum for comments on earlier versions of this paper, only some of which are integrated here. I am also grateful to Karen Spalding and Elsie Chandler for sharing their knowledge of imperialism with me.

the development of a national economy (Kolko, 1963). Since narcotics were the first of five categories of drugs to be addressed by federal legislation, followed by marijuana, barbiturates, amphetamines, and hallucinogens, the Harrison Act may well have set both jurisdictional and ideological precedents for the subsequent management of the use of recreational drugs of quite different pharmacological and behavioral properties.

FORMULATION OF THE HARRISON ACT

Many sociologists have analyzed the way in which drug laws create a legal class of drug offenders (Becker, 1963; Lindesmith, 1965; Schur, 1965:120-179, 1962; Dickson, 1968; Duster, 1970; Carey, 1968:172-199). Most writers refer to the Harrison Narcotics Act as the prototype of such federal legislation. If there is any explanation of the act itself, apart from oblique references to it as an international treaty obligation, the act is viewed as an attempt by the federal government to deal with a real drug problem in the United States. The assumption that the law was an attempt to deal with a domestic problem steers the focus to determining and debating the magnitude of drug use previous to its passage in 1914. None of the writers who have made that assumption have examined the circumstances surrounding the development of the Harrison Act or analyzed the three acts to which the Harrison Act is appended. Indeed, the narcotics legislation appears as though it dropped out of nowhere into the laps of an unsuspecting and possibly reluctant public and Congress.

Here I shall demonstrate that the Harrison Act, far from being a national obligation to follow an international treaty, resulted from the United States' own attempts to regulate international trade in opium. Both international conventions and domestic legislation regulating drug use were projects formulated and advocated by the State Department. I will argue that the State Department's interest in the control of opium traffic was *not* a response to a domestic problem of drug abuse, but rather a policy which grew from domestic, racist, anti-Chinese feelings and from the United States' colonialist policy in Southeast Asia, particularly in the Philippine Islands.

Domestic Racism

Although the State Department did not develop a policy concerning opium trade until the turn of the 20th century, the foundations of the department's particular racist, anti-Chinese character were set during the 1800s (Isbell, 1963; Morgan, 1976; Helmer, 1975).

In America, public attention was slowly drawn to the practice of opium smoking as distrust of Chinese immigrants intensified. Racism stemmed from both economic and moral conflicts between Americans and Chinese. The economic and cultural basis of American's abhorrence of the Chinese was rooted primarily in the changing role of the Chinese in American commerce. Between 1852 and 1870, some 70,000 Chinese laborers were brought to the western states to work on railroads. They were then experienced as harmless, hard-working, honest people.

By the 1860s, the railroads were being completed, and the Chinese turned to more ordinary commercial pursuits in coastal cities, in urban areas where their economic pursuits and cultural practices could be observed and compared to those of Americans by Americans themselves. Economic competition arose between the two groups in running shops, laundries, and restaurants. Their clan organization of life and their habits and practices were distinctly different from those of Anglo-Saxons. Attitudes toward the Chinese began to change radically: economically they were cheap labor; morally their life-style was substantially different and viewed as threatening. The Chinese became regarded as dirty, immoral people—involved in strange criminal activities under the guise of extended clan relationships. During the depression of the 1870s, there were extensive race riots directed against Chinese citizens in California and Canada. By 1888, fear of the "yellow peril" culminated in the Chinese Exclusion Act, which severely restricted the number of Chinese permitted to immigrate to America.

In terms of legislation, both local and federal, racism against the Chinese was directed specifically to their practice of opium smoking (Terry and Pellens, 1928:749). In part, this practice was strange to Americans and was increasingly reacted to with disgust and horror. It seemed to symbolize the strangeness of a group that looked distinctive and maintained a distinctive organization of life. Moreover, by the 1860s, the practice seemed to be spreading to marginal elements of both the black and the white populations, a development which was viewed as especially alarming (for documentation, see Terry and Pellens, 1928:746). The racial element in this legislation is reflected in the fact that the laws ignored the major use of opium at this time, which was for the relief of pain and not for recreational purposes.

Opium and Domestic Revenue

On the federal level, interest in opium originally involved its practical, financial facets rather than moral revulsion. According to a report of a State Department's appointed Commission on Opium, the federal government's initial interest in opium was to obtain some revenue from tariffs on its importation (Terry and Pellens, 1928:745).

During the 1860s, the government began placing heavy ad valorem taxes on imports of smoking opium. While other forms of opium were only lightly taxed, the importation of smoking opium became more and more restricted by import duties. High tariffs led to extensive smuggling operations along the Pacific Coast and Canada, and customs officials were increasingly unable to restrict shipments. Tariffs were subsequently lowered, but clandestine operations persisted (Terry and Pellens, 1928:747-748).

By 1880, the United States signed a treaty with China prohibiting the exportation of smoking opium from China to Chinese citizens. Apparently, smoking opium could be, and was, imported by Anglo-Saxons who would sell the opium to the Chinese. Moreover, smuggling operations continued, and in 1888 the Secretary of the Treasury, under pressure from customs officials, introduced a bill in Congress to prohibit altogether the importation of smoking opium; it failed to pass. Another strategy was employed by the federal government to regulate commerce in smoking opium in the hopes of gaining some revenue. A tax on all opium manufactured for smoking purposes in the United States was levied under the Internal Revenue Act of 1890. This act also restricted the manufacture of smoking opium to United States citizens. No licenses were ever taken out under this act.

It is noteworthy that the higher grades of opium used for the manufacture of morphine and the relief of pain were taxed very lightly by comparison with the lower grades of opium used for smoking. Because of the marginal position of the Chinese who dominated the production, distribution, and use of smoking opium, revenue could be derived more easily by taxing them than by taxing the Anglo-Saxon-controlled opium industry, which had a large and acceptable market in morphine and patent medicines and a highly organized lobby in Congress.

However, by the end of the century, these efforts by the federal government to obtain revenue from commerce in opium had proved to be rather ineffectual. Indeed, the government was losing money in its tariff and tax policy: restrictive policies only encouraged smuggling, and the cost of administering the law was higher than any derived income.

Since most shipping, including smuggling, was under British control, it became necessary for the United States to negotiate a treaty with Great Britain in order to obtain some revenue from commerce in opium. This is so because revenue from taxing the cultivation and exportation of opium from India had become increasingly important to Britain as the 19th century progressed (Hobsbawm, 1968:110-122). Originally Britain had imported textiles from India; with the rise of British domestic textile industry, however, this importation became more restricted. As the industry grew to the point of requiring a market beyond the domestic one, the British destroyed much of the

Indian manufacture and thus obtained a market for its surplus cloth. A similar tactic was employed in the opening of Chinese ports to foreign trade during the Opium Wars. Nonetheless, Britain still imported vast amounts of tea and spices from the two countries, and their value, in terms of price, outreached India's and China's demand for British-made products. Such circumstances contributed to a balance of payments that eroded Britain's economy by creating a deficit in her outlay of gold. Thus the revenue-producing monopoly of opium cultivation and commerce became, by the turn of the century, a very important feature in the maintenance of the gold standard.

In view of the importance of the opium trade to the British economy, England could not be expected to accede to American requests for regulation. Not until the turn of the century, when America emerged as a colonial power in the Far East, was the United States able to obtain British cooperation in this area.

Colonialism and the Opium Problem

The State Department took up the opium issue as an integral part of its foreign policy when America emerged as a colonial power in the Far East with the acquisition of the Philippine Islands during the Spanish-American War of 1898 (Williams, 1969). Rule over the Philippines involved the United States in the affairs of colonizers in Asia more directly than before and particularly in the manifold manifestations of the British monopoly of opium trade in China and India.

The major benefit derived from colonizing a territory is acquisition of control over its economic resources—that is, establishment of commercial relations between the two lands such that the colonizer accrues a substantial profit. (To simply administer a territory entails a loss of revenue.) To accrue any profit from the Philippine Islands, the United States had to develop some strategy for redirecting trade to ensure that raw materials would be sent to the States and that American industry would have a market in the islands for its commodities.

A purely military strategy for reorienting commerce was not feasible because any disruption that involved British commercial interests ran the risk of military or economic retaliation on the part of England. If the United States was to profit at all from its rule of the Philippines, then it would have to obtain Britain's consent.

But why did the State Department select opium as the commodity to begin diplomatic discussions with England? Economically, one reason for the State Department's interest may well have been the clear fact that opium was a highly lucrative commodity. In 1912, for example, the State Department's Opium Commission reported that the annual aggregate amount of revenue derived from nations participating in opium monopolies was some one hundred million dollars (Terry and Pellens, 1928:640). Opium was the most profitable commodity handled by the already established commercial class in the Philippines. If the opium trade could be regulated through tariffs, the United States could obtain a portion of the revenues connected with the commerce.

Legitimation for United States intervention was provided by American missionaries in the Philippines, who characterized the Chinese commercial classes importing opium as wicked corruptors of an innocent native population. For the missionaries, disruption of the opium trade would help to Westernize the population, while for the State Department it was a way to dislodge the Chinese control of commerce under the pretense of benevolence. In addition, the State Department hoped that its support for an international humanitarian movement against smoking opium would win trade concessions for American merchants from the Chinese government. The Chinese government favored this movement because of its own opposition to the importation of opium and to the foreign intervention in its domestic affairs which accompanied the opium trade.

In 1903, the State Department initiated the first federal actions toward regulating the *use* of smoking opium by appointing a commission of inquiry to investigate the problem of the Chinese and opium smoking in the Philippines (Terry and Pellens, 1928:631). Within a year, the commission presented a plan to regulate the use of smoking opium in the islands by prohibiting the use of opium except for medical and scientific purposes. The commission noted that this form of regulation would not constitute a commercial monopoly for profit, which the British enjoyed vis-à-vis its colonies; however, by taxing the distribution of opium for legitimate purposes, the American government was assured of some revenue.

Because of the smuggling problems likely to follow such action, the State Department quickly realized that the Philippines project depended heavily on the successful regulation of opium trade throughout Asia. Such control had to be obtained through the cooperation of Great Britain. Furthermore, other European nations holding colonies in Southeast Asia were interested in limiting England's opium monopoly by some method other than warfare or economic restriction and without jeopardizing the already shaky gold standard. An international treaty limiting the sale, traffic, and possibly the cultivation of opium would be a solution to the persistence of smuggling both in the Philippines and in the United States. For the project to be successful, however, the consent of Britain had to be obtained, and in 1906 the State Department began corresponding with England on the possibility of holding an international convention.

England was initially reluctant to participate in such a convention, because any interference with the importation of opium into China would involve a great sacrifice of revenues (Terry and Pellens, 1928:632). However, pressured by Parliament to restrain the sale of smoking opium in China, England finally consented in 1908. Invitations were sent by the State Department to European nations holding Asian colonies, and each country agreed to appoint a commission to determine the parameters of the opium smoking problem in both their homelands and foreign territories. In February 1909, the nations would meet for discussion in Shanghai.

The State Department as an International Moral Entrepreneur

The State Department took up leadership in calling together the Shanghai conference and the subsequent International Opium Conference to regulate international commerce in smoking opium because America had much to benefit from such agreements and little to lose in terms of national revenue. Since soil and climatic conditions tended to make the cultivation of the opium poppy in the States an unprofitable enterprise, America was dependent upon the international market for its supplies of crude and processed opium. The nation depended on European manufacturers for most finished preparations of alkaloids and on European middlemen for crude opium. Drugs from the Far East and South America were shipped first to London and Amsterdam. Cocaine, codeine, and morphine were drugs typically imported from Europe by the United States. Therefore the United States would lose little revenue from any restrictions on the manufacture, processing, and cultivation of opium.

In narrow economic terms, power might have derived from a nation's control of international traffic in particular drugs. However, America's dependence on international markets gave the State Department little bargaining power during the conventions. Its leverage at this time derived instead from America's growing military and economic strength. To obscure its economic motivations from its own citizens, the State Department claimed that its policies derived from moral considerations. One way in which the State Department could support its claim to moral leadership during the bargaining sessions was to demonstrate that America had already taken up corrective legislation of the opium problem within its own national boundaries.

Following this strategy, the State Department drew up and introduced into Congress a series of bills in preparation for the forthcoming Shanghai Convention in 1909. The result was the first federal legislation attempting to control the use of opium in the United States, the act of February 9, 1909. While the law was entitled "An act to prohibit the importation or use of opium for other than medical purposes," its main objective was to prohibit importation of smoking opium. The quantity of opium appropriated for medical purposes was to be determined by the Secretary of the Treasury. Penalties for violations in the form of fines or imprisonment were also provided. Finally, specific ports were designated as legal ports of entry.

The forthcoming International Opium Convention at The Hague was planned, again by the State Department, to limit further international and domestic manufacture and distribution of smoking opium. The convention, however, was temporarily postponed by Britain's refusal to attend. Britain insisted that the manufacture, sale, and importation of morphine and cocaine be restricted as was smoking opium. Morphine and cocaine were commodities produced mainly by Germany. Britain declared that, if she were to give up a substantial portion of her revenues from the smoking opium trade, other countries should not profit from increased sales in morphine and cocaine to her colonies and to her major consumer, China. After considerable negotiation the interested nations accepted her proposal, for without Britain's participation in the treaty, the expected regulation would be ineffectual. In this manner, morphine, cocaine, and heroin were added to the provisions of the International Opium Convention at The Hague (Terry and Pellens, 1928:640-644).

After the Hague Convention in 1912, the State Department again advocated domestic legislation to show that the United States took the international treaty seriously and that for Western nations it would set an example of model domestic legislation fulfilling the treaty provisions. Because of America's constitutional framework, the State Department had difficulties in devising a strategy whereby the federal government could regulate manufactures and commerce beyond the boundaries of interstate commerce. Such legislation was mandatory, however, to permit ratification of the Hague Convention. The delegates sadly noted that "The one nation which has not been vitally affected by the international movement initiated by the United States is the United States itself, except in the Philippines. . . . In spite of repeated urging by the executive, the Congress has so far failed to favorably consider carefully drafted measures aimed to bring the continental United States into line and in accord with the principles now embraced by the International Opium Convention" (Terry and Pellens, 1928:646).

After lengthy debate and amendments by Congress, three bills were passed in 1914. Collectively they are known as the Harrison Acts. The first two acts further elaborated the 1909 law by restricting the importation and transshipment of smoking opium to nations also prohibiting its importation. The third bill, known as the Harrison Narcotics Act, aimed to control the manufacture, distribution, and sale of all forms of opium and coca leaves in the United States.

Although the State and Treasury Departments had hoped that the laws and treaty would end smuggling and provide revenues, the drug-producing nations never effectively established control over the cultivation or distribution of opium. The State Department did achieve some semblance of moral leadership, but the domestic problem of smuggling was not resolved, and the colonial concern with the Philippine opium trade was directed to other issues during World War I.

Here I have attempted to show that the State Department was a particular sort of moral entrepreneur in the formulation of American drug policy. Its interest in the control of the drug traffic was not a response to a domestic drug problem, but rather grew from the State Department's linking of domestic, racist, anti-Chinese feelings to its colonial endeavors in Southeast Asia, particularly in the Philippines. Its selective attention to domestic and international control of smoking opium constituted a moral condemnation of Chinese drug use rather than any condemnation of opium use in general. Indeed, morphine, cocaine, and heroin were added to its concern with smoking opium for internationally rooted economic and political reasons rather than from any pressing concern with their use in the United States.

IMPLICATIONS FOR THE SOCIOLOGY OF LAW

This analysis of the Harrison Narcotics Act has major theoretical implications for the sociology of law.

Previous sociological analyses of moral crusades to enact criminal legislation have been based on two concepts, "the moral entrepreneur" and the "symbolic crusade." As defined by Becker (1963), the moral entrepreneur is a structurally unlocated, morally self-righteous absolutist who campaigns to prohibit activities that others enjoy. Dickson (1968), in an analysis of marijuana legislation, has argued that a government agency can initiate moral crusades to advance its own bureaucratic goals, and he thus has advanced Becker's analysis by introducing the organizational context in which crusades emerge. Finally, Gusfield (1963) has distinguished symbolic from instrumental crusades on the basis of their goals (status rather than economic benefits).

Although the initial crusade against Chinese importation of smoking opium may have had some symbolic content, it grew out of an ethnic conflict that was largely economic in content and origin. In that the stigmatizing of an ethnic group's way of life can provide direct economic benefits to the stigmatizers, Gusfield's distinction between symbolic and instrumental crusades may be overdrawn (see Morgan, 1976).

Although the economic concerns of California's petty bourgeoisie and working class may have sparked an initial interest in limiting the importation of opium, neither the Harrison Act nor the international treaty can be explained by these concerns. Although there was some domestic interest in the opium smoking practice of the Chinese, the Chinese population was small and scattered, so that legislation emerged locally, was rarely systematically enforced, and reflected a narrow, economically rooted racism more than any national concern with opium. The act was instead a creation of the State Department, which, subservient to American commercial interests, was orchestrating an imperial expansion into the Pacific. Narcotics legislation was part of its conflict with the dominant imperial power of the time, Great Britain.

In attempting to create support for the act, the State Department did bring Chinese use of opium to public attention, and it thus tried to frame the opium issue in terms of a domestic drug problem, but not because of a concern with domestic drug use. The State Department also made use of moral arguments and, in that sense, might be considered a moral entrepreneur. But this reliance reflected only the State Department's need to legitimate its activities to a citizenry among whom anti-imperialist sentiment was widespread, and its attempt to curry favor with the Chinese government. Its aims, as distinct from its propaganda, were economic, not moral.

Other discussions of the Harrison Act have assumed that the act was passed in response to a domestic problem of drug use (Isbell, 1963; King, 1961; Cantor, 1961; Mauer and Vogel, 1967; Schur, 1962, 1965)—in particular, to the nonmedical use of opium—and go on to discuss the effects of Prohibition (Schur, 1971). In fact, the law grew out of international, rather than domestic, concerns.

Sociologists have traditionally slighted the role of economic interests in discussions of narcotics legislation in favor of an emphasis on moral concerns because of their desire to establish the harmful effects of the legislation on drug users (in itself a legitimate issue). This emphasis has focused attention on the population of drug users themselves. The assumption is implicitly made that prior to the act there was a known group of people who were considered by the moral entrepreneur as a problem in some aspect of their behavior. The origin of the law is then located in the efforts of moral entrepreneurs to deal with this problem.

Sociologists have become cynical about these efforts because of the harmful social consequences of the legislation and thus have relied on the vague premise of status concerns to discredit the reformers. Thus the analysis remains fixed at social psychological explanations of the reformer's concerns.

A full understanding of the legislation, however, cannot be achieved through an analysis limited to this level. Whatever the motivations of individual moral entrepreneurs, their concerns are unlikely to be translated into legislation without the backing of economically powerful groups. These groups may utilize moral arguments as propaganda, which could lead the researcher to a misplaced emphasis on moral preoccupations.

To avoid this misplaced emphasis, it is necessary to ask who benefits from the legislation. This question draws attention to the role of broad economic, political, and social groups and events and leads to a more structural explanation of the criminal prohibition.

REFERENCES

ALLEN, F.A. (1965). "Current tendencies in narcotics legislation." In D.M. Wilner and G.G. Kassenbaum (eds.), Narcotics. New York: McGraw-Hill.

BECKER, H.S. (1963). Outsiders: Studies in the sociology of deviance. New York: Free Press.

CANTOR, D.J. (1961). "The criminal law and the narcotics problem." Journal of Criminal Law, Criminology, and Police Science, 51(January):512-527.

CAREY, J. (1968). The college drug scene. Englewood Cliffs, N.J.: Prentice-Hall.

DICKSON, D.T. (1968). "Bureaucracy and morality: An organizational perspective on a moral crusade." Social Problems, 56(spring):143-156.

DUSTER, T. (1970). The legislation of morality: Law, drugs and moral judgement. New York: Free Press.

EMBREE, S. (1973). "The politics of expertise: A profession and jurisdiction." Unpublished Ph.D. dissertation, New York University.

GUSFIELD, J.R. (1963). Symbolic crusade: Status politics and the American temperance movement. Urbana: University of Illinois Press.

HELMER, J. (1975). Drug use and minority oppression. New York: Seabury.

HOBSBAWM, E.J. (1968). Industry and empire: The making of modern English society (Vol. 2, 1750 to the present day). New York: Random House.

ISBELL, H. (1963). "Historical development of attitudes toward opiate addiction in the United States." In S. Farber and R. Wilson (eds.), Conflict and creativity. New York: McGraw-Hill.

KING, R. (1961). "An appraisal of international, British, and selected European drug laws, regulations, and policies." In Drug addiction: Crime or disease? Interim and final reports of the Joint Committee of the American Bar Association and the American Medical Association on Narcotic Drugs. Bloomington: Indiana University Press.

KOLKO, G. (1963). The triumph of conservativism: A reinterpretation of American history, 1900-1916. Chicago: Quadrangle Books.

LINDESMITH, A.R. (1965). The addict and the law. Bloomington: Indiana University Press.

MAURER, D., and VOGEL, V. (1967). Narcotics and narcotic addiction. Springfield, Ill.: C.C. Thomas.

MORGAN, P.A. (1976). "The legislation of drug law: Economic crisis and social control." Paper presented at the meeting of the Society of the Study of Social Problems, New York.

MUSTO, D. (1973). The American disease. New Haven, Conn.: Yale University Press.

SCHUR, E. (1962). Narcotic addiction in Britain and America: The impact of public policy. Bloomington: Indiana University Press.

——— (1965). Crimes without victims: Deviant behavior and public policy. Englewood Cliffs, N.J.: Prentice-Hall.

——— (1971). Labeling deviant behavior: Its sociological implications. New York: Harper and Row.

TERRY, C.E., and PELLENS, M. (1928). The opium problem. New York: Committee on Drug Addiction, with the Bureau of Social Hygiene.

WILLIAMS, W.A. (1969). The tragedy of American diplomacy (rev. ed.). New York: Dell.

Chapter 9

THE MOVEMENT TO LEGALIZE ABORTION:
A HISTORICAL ACCOUNT

DREW HUMPHRIES

Beginning in the mid-sixties, legislature after legislature in the United States liberalized state anti-abortion laws until in the early seventies the U.S. Supreme Court held that abortion was legal in all the states. For many observers of legal reform, these achievements of the abortion movement represent the importance of popularly expressed aspirations. The abortion movement might, accordingly, be considered as a symbolic crusade (Gusfield, 1966), that is, an instance of collective action undertaken by a status group, the urban middle class, in an attempt to liberalize abortion law and thereby enhance its prestige and address more practical concerns over unwanted pregnancies. It is true that the abortion movement appealed to the subtle status resentments on the part of this group: restrictive law did inhibit the expression of permissive attitudes toward sexuality, did denigrate waning commitments to family life, and did symbolize the degrading and inferior position of women with regard to the law (Blake, 1971; Cisler, 1970b). Moreover, estimates of the number of illegal abortions performed in this country highlight the importance of women's more instrumental interests in legalization.

However, the abortion movement in the United States and especially in New York State can only be partly understood as a middle class symbolic crusade. While public opinion surveys administered throughout the sixties indicate that a majority expressed favorable attitudes toward expanding the set of reasons for terminating pregnancy, only a minority agreed that termination of pregnancy should be at the discretion of prospective parents and their physicians (Blake, 1971). New York enacted a repeal law in 1970 and made abortion a matter to be decided on by the doctor and the woman. Consequently, legislative action on the New York repeal bill went beyond popularly expressed aspirations representing the interests of a minority.

Furthermore, the abortion movement did not suddenly emerge in the sixties as the unique expression of even this minority's concerns. The movement can be traced to the international family planning and American birth control movements, whose attention was focused on the eradication of poverty and oversized families. These precursors of the present-day abortion movement gradually redefined the legal prohibition as socially problematic in contrast to the traditional understanding of abortion as an immoral act. Moreover, for nearly half a century, these precursor movements maintained that the dangers of outlawing abortion outweighed the disadvantages of legalizing an allegedly immoral act.

The abortion movement is more adequately understood from the vantage point of history. It involved professionals who redefined the meaning of the prohibition, on the one hand, and industrial philanthropists who funded such efforts, on the other. First, population experts, doctors, lawyers, academics, and intellectuals identified the social problems associated with antiabortion law, deeming them dangerous enough to justify a legal challenge in the late sixties and early seventies. Such professionals perceived the ills of antiabortion legislation in light of professional goals: population stabilization, extension of civil rights, and the assertion of medical prerogatives.

Second, some philanthropists envisioned population growth as a problem in its own right from a very early date. Research and action programs designed to bring birth rates under control were supported by foundations. These programs, however, also expressed the laudable hopes of reformers intent on ameliorating human misery. In practice, such programs were limited in their effects, for, without accompanying social reorganization, fertility control tended to maintain the existing standard of living for the affluent while reducing only the most visible signs of poverty.

This historical analysis begins with the predecessors to the present-day abortion movement, detailing how the international family planning and the American birth control movements defined the dangers of antiabortion law. It then describes the present-day abortion movement as the modern organizational form disseminating previously formulated definitions of abortion. Finally, this paper presents the outlines for an alternative approach to the study of legal reform.

EARLY MOVEMENTS AND TENDENCIES

International Family Planning

The philanthropic model for social change involves identification of problems, creation of experts equipped with the skills necessary for their amelioration, and the institutionalization of experimental programs, initially funded by foundations and then gradually financed by governmental agencies. This model, pioneered by the Rockefeller Foundation, summarizes that foundation's involvement with the population problem.

The Rockefeller Foundation has long been aware of the population problem, seeing it as the inevitable result of a falling death rate, the reduction of famine, and the successful prevention of disease. From 1921 to the mid-sixties, the Rockefeller Foundation spent $4.5 million on population research alone. In 1947, the International Health Division of the foundation proposed renewed efforts in this area. Encouraged by John D. Rockefeller III, then a trustee, the foundation sponsored a research team to survey the population explosion in the Far East. The team returned with a proposal for a large-scale research program. However, the proposal was not accepted by the foundation's board because there was no birth control technique then available for mass distribution and because the board considered that such proposals would encounter denunciation from the Catholic Church. It was agreed, nonetheless, that the foundation would increase grants for population research.

John D. Rockefeller III had more ambitious plans in this area and took on the mission of arousing governmental, intellectual, scientific, and academic interest in finding a solution to what he considered a vastly neglected problem. In 1952, he personally contributed over a million dollars to start a new foundation, the Population Council, to carry out the program recommended by the original Rockefeller survey team (Williams, 1964).

Reproduction, in the Population Council's scheme of things, was seen as the critical variable in raising the standard of living in underdeveloped nations. It now spends three million dollars annually on outreach and action programs (Rockefeller Foundation Quarterly, 1968) in an effort to convince the "uneducated" that their best interests rest in the consistent use of birth control. The full extent of the Population Council's activities are not known, although it has been a conduit for United States governmental as well as private funds to overseas population control and family planning projects (U.S. Agency for International Development, 1967). These programs, however, were seriously limited by the underdevelopment of birth control technology until the sixties when the "pill" and the intrauterine device (IUD) became available for mass distribution.

Programs supported by the Population Council were shaped by the International Planned Parenthood Federation (the worldwide organization that includes the Planned Parenthood Federation of America), which annually brings together demographers, population experts, and family planners to discuss how best to confront the issue of overpopulation. In 1962 the International Planned Parenthood Federation took up the topic of abortion. Here, the abortion question was framed in terms of the population crisis. "If people, because of their particular situation chose to adopt a particular form of behavior, the ignoring of that behavior will not change its importance or its role" (International Planned Parenthood Federation, 1964:746). Participants went on to cite with approval that, in India, sterilization was available to meet the crisis and that, in Japan and Eastern Europe, legalized abortion had affected population growth. Officials were urged to recognize the reality of the situation and to begin the "total, complex process of movement toward a stable population" (International Planned Parenthood Federation, 1964).

In 1967, the International Planned Parenthood Federation conference went further, and the session devoted to the "World Wide Problem of Abortion" concluded by favoring legalization of abortion. Although "abortion was already a widely used method of birth control," the session concluded that it could not be recommended as an explicit method of family planning (International Planned Parenthood Federation, 1967:129-153). Such routine birth control techniques as the pill and the IUD, methods preferred by the International Planned Parenthood Federation, were to be made more effective by legalizing abortion as a backup measure. In this way, legalized abortion on a worldwide scale would provide international population planners with a greater range of methods to stabilize population growth.

This formulation of the abortion problem received explicit recognition in the United States only when the American population crisis became an issue. While specific dimensions of the United States crisis are subject to debate, it can be generally defined as a population growth rate which at some time will outstrip the resources necessary to sustain the country at its present level of economic development. On the one hand, experts saw the situation complicated by the wasteful use of natural resources and by the heavy reliance on inefficient technology (Ehrlich and Holdren, 1970). On the other hand, experts saw the crisis complicated by the reluctance of public officials to deal with the issue of overpopulation as a matter of public policy (Mayer, 1970).

While some organizations, like Zero Population Growth, urged drastic and immediate action, other more moderate organizations such as Planned Parenthood World Population and the Population Council urged a gradual slowing of the growth rate. Frank S. Notestein (1970), president emeritus of the Population

Council and a member of Planned Parenthood-World Population's board of directors, reiterated the value of family planning in the accomplishment of this task. "Family Planning," he wrote, "represents a new and important freedom in the world. . . . It is a matter of major importance that this kind of new freedom to choose, now existing for the bulk of the population, should be extended to its most disadvantaged parts" (1970:22). The importance of extending family planning services to the most disadvantaged lies in the rising number of "unwanted births" found among low income groups and, partly as a consequence of this, among black groups. While Notestein favored liberalization of abortion law, he rejected abortion as a population stabilization technique per se but added ambiguously that "easy abortion will further reduce the birth rates" (1970:22).

Kingsley Davis sharply criticized Notestein's family planning approach, calling it a euphemism for distributing contraceptives and, as such, a major obstacle to real population control. According to Davis (1967), real population control required attention to the low motivation to use birth control and to the underlying causes of high fertility. Davis' critique provoked a response from Bernard Berelson (1969) of the Population Council, who compiled an exhaustive list of alternatives—some voluntary, some involuntary—which could deal with the issues of control raised by Davis. In doing so, Berelson placed the issue of legalization in the context of an elaborate strategy deliberately intended to curb population growth. And although Notestein urged abortion and contraception as "new freedoms," it is apparent that, when the argument is challenged, the defenders of family planning fall back on population control as the underlying rationale.

The American Birth Control Movement

Margaret Sanger, founder of the National Birth Control League and the later American Birth Control League, rejected abortion as a birth control technique in 1928, arguing that the legalization of contraception would put an end to what she called the "desperate remedy" (1928). This official stance safeguarded the fledgling birth control movement, although in later years the American Birth Control League admitted to having maintained cooperative relations with the more venturesome National Committee on Maternal Health (Hartman, 1967:19). This committee, a private organization under an exclusively medical leadership and housed in the New York Academy of Medicine, was founded in 1930 and took a more aggressive position on abortion. Dr. Robert L. Dickenson, a medical specialist on conception and contraception (at the New York Academy of Medicine) and the voluntary leader of the committee for 11 years, tied birth control to abortion, seeing in the legalization of both some answers to marital problems and subnormal sexual functioning (Himes, 1970:318).

The National Committee on Maternal Health sponsored Frederick Taussig's classic work on abortion, *Abortion: Spontaneous and Induced* (1936), which in part reported on the Soviet experiment with legalized abortion. The Soviet law functioned to eliminate illegal abortion and to reduce maternal mortality and morbidity, to rationalize population growth in relation to labor force needs, and to emancipate women by legalizing the procedure (Field, 1956:421). Taussig focused on the first, the public health benefits, which later became the central issue in the birth control movement's formulation of the problem of abortion. This public health argument can be summarized simply: when the therapeutic abortion rate (i.e., of legal abortions) declines, the criminal abortion rate climbs, and its increase can be estimated from the greater incidence of maternal mortality and morbidity. It follows quite naturally that, by relaxing the abortion prohibition, the dangers of illegal abortions can be brought under control. Taussig recommended that abortion be allowed when certified by two doctors and when a woman had a predisposition to disease, mental or physical, or when she had become pregnant unwillingly as in the case of rape.

The National Committee on Maternal Health (1944) went on to sponsor an abortion conference in 1942. This conference reiterated Taussig's public health formulation and cited the needless destruction of maternal and fetal life at the hands of criminal abortionists. Originally convened to draft a relaxed abortion law, the conference issued only two mild resolutions: first, that both reproduction and the problem of abortion be opened up for public discussion and, second, that another conference be held to further that discussion. A second conference was thus convened in 1954 under the auspices of the Planned Parenthood Federation of America, the organization which had inherited from the American Birth Control League the leadership mantle for birth control in this country and which enjoyed membership in the International Planned Parenthood Federation. Dr. Alan Guttmacher, president of the Planned Parenthood Federation of America, opened the conference and directed the discussion to issues surrounding the public health argument (Calderone, 1958). This conference went further than the 1942 conference by recommending that the American Law Institute draft a model abortion law. This was done in 1959, and the draft was presented to the federation's delegates in 1962 (American Law Institute, 1962:189-191).

The American Law Institute and the Model Penal Code

The American Law Institute is a private voluntary group composed of jurists and attorneys; its recommendations, the Model Penal Code, may influence legislative reform, but they do not determine legislative action. Planned Parenthood was unable to participate officially in the institute's deliberations on the model abortion laws. Instead, trends internal to the legal profession can more adequately account for the willingness of the institute to support liberalization. These trends include the attack on legal moralism and the tenor of legal policy advanced under positive law.

Legal moralism expresses the view that private behavior is within the range of activity properly subject to criminal sanction. Lord Devlin, one of its modern defenders, has argued that "society cannot ignore the morality of the individual any more than it can his loyalty; it flourishes on both and without either it dies" (1970:22). The law, the argument proceeds, should criminalize vicious, offensive, or otherwise immoral activity (Schur and Bedau, 1974:84-94). Such criminalization is justified on the grounds that people are unable to make informed judgments about participating in immoral activity because of weakness of will or inadequate information (Schur and Bedau, 1974:85).

Arrayed against legal moralism are academic jurists and social scientists who, in advancing positive law, have shaped the rationales favorable to an attack on moral prohibitions. Social scientists recreated abortion—along with homosexuality, gambling, and prostitution—as a victimless crime, that is, an exchange between willing partners of strongly desired goods or services, a consensual transaction (Schur, 1965). Moreover, academic jurists questioned the utility of prohibiting such consensual transactions, seeing in these attempts a crisis of overcriminalization (Kadish, 1968). The crisis threatened the legitimacy of law and was defined in terms of inadequate prosecution, dead-letter laws, discriminatory enforcement, and routine violation. Sanford Kadish (1968), one of the proponents of this position, has argued that the failure to prosecute contradicts the "moral message of the law," disparaging it and leaving it open to charges of legal hypocrisy. Casual violation, he continued, creates an "unhealthy disrespect for law," and discriminatory enforcement not only singles out target groups but reflects complicity and corruption on the part of law enforcement officials.

Moral legal policy, according to the logic of positive law, is to be evaluated pragmatically and amorally. The effectiveness of such policy is to be measured by how well it promotes legitimacy, general respect for authority, and conformity to legal norms. If a policy such as legal moralism fails to foster enforceability and, thereby, legitimacy, it should, according to positive law advocates, be revised. This focus on enforcement as a pragmatic goal is, however, amoral; few judgments regarding the desirability of a behavior—whether abortion, prostitution, or gambling—are made. One simply suspends moral judgment and relies on the assessment of practical consequence as a guide for legal policy. Here, the appraisal of facts, as well as the cost-benefit analysis, plays a critical role in legal policy, for such appraisals determine the meaning of practical consequence (Skolnick, 1968:618).

The American Law Institute approached construction of the Model Penal Code from the positive law viewpoint of regulation. Since it is impossible to regulate behavior that is prohibited, the institute sought to control the dangerousness or the offensiveness of prohibited activities by placing them under suitable regulations (Schwartz, 1962:669-686). In the case of abortion, the criminal sanction was to punish nonmedical, nonaccredited persons who performed abortions: it was a third-degree felony if performed prior to the 26th week of pregnancy, a second-degree felony if performed after the 26th week. Here the criminal sanction was applied to mitigate the public health dangers of illegal abortion and to give the medical profession a monopoly on abortion services under specific conditions—namely, when the pregnancy jeopardizes the physical or mental life of the woman, when the child might be born with a grave mental or physical defect, or when the pregnancy has resulted from rape, incest, or felonious intercourse.

The National Committee on Maternal Health and Planned Parenthood Federation of America specified the dangers of abortion in terms of public health problems. The American Law Institute adopted the model abortion law in 1962, thus responding to the public health definition of abortion and the positive law approach to legal revision: the waste of maternal life at the hands of criminal abortionists outweighed any benefit derived from the prohibition.

The Medical Community and Medicalized Abortion

Just as trends internal to the legal profession can account for their support of decriminalization, the shift toward liberalization within some parts of the medical community can be explained by events endemic to the profession. The medical community, as distinct from lawyers and family planners, grappled with the abortion problem on a firsthand basis and thus defined it in terms of occupational interests. During the 1940s and 1950s, medical opinion considered the performance of therapeutic abortion as a liability since it subjected hospitals and doctors to the risk of prosecution under restrictive law, civil suit, and adverse publicity. Therapeutic abortion, according to medical opinion, was indicated only when pregnancy complicated severe illness (Guttmacher, 1954:13-16). Medical science, however, advanced in this period such that severe illness could be treated without terminating a pregnancy. While therapeutic rates dropped for New York hospitals, therapeutic abortions performed on psychiatric grounds increased (Calderone, 1958).

This trend when recognized in the mid-fifties was swiftly and firmly curtailed. Psychiatric requests were discredited by reinterpreting them as symptomatic of underlying disorder for which counseling and psychological therapies were indicated, not termination of pregnancy (Lidz, 1954; Mandy, 1954; Dunbar,

1954). Therapeutic abortion committees regulating the therapeutic abortion rate became the rule. These committees insulated physicians from the importunities of patients and curbed the activities of overly liberal or sympathetic doctors (Packer and Gampell, 1959). The therapeutic rate, consequently, continued to decline in the late fifties, stabilizing at rates low enough to be acceptable to therapeutic abortion committees (Calderone, 1958).

Between 1963 and 1964, however, the rubella epidemic swept across the nation, and in New York the therapeutic rate doubled. Over half of these New York abortions were performed for the purpose of preventing the birth of deformed infants (Lader, 1966:29). Medical opinion and, to a certain extent, legal opinion condoned these terminations. First, from the viewpoint of medicine, such requests were not as easily discredited as the psychiatric ones mentioned above. The rubella epidemic had subjected an estimated 15,000 to 20,000 women contracting the disease during the first trimester of pregnancy to the very serious possibility of bearing a deformed infant (Callahan, 1970:101-104). None of these women could be held morally responsible for having contracted the disease, nor could their motives be easily maligned. While it is true that many New York hospitals were suspicious of these requests, they nevertheless allowed them (Lader, 1966:36-39).

Second, these abortions conformed more to the legitimate use of medical services than did the psychiatric abortions. Although the pregnancies did not technically intensify the illness, rubella complicated the pregnancy and jeopardized the normalcy of the pregnancy and fetal development. The pregnancies evidenced, in other words, a pathology which the medical profession, if it asserted its own traditional prerogative to define the terms of its own work, could easily treat. In doubling the therapeutic rate, the medical community asserted these prerogatives and, in doing so, actively "medicalized" abortion, cautiously embracing it as part of the domain of medical service.

New York courts, in addition to the American Law Institute, agreed with the need to so "stretch" the antiabortion law. In 1963, the court reversed the burden of proof in criminal abortion trials, henceforth requiring the prosecution to demonstrate beyond a reasonable doubt that the abortion was *not* necessary under the statute (*People* v. *Harrison*). Furthermore, lawyers of a civil libertarian persuasion were actively encouraging doctors to stretch the law. Morris Ernst and Harriet Pilpel, New York attorneys long affiliated with the birth control movement, asserted that the problem facing the medical community was not the restrictive law but doctors' bias against insisting on their rights within it. The law, argued Harriet Pilpel, was only as strict as the doctors made it. Morris Ernst continued, "one might even go so far as to argue that the figures on illegal abortion reveal that the failure of the legitimate medical profession to take over in this area constitutes as great a threat to life as many of the major diseases we as a nation are trying to eradicate" (Ernst, 1962:21-23).

THE PRESENT-DAY ABORTION MOVEMENT

The Association for the Study of Abortion

Creation of the Association for the Study of Abortion (ASA) in 1965 marked the beginning of an organized abortion movement in this country. In 1964 the Society for Ethical Culture met in upstate New York to discuss the abortion problem, namely, the limits set by hospital administrators on therapeutic abortion in instances of possible fetal deformity. The position of this humanist group is best summarized by Israel Margolies (1970:30), who suggested that "the truly civilized mind would be hard put to devise a greater sin than to condemn a helpless infant to a life of permanent deformity or the twilight world of slum or orphanage, or to the cold environment of a home in which it is not welcome. If there is to be talk of sin, then here is where it is to be found." Out of this original meeting, a steering committee was formed which then organized the ASA as the only national nonprofit, tax-exempt organization devoted to the single issue of abortion legalization (Kimmey, 1970).

The leadership of the ASA has remained stable, and, although it represents diverse ideological orientations in defining the abortion problem, these definitions are compatible. Dr. Robert Hall, associate professor of clinical obstetrics and gynecology at the Columbia Presbyterian Medical Center, assumed the presidency of ASA just after it was created. Dr. Hall (1965:531) had expressed his position on abortion:

> Birth control measures are primarily medical matters. The obstetricians' obligation to provide abortion, sterilization, and contraception are inadequately and inequitably met at the moment. The obstetricians of America must individually and collectively review these vital issues in an effort to establish a more uniformly humane birth control ethic.

In fact, Dr. Hall (1970b) considered abortion a form of birth control, all aspects of which should be under medical supervision. The task was to move the medical profession toward a position more conducive to the provision of birth control.

Dr. Jimmey Kimmey, professor of political science at Barnard College in Manhattan prior to becoming the executive director of the ASA, brought a nonmedical, non-birth-control orientation to the abortion movement. The major impact of abortion liberalization, she indicated, is "in the area of civil rights." It is, according to Dr. Kimmey, part of the overall extension of civil rights that minority groups have been involved in since the early sixties; it includes the protection of existing rights and the extension of new rights to individuals. Accordingly, abortions should be removed from the back alleys and from doctors' offices and be performed in hospitals where the rights of women can be protected under medical standards of safety and competence. Furthermore, Dr. Kimmey rejects abortion as a means of population or birth control, because, as she indicates, "contraception is as effective as it needs to be" (Kimmey, 1970).

The leadership of the ASA tied the association to the older, more powerful birth control movement. Dr. Alan Guttmacher of Planned Parenthood World-Population and Dr. Christopher Tietze of the National Committee of Maternal Health and the Population Council are both on its board of directors. In the American birth control movement, abortion had been cautiously related to birth control, but the movement had defined the social evils of abortion in terms of how the prohibition contributed to maternal morality and morbidity. Dr. Hall, however, was less inclined to rely on the public health argument, urging instead that doctors provide such services as are necessary to birth control.

The ASA was also connected to the various Rockefeller granting foundations and to the Population Council, since these were the agencies which funded its programs. In the population stabilization and family planning movement, abortion was explicitly considered a birth control technique and advocated along with a range of strategies to curtail population growth. Dr. Kimmey, however, rejected this rationale for legalizing abortion, and the ASA has never urged legalization on this basis. Nonetheless, the two views are compatible. Dr. Notestein (1970) of the Population Council does speak of family planning as a new freedom in need of extension to all groups.

The ASA can be described as a legal-educational organization. It helped coordinate at the national level the many cases challenging restrictive state laws, and it kept tabs on the appellate court decisions which were to force the U.S. Supreme Court to deal with the abortion issue in the *Wade* v. *Roe* decision of 1972. In its legal attacks on antiabortion law, the ASA has been able to rely on the services of Harriet Pilpel, attorney with Greenbaum, Wolff, and Ernst, who is a noted specialist in laws affecting population, family planning, and abortion. The law firm itself has important connections to the birth control movement: Morris Ernst, senior partner, was counsel to Margaret Sanger during the years of the birth control fight, and Harriet Pilpel argued the landmark birth control case, *Griswold* v. *Connecticut*, before the U.S. Supreme Court (Pilpel, 1970).

In addition, the ASA has also been able to rely on the legal assistance of Roy Lucas, founder of the James Madison Center for Constitutional Law. Just after finishing law school, Lucas came to the ASA with a paper on the unabridgeable right to abortion (Lucas, 1968) and has continued to assist the abortion movement. In New York, Harriet Pilpel and Roy Lucas collaborated in filing one of the constitutional challenges to the New York statute, *Hall* v. *Lefkowitz*, which argued that the statute violated doctors' rights to practice medicine. This suit along with three others were consolidated in a single challenge in October of 1969 and were scheduled to be heard by the Statutory Court in April of 1970. The timing of this suit forced the New York State legislature to act: if the Senate and the Assembly were to keep some measure of control over the terms of abortion legalization in New York, they had to act on pending bills prior to April of 1970.

The ASA also served as an educational resource for local or state groups which were concerned with changing the abortion laws but which on the basis of their own efforts were unable to attract the funds necessary to finance legal reform. The ASA consolidated local mailing lists and disseminated information across the country free of cost. Newsletters, bibilographies, lists of conferences and symposia as well as commentaries on the state of the movement went out from the New York office of the ASA to newly forming state and local proabortion groups (Kimmey, 1970). This informational function is important, since the ASA in effect refined and distributed the ideology of abortion already formulated by the birth control movement and the population control movement.

To this end, the ASA held its first abortion conference in 1968 (Hall, 1970a) and invited the abortion "experts." From law came Harriet Pilpel, Roy Lucas, and Herman Schwartz; from medicine came Robert Hall and Alan Guttmacher; from sociology came Edwin Schur; and from demography came Bernard Berelson and Christopher Tietze. John D. Rockefeller III gave the keynote speech, in which he outlined the moral basis for abortion law change. Abortion, he began, is the lesser evil. "It is morally justified by the greater evils that in all too many cases flow from the absence of abortion—the unwanted child, the unwanting mother, the medical risks of nonprofessional practices, disrespect for the law" (Hall, 1970a, vol. 1, p. xciii).

Rockefeller outlined the fundamental issue for the ASA conference: whether to support abortion law reform proposals following the American Law Institute's Model Penal Code or whether to support repeal proposals which would eliminate abortion laws altogether, replacing them only with the requirement that a duly licensed physician perform the procedure. Experience with the reform laws enacted from 1966 to 1968 was disappointing: there was a wide variation in the permissiveness of the mental health provisions; reform laws did not reduce the incidence of criminal abortion; such laws maintained physicians in the role of "abortion broker"; they did not protect the privacy of women; and they tended to give the state rather than the woman and her doctor the right to determine when and if an abortion was to be performed at all. These specific objections to reform were raised during the ASA conference, and they reflected the sentiment expressed by Rockefeller: repeal would "give us a true basis for eliminating the social evils" of abortion and "will inevitably be the long range answer" (Hall, 1970a, vol. 1, p. xx).

The Modern Abortion Movement: Left, Right, and Center

The question confronting the abortion movement was whether to continue its endorsement of the American Law Institute's model reform law or to shift its support to the more permissive repeal proposals. How each organization decided the question defined the political makeup of the abortion movement: the right wing position within the abortion movement supported reform, and the left wing position endorsed repeal. The center of the movement was made up of organizations which in some way or another endorsed both reform and repeal. By so depicting organizations within the abortion movement, it will become clear that when New York enacted repeal in 1970 it was writing into law the views of the center organization in this movement.

The center position involves, on the one hand, support for repeal on the part of activist groups in the lobby and, on the other hand, an ambiguous commitment to reform and to repeal on the part of the prestigious nonprofit organizations. Planned Parenthood World Federation and its New York affiliate endorsed the American Law Institute's reform for New York state, while the closely related Association for the Study of Abortion endorsed both repeal and reform. Dr. Robert Hall (1970b), president of ASA, founded the Abortion Reform Association (ARA) as a national activist group, although it concentrated much of its activity in New York. Dr. Hall became its vice president, and Dr. Kimmey (executive director of ASA) attended its board meetings so that the two organizations could work closely together (Kimmey, 1970). The ARA, as the activist front for ASA, came out for repeal in 1970 when such bills were introduced in the New York state legislature.

Furthermore, the National Association for the Repeal of Abortion Laws (NARAL), founded in 1969 by journalist Lawrence Lader, hoped from its inception to organize individuals and groups who had become "disillusioned with the ineffectiveness of reform laws" and to rechannel such energies as existed toward securing passage of repeal legislation (National Association for the Repeal of Abortion Laws, 1969:4). Again NARAL was a national organization attempting to elicit the kind of support for repeal that the ASA had activated on behalf of reform. ASA, however, was not opposed to such organizing. In fact, the ASA maintained cooperative relations with NARAL throughout: ASA supplied NARAL with literature and kept the organization up to date on where each state was in relation to abortion law change. And

NARAL, together with the ARA, constituted the activist arm of the abortion lobby's center groups. In 1970 both the ARA and NARAL participated along with approximately 50 other groups in New York's registered lobby for repeal, the Committee to Pass the Cook-Leichter Bill.

The left wing of the abortion lobby, represented by New Yorkers for Abortion Law Repeal (NYALR) was feminist in character and refused to support any legislation which would distinguish abortion from any other medical procedure (Cisler, 1970a). Here, the ills of the antiabortion law were defined in terms of their oppressive effect on the rights of women. Lucinda Cisler, president of New Yorkers for Abortion Law Repeal, wrote, "Without the full capacity to limit her own reproductive capacity, a woman's other freedoms are tantalizing mockeries that cannot be exercised" (1970b:278). NYALR rejected reform proposals because under such laws "abortion must be regulated, meted out to deserving women under an elaborate set of rules designed to provide safeguards against abuse" (Cisler, 1970b:278). The unabridgeable right to abortion was urged in the form of repeal. "Repeal," Cisler wrote, "is based on the quaint idea of *justice;* that abortion is a woman's right and that no one can veto her decision and compel her to bear a child against her will" (1970b:278).

NYALR did not joint the Committee to Pass the Cook-Leichter Bill and attempted to remain instead an independently radical and feminist group. NYALR associated itself with the community control movement to restructure health care in New York City. The Student Health Organization, the Medical Committee for Human Rights, and the Women's Health Collective of New York City all called for a major transfer of power in the regulation of health care; services related to women should be regulated by women (Ehrenreich and Ehrenreich, 1970). In this way, abortion law change, from a radical perspective, became an issue around which those interested in structural reform (Gorz, 1967), especially in the area of health care and abortion services, could rally.

NYALR also associated itself with radical law, relying on the strategy of New Left attorneys to articulate demands for structural change at the level of law. A handful of radical lawyers, all women, brought suit in New York District Court challenging the constitutionality of the New York prohibition. *Abramowicz* v. *Lefkowitz* was the suit brought on behalf of women plaintiffs, and for this reason it was called the "women's case." This case was intended to be the focal point for radical organizing, a weapon combatting the state's legal oppression of women and a means to demonstrate the state's cynical indifference to their rights. It also represented, according to its instigators, the first time that women were the "vanguard of attack against the oppressive police and governmental actions for declaration of women's rights to control their own bodies and destinies" (Schulder and Kennedy, 1971).

The feminist influence, aside from its visible signs in mass demonstrations and guerrilla theater, was devitalized by the stronger center groups in the abortion lobby. One way that this occurred was through the center's control over information. Planned Parenthood and the ASA along with NARAL provided the literature for the Committee to Pass the Cook-Leichter Bill and also provided literature for the general public. This control amounted to a monopoly over the definition of the abortion movement's aims. Although many feminists rallied, demonstrated, and got petitions signed, their unique view defining the right to abortion as involving both structural change and the advancement of women was lost.

Finally, the right-wing position was represented by the official political organization of physicians. The New York State Society of Medicine stood with its national affiliate, the American Medical Association (AMA), and refused to budge from its support of reform. And even this reform position was far more conservative than that originally advanced by the American Law Institute. The AMA's reform proposal required "documented medical evidence" supporting a physician's belief that the effects of a continued pregnancy risked a woman's health. In contrast, the American Law Institute recommended in such situations that only the "physician's reasonable belief" should be required. The AMA also required that the criterion for abortion in instances of fetal deformity be an "incapacitating" defect rather than a "grave" one as recommended by the institute. Finally, the AMA rejected all grounds for abortion which would permit performance of the operation for humanitarian reasons: its proposal accepted action in situations of rape or incest but only because these situations "constituted a threat to the mental or physical health of the patient." The state medical society, in contemplating reform, insisted throughout on specific standards for terminating pregnancy, for the conduct of physicians who might engage in abortion practices, and for the operating procedures of clinical services (New York State Journal of Medicine, 1971:1368).

This right-wing position may well have represented the fears of doctors over the likely consequences of liberalization. Such fears include (1) the possible "tainting" of the medical profession if it were to become involved in running "abortion mills," (2) the desire to protect physicians from patient-initiated suits by insisting on strict standards of conduct for doctors, and (3) the concern over unscrupulous doctors who might use the liberalized law to profiteer. This position, like the feminist one, was devitalized by the center groups who could point to support of equally prestigious medical organizations like the American College of Obstetrians and Gynecologists, the American Psychiatric Association, and the American Public Health Association.

The 1970 New York repeal law reflected the views of the abortion movement's center position, which can be traced historically to various organizations representing class concerns over the control and allocation of abortion services. Industrial philanthropy and the international family planning movement framed abortion services within the context of neo-malthusian programs of population control. The American birth control movement detailed the public health dangers of the prohibition and stressed the need for medical control over and greater allocation of services. The public health dangers, moreover, were easily translated into the cost-benefit calculations of positive law such that regulation rather than prohibition promised the greatest measure of control. Furthermore, physicians cautiously embraced abortion as a legitimate medical service by asserting their prerogative to control medical services.

This process of redefinition was complete prior to formation of the organizations constituting the present-day abortion movement, i.e., the ASA, the ARA, and the NARAL. These organizations can, consequently, be seen as linking their historical precursors to the numerous state and local groups dedicated to liberalization. The movement provided this link by refining the rationales developed earlier and by disseminating these rationales to a larger public. These local and state groups may well have appealed to the symbolic concerns of the middle class as well as women's practical concerns over contraception failure and unwanted pregnancy. However, the movement's history indicates the greater importance of instrumental concerns on the part of industrial philanthropists and professionals regarding control of abortion services.

CONCLUSION

This study has attempted to clarify the sources of support for legalization of abortion by emphasizing the role of professionals in the long process of legitimating the issue as a social problem. This process has been called the "professionalization of reform" (Moynihan, 1965) and not only preempts public discussion of morality but also urges the adoption of amoral pragmatic standards by legislatures and courts in their effort to assess the requisites of order. The question of legitimacy with regard to the criminal law is reduced by professionals to the mere issue of enforcement efficiency; order is measured on the basis of cost-benefit analysis, science providing the most effective solution. This supersedes the discussion of moral order, because professionals in suspending such judgments emphasize the detrimental effects of moral pro- hibitions. From this perspective, the abortion movement's accomplishments represent the emergence of a technocratic morality borne by professionals and signals the decline of moral crusades.

However, this account should not be interpreted as discrediting the import of culture in the legalization of abortion or the role of more popularly expressed aspirations, especially among urban middle class women. As was noted in the introduction to this paper, these women embodied in their behavior and attitudes toward abortion a cultural transformation associated with permissive views on sexuality, lessening commitments to family life, and a sensitivity to female liberation. These concerns should, however, be placed in perspective: they served as the more or less spontaneous counterpart to professionals' support for legalization and expressed popularly what the international family planning movement and the birth control movement had historically urged within professional circles.

This account of the abortion movement, moreover, may portend the character of reform efforts aimed at decriminalizing other moral prohibitions. Gambling laws have been modified, legalizing state lotteries among other gaming practices. Marijuana laws have also been reformed: possession of a small quantity has been legalized or reduced to a misdemeanor in some states and to a finable offense in others. Prostitution laws are under attack, and advocates of decriminalization urge regulation rather than prohibition. These instances of decriminalization may well reflect a combination of concerns similar to those associated with the abortion movement: philanthropic interests in voluntary forms of social control, professionals' desires to more adequately control services, and the status resentments and practical interests of the urban middle class. Moreover, further empirical research may well reveal that the reliance on technocratic standards for determining the requisites of order and legitimacy lies at the basis of decriminalization movements.

In addition, evidence presented here has implications for the study of legal reform. This study shows that legal reform movements are most adequately approached from a historical perspective. Had this study begun the analysis of the abortion movement during the period of its organizational formation in the mid-sixties, it may have simply interpreted the movement as a symbolic crusade and focused on the immediate maneuverings of special interests. The historical emphasis, however, draws attention to the lengthy process of redefinition and to its professional and philanthropic sources and indicates that middle class symbolic concerns provided the window dressings of popular support for the professionally oriented movement. This approach frames the immediate activities of the proabortion organizations within the context of philanthropic and occupationally expressed concerns rather than in the context of competing interest groups.

This approach, however, does not lend itself to facile conspiratorial accounts of legal reform. Definitions about the ills of the abortion prohibition emerged autonomously within specific professions. The convergence of definitions reflects the way pervasive and underlying contradictions can be experienced differentially and reformulated as distinct social problems within independent professions. Academic jurists perceived the "crisis of overcriminalization," physicians experienced the effects of the rubella epidemic, industrial philanthropists and population experts identified the problem of overpopulation, and family planners saw the debilitating consequences of oversized families. The contradiction underlying these diverse perceptions turned on the former but implicit pronatalist policy of the United States on the one hand and the state's commitment to ameliorating social and economic inequities on the other. The policies were incompatible, creating dilemmas which were experienced quite differently by professionals involved in diverse occupations.

Finally, insofar as the historical perspective shifts the focus of analysis from interest groups to more permanent class-linked formations, the functions of lobbying and public education organizations are clarified. Industrial philanthropists are in a position to take the initiative in defining social problems. They can advance "seed money" to launch experimental programs and to endow public education organizations, thereby providing the necessary resources for legal change. By financing organizations whose goals are compatible with their own, they can create the forum around which various occupational interests may coalesce. This is not to denigrate organizational commitments to their recommended values or freedoms. Rather, it is to indicate that philanthropic interests may be expressed in the name of public freedoms defined by such organizations. Consequently, as the main activities of reforming organizations, public education and lobbying veil the role of philanthropy and highlight the role of interest groups in the process of legal reform. To the degree that class linkage is obscured, the visibility of interest group activity increases, validating the perception that the process of legal reform conforms to the pluralist scenario.

REFERENCES

American Law Institute (1962). Model penal code: Proposed draft. Philadelphia: Author.
BERELSON, B. (1969). "Beyond family planning." Studies in Family Planning, 38(February):1-16.
BLAKE, J. (1971). "Abortion and public opinion: The 1960-1970 decade." Science, 171(February):540-549.
CALDERONE, M.S. (ed., 1958). Abortion in the United States: Proceedings of Planned Parenthood's Conference on Abortion. New York: Hoeber-Harper.
CALLAHAN, D. (1970). Abortion: Law, choice, and morality. London: Macmillan.
CISLER, L. (1970a). Personal interview, New York City.

――― (1970b). "Unfinished business: Birth control and women's liberation." In R. Morgan (ed.), Sisterhood is powerful. New York: Vintage.

DAVIS, K. (1967). "Population policy: Will current programs succeed?" Science, 158:730-739.

DEVLIN, Lord P. (1970). The enforcement of morals. New York: Oxford University Press.

DUNBAR, F. (1954). "A psychosomatic approach to abortion and the abortion habit." In H. Rosen (ed.), Abortion in America. Boston: Beacon.

EHRLICH, P.R., and HOLDREN, J.P. (1970). "The people problem." Saturday Review, (July):42-43.

EHRENREICH, J., and EHRENREICH, B. (1970). The American health empire: Power, profits, and politics. New York: Random House.

ERNST, M. (1962). "There is a desperate need of medical wisdom to deal with the problem of abortion." New Medical Materia, (July):21-23.

FIELD, M. (1956). "The relegalization of abortion in the Soviet Union." New England Journal of Medicine, 255:421-448.

GORZ, A. (1967). Strategy for labor. Boston: Beacon.

GUSFIELD, J. (1966). Symbolic crusade: Status politics and the American temperance movement. Urbana: University of Illinois Press.

GUTTMACHER, A. (1954). "The shrinking non-psychiatric indications for therapeutic abortion." In H. Rosen (ed.), Abortion in America. Boston: Beacon.

HALL, R.E. (1965). "Therapeutic abortion, sterilization, and contraception." American Journal of Obstetrics and Gynecology, 91:518-532.

――― (ed., 1970a). Abortion in a changing world (2 vols.). New York: Columbia University Press.

――― (1970b). Personal interview, New York City.

HARTMAN, C.G. (1967). "Acceptance speech on receiving the Margaret Sanger Award in Medicine." Advances in planned parenthood (International Congress series no. 138). Amsterdam: Excerpta Medica.

HIMES, N.E. (1970). Medical history of contraception. New York: Schoeken.

International Planned Parenthood Federation (1964). Proceedings, seventh conference, Singapore, February 10-16, 1962 (International Congress series no. 72). Amsterdam: Exerpta Medica.

――― (1967). Proceedings, eighth international conference, Santiago, Chile, April 9-15, 1967. London: Author.

KADISH, S. (1968). "Crisis of over-criminalization." American Criminal Law Quarterly, 7(fall):17-34.

KIMMEY, J. (1970). Personal interview, New York City.

LADER, L. (1966). Abortion. Boston: Beacon.

LIDZ, T. (1954). "Reflections of a psychiatrist." In H. Rosen (ed.), Abortion in America. Boston: Beacon.

LUCAS, R. (1968). "Federal constitutional limits on the enforcement and administration of state abortions laws." North Carolina Law Review, 46:730-777.

MANDY, A.J. (1954). "Reflections of a gynecologist." In H. Rosen (ed.), Abortion in America. Boston: Beacon.

MARGOLIES, I.R. (1970). "A reform rabbi's view." In R. Hall (ed.), Abortion in a changing world (vol. 1). New York: Columbia University Press.

MAYER, L.A. (1970). "U.S. population growth: Would fewer be better?" Fortune Magazine, (June):80-83, 164-168.

MOYNIHAN, P. (1965). "The professionalization of reform." Public Interest, 1:1-16.
National Association for the Repeal of Abortion Laws (1969). NARAL Newsletter (summer).
National Committee on Maternal Health (1944). The abortion problem: Proceedings of the conference held under the auspices of the National Committee on Maternal Health, June 19-20, 1942. Baltimore: Williams and Williams.
New York State Journal of Medicine (1971). "Report of the Reference Committee on Abortion to the New York State Society of Medicine, House of Delegates, Milton J. Greenberg, M.D., Chairman." (June):1368.
NOTESTEIN, F.S. (1970). "Zero population growth: What is it?" Family Planning Perspectives, 2:20-23.
PACKER, H.L., and GAMPELL, R.J. (1959). "Therapeutic abortion: A problem in law and medicine." Stanford Law Review, (May):417-455.
PILPEL, H. (1970). Personal interview, New York City.
Rockefeller Foundation Quarterly (1968). "Editorial: Problems of population." 3:43-44.
SANGER, M. (1928). Motherhood in bondage. New York: Brentano.
SCHULDER, D., and KENNEDY, F. (1971). Abortion rap. New York: McGraw-Hill.
SCHUR, E. (1965). Crimes without victims: Deviant behavior and public policy. Englewood Cliffs, N.J.: Prentice-Hall.
SCHUR, E., and BEDAU, H. (1974). Victimless crimes: Two sides of a controversy. Englewood Cliffs, N.J.: Prentice-Hall.
SCHWARTZ, L.B. (1962). "Moral offenses and the Model Penal Code." Columbia Law Review, 63:669-686.
SKOLNICK, J. (1968). "Coercion to virtue." Southern California Law Review, 41:588-641.
TAUSSIG, F. (1936). Abortion, spontaneous and induced: Medical and social aspects. St. Louis: Louis C.V. Mosby.
United States Agency for International Development (1967). "Assistance for family planning programs in developing countries." Washington, D.C.: Author.
WILLIAMS, G. (1964). "The Rockefeller Foundation: How it operates." Atlantic Monthly, (April):106-118.

PART IV.

PROCESS:
CORRECTIONS AND PUNISHMENT

Chapter 10

THE AFTERMATH OF EXTREME TACTICS
IN JUVENILE JUSTICE REFORM:
A CRISIS FOUR YEARS LATER

A L D E N   D.   M I L L E R
L L O Y D   E.   O H L I N   a n d
R O B E R T   B.   C O A T E S

The largely successful reform that took place in Massachusetts youth corrections in the early 1970s was followed by a rise in counterreform pressures to a point where in 1976 the system faced a significant crisis. In our research study a simulation of this process through its various phases pointed to the need for a resurgence of liberal power in some form if the reforms already achieved were to be safeguarded and consolidated. This chapter first briefly summarizes the history of these reforms and the principal mechanisms involved in them. It then presents more detailed data on the state of the Massachusetts youth correctional system and its political relationships in 1976. We advance the proposition that the use of extreme tactics by both conservatives and liberals played a crucial role in the process of reform and counterreform. Finally, we consider how the system responded in an attempt to preserve the gains of such tactics and offset their dysfunctional consequences.

In the mid-1960s, a liberal group attacked the conservatively run youth corrections system in Massachusetts by investigating it publicly, provoking the

AUTHORS' NOTE: *This paper was prepared under grants from the National Institute of Juvenile Justice and Delinquency Prevention, Law Enforcement Assistance Administration, U.S. Department of Justice, and from the Massachusetts Committee on Criminal Justice. Points of view or opinions stated in this document are those of the authors and do not necessarily represent the official position of the funding agencies.*

conservatives to respond by employing the extreme tactic of dismissing their critics (Ohlin, Coates, and Miller, 1974). The critics included members of the crucial "formal decision-making group," those people concerned with the prerogatives of decision making, as opposed to the substance of the decision outcomes. Made up largely of legislators and members of the governor's office, the formal decision-making group functioned as a swing power between the liberals and the conservatives. Consequently, the conservatives' dismissal of their critics, including the formal decision makers, alienated the crucial support of that group from the conservative cause so that the liberals could resume their investigations and topple the conservative regime, replacing it with their own reform regime, which they subsequently replaced in turn with a new community-based regime. In the course of effecting this second replacement, however, the liberals themselves employed extreme tactics which alienated the formal decision-making group, as the conservatives had done earlier. These tactics consisted of closing the training schools, which threatened the vested interests of members of the conservative coalition. The conservatives now sought support for counterreform through their relationships with members of the formal decision-making group. In response, the liberal coalition, like the conservatives before them, sought to reject the right of the formal decision-making group to criticize.

A particularly telling incident that proved to be a crucial precipitating event in the emerging crisis involved a legislator seeking to investigate the complaint of a fire hazard at a detention center. When he was rebuffed, he retaliated by holding formal hearings on some of the department's programs and was publicly accused by the commissioner of being a racist and of promoting a witch hunt. On hearing this accusation, the legislator, who wore a pacemaker, slumped over the table. He quickly recovered, but the legislature as a whole rallied in his support, rejecting this challenge to its right to investigate. Although the liberally oriented leadership had up to this time kept active conservative forces within the legislature firmly under control, this precipitating incident decimated that control. Despite this, the liberals were able to complete the implementation of their new programs. However, the possibility of backlash and restoration of the old conservative regime grew steadily and visibly in the background. The 1976 crisis may thus be seen as a legacy following from the unleashing of conservative discontent by the liberal alienation of the formal decision-making group in 1972.

In 1973 and early 1974 we developed a mathematical simulation of the reform struggle (Miller, 1976; Miller, Ohlin, and Coates, 1975). It reproduced the history of the Massachusetts Department of Youth Services (DYS) from the mid-sixties to that point and also projected several years into the future, as far as 1976. The simulation, both in its re-creation of history and its projection into the future, was based on 16 nominal scale variables, four logical principles growing out of the definition of the variables, and five empirical principles. The empirical principles, related to a wide range of sociological theories, suggest first that substantial change in a social relationship is likely to require simultaneous attention to both the internal dynamics and the environment of a relationship, since these are interdependent (Miller, Ohlin, and Coates, 1976; see also Coser, 1956; Thompson, 1967; Etzioni, 1963). Second, the principles suggest that a functioning correctional system, because of its relationship to the supporting interest group structure, tends to reinforce that structure and thus to protect itself from change. However, this self-protective resistance to change can be overcome by interrupting the operation of the system, as with a public and scandal-producing investigation into program practices (Miller, Ohlin, and Coates, 1976; see also Blumer, 1951; Turner and Killian, 1957). Third, the principles suggest that the formal decision-making group operates as a swing power between the liberals and the conservatives and that neither the liberals nor the conservatives can win without its help (Miller, Ohlin, and Coates, 1976; see also Dahrendorf, 1959).

The principles further suggest that while the formal decision-making group by definition does not respond to the substantive policies of the correctional system, but rather to the political dynamics that underlie it, the liberals and conservatives do respond to such policies. When things get beyond their control, that is, when challenges become seriously threatening or when their programs strike immovable barriers, liberals and conservatives tend to resort to extreme tactics. By contrast, when things are going very smoothly they tend to relax and do nothing. (To avoid misunderstanding, we should observe that members of the formal decision-making group may also be members of the liberal or conservative groups, and as such they too may become concerned with the shape of the correctional system itself; Miller, Ohlin, and Coates, 1976; see also Smelser, 1963.)

Finally, of particular importance here is the fact that the five principles yield an expectation that extreme tactics such as closing the training schools and at the same time rejecting the legislature's right to oversee and criticize can be expected to result in two things. First, the immediate objective may well be met—in the Massachusetts case, the training schools were closed, and a community-based system was implemented. Second, the long-run objective—in this case the objective of making the reforms secure against return to a custodial model—may fail. The projected long-run failure is predicated on the mechanism described in the brief historical synopsis above. Extreme tactics alienate the crucial support of the swing power, the formal decision-making group. When that group switches sides, it gives the other side sufficient support to gradually build up a challenge to the reforms and eventually topple them. This process is often slow enough to permit the reforms to be completely implemented in the meantime and thus to provide some evidence of success (Miller, Ohlin, and Coates, 1976; see also Gamson, 1961).

That a reform actually took place in the short run in Massachusetts is clear. In 1970 nearly all the youth were in training schools, and their contact with the community was minimal. By 1975 only 10% of those not on traditional parole were in secure settings; 23% were in group care, 19% in foster care, and 56% in nonresidential programs. Some of the youth who were in nonresidential programs were also in residential programs. In 1973, during the transition, we compared the new community-based programs that were beginning at that time with the traditional institutional programs and with experimental, therapeutically oriented programs that were started within the institutions before the institutions closed. We asked youth in the various programs whether the staff would reward them for good behavior. There was no difference among the three types of programs; approximately three-quarters of the youth in each agreed that the staff would reward them for good behavior. However, we then asked whether the youth themselves would reward each other for good behavior; 37% in the institutional cottages, 60% in the experimental cottages, and 80% in the community-based programs thought so. We also asked whether youth thought that the cottage was more concerned with keeping them under control than with helping with their problems; 61% of the institutional cottage youth thought so, while 30% of the youth in experimental cottages and 14% of those in community-based cottages thought so.

Clearly the reforms placed youth in more contact with the community and gave them more of a sense that they were being supported. According to preliminary data, this feeling did not translate into lower recidivism rates, but neither were the rates increased. About half of the youth whose records have so far been checked reappeared in court within six months under the old system, under the new system, and during the transition period. Under both systems, youth in the more open settings were the ones who recidivated less, while youth in the most secure settings were the ones who recidivated most.

Nonetheless, by 1976 a crisis had developed around the feeling of the courts and police that there was not enough secure care, and numerous proposals were being considered in the legislature to increase the custodial nature of the youth correctional system. Prominent program staff were suggesting that there was a need for more secure care facilities to take all the youth who were hard to handle in the more open programs. They warned that, if more secure care was not provided, the conservative judges and legislature would destroy the reforms totally. A task force of persons was assembled from throughout the criminal justice system and related agencies, headed by an official from the attorney general's office, to consider the issue of secure care. During this period we began a final survey of DYS staff and the staff of programs contracting services to DYS youth. We were interested in whether these people could tell us anything that would suggest whether or not any resurgence of liberal power was likely —whether or not the reforms were salvageable.

We began the interviews with an explanation of what we were doing. We said that we were doing a study of the youth correctional system and the problems of youth in trouble. We wanted the help of the respondents in learning more about this subject. We explained that it was important to know how the respondents felt about these topics and that there were no right and wrong answers to our questions. We stressed that, although most of our questions were in multiple choice form, we welcomed answers other than those listed. We explained that the interview would begin with questions about what the respondent liked and disliked in youth corrections today. It would then move to questions about the politics of youth corrections, the programs and the youth themselves, and finally the respondent and his most important experiences. We suggested that some questions might seem difficult to some respondents, but that we needed their help anyway on the questions that they could answer. Furthermore, all the questions were about actions and arrangements that at one time or another during the past decade had critically limited the possibilities for working constructively with youth. At times the staff had limited opportunities to do liberal things; at other times, to do conservative things. In either case they had had significant effects in determining what was done in youth corrections.

We also pointed out that our questions were about the present. Some of the questions simply asked for descriptions of the way things were now, and others asked about implications for the future. By the future we meant the immediate or short-run future. We stressed that the answers of individual respondents would be kept confidential.

Our data consist of 109 computer-analyzed interviews and a number of interviews using exclusively open-ended questions. Of the computer-analyzed interviews, 72 were of staff in programs, 18 were of regional office staff, and 19 were of staff in the central office of DYS in Boston. It was possible to do an interview in about 35 minutes, but we typically spent an hour, sometimes two, encouraging a conversational tone and taking down marginal notes as well as the formal answers.

The first two questions provided a partial basis for categorizing respondents.

A. *What do you like most about the way things are now in youth corrections?*

B. *What do you dislike most about the way things are now in youth corrections?*

We divided respondents as to whether they expressed concerns about youth needs, staff needs, community needs, or other needs or whether their concerns were not easily characterizable on this basis. The results were 62% expressing primary concern about youth needs, 4% expressing concern about community needs, 14% expressing concern about staff needs, 17% expressing concern about other needs, and 2% not having concerns characterizable on this basis.[1] The preponderance of concern about youth needs and the lack of concern about community needs suggest the liberal character of this group of respondents from the staff of the system. (We define "liberal" in question 1a below.)

We then asked directly about interest group identity:

1. *Let's talk first about who is concerned about youth corrections. We will be asking about three broad categories of concerned people. It may be that some people you know of belong to more than one of the categories.*

a. *Who are the liberals—people or groups of people who believe that the corrections system has an obligation to protect society, but that its primary obligation is to provide services to its youth?*

b. *Who are the conservatives—people or groups of people who believe that the corrections system has an obligation to provide services to youth, but that its primary obligation is to protect society?*

c. *Who are the formal decision makers—people or groups of people who are concerned with the question of who formally decides such things as budget, appointments and jobs, contracts, changes in fiscal authority, and things like that as they relate to youth corrections?*

d. *How would you characterize yourself? Do you belong to any of these groups? Indicate as many as apply.*

1. *Liberals*

2. *Conservatives*

3. *Formal decision makers*

4. *None*

The diversity of people perceived as being liberal was greater than those seen as being in either the conservative or formal decision-making camps. We note here the most frequently mentioned types. Among the liberals five main categories were identified: program staff, regional office-based youth workers, DYS administrators, other administrators, and private pressure groups. Fifty-one percent of the respondents mentioned the program staff, 45% the regional youth workers, 45% the DYS administrators, 42% other administrators, and 36% private pressure groups. There were three main categories of conservatives. Sixty-five percent of the respondents mentioned judges, 59% mentioned police, and 45% mentioned probation officers. Forty-six percent mentioned legislators as members of the formal decision-making group, as was expected. However, 72% mentioned DYS administrators as members of this group. This was surprising, since in the past the DYS administration had been decisively dominated by persons like Jerome Miller, whose interests were unambiguously liberal and not in the least of a formal decision-making nature. Miller and his associates had even entertained the idea of having the agency itself go out of business if its work could be done better by other child-related agencies. The administrators who were being named now as members of the formal decision-making group were largely a mixture of former liberals and others new to youth corrections but having liberal credentials such as experience in promoting reform elsewhere in the human services system. On the surface this development appeared to reflect the end of the reform: the reform constituency seemed to be dissolving, and its members were drifting into other interest groups. More careful analysis of responses to other questions, however, led to another possible interpretation, which we will come to shortly.

To complete the data from this question of interest group identity, our respondents identified *themselves* as 58% liberal, 9% conservative, 4% formal decision maker, 10% a mixture of liberal and conservative, 5% a mixture of liberal and formal decision maker, 4% a mixture of conservative and formal decision maker, 6% a mixture of all three, and 3% none of these.

Then we asked a question about how the actions of the interest groups combined and interacted:

2. *The actions of these interest groups are only a few among many factors competing, sometimes unsuccessfully, to affect correctional policies, programs, or organization. Still, thinking back over the actions or tactics of the liberals, conservatives, and formal decision makers you have been describing, how do they* combine *or* interact *to affect future correctional policies, programs, or organization? Are the actions of some groups more important than others? Which of the following best describes the way the actions of the three groups are combining now to affect the future?*

19% 1. *To consolidate or solidify a liberal system*

 7% 2. *To reform the existing system to make it more liberal*

 3% 3. *To replace the existing system with a more liberal one*

29% Subtotal

 3% 4. *To consolidate or solidify a conservative system*

28% 5. *To reform the existing system to make it more conservative*

 9% 6. *To replace the existing system with a more conservative one*

40% Subtotal

14% 7. *To investigate how youth are handled within specific correctional programs*

16% 8. *Other*

100% Total

N = 95

The first three response alternatives reflect the way in which interest group actions combine and interact in a liberal direction, while the second three reflect similar tendencies in a conservative direction. The seventh category points to the crisis that interrupts the system to overcome its resistance to change, and the eighth, "other," consists largely of combinations of the above categories. We see at once that only 29% of our respondents gave answers suggesting movement in a liberal direction. Further, of the three response categories that reflect a liberal direction, the only one that occurred frequently was the "consolidation" category. These responses represent a considerable retrenchment from a few years ago when the key responses would have been "reform" and "replace" —reflecting liberal reform within the institutions until 1972 and replacement of the institutions with community-based care after that. In 1976 our respondents even saw strong possibilities of positive conservative reform: 40% gave one of the three responses reflecting movement in a conservative direction; 28% gave responses in the conservative reform category. Most of the responses indicating a conservative direction, unlike those representing a liberal direction, describe aggressive, positive change. The 16% of persons giving "other" as a response frequently indicated a combination of the first and fifth response categories, liberal consolidation and conservative reform, or they simply explained that the liberals were protecting their programs by giving a little to the conservatives while maintaining the basic liberal direction or that the pendulum was swinging back from an extreme liberal position to a more moderate one. All in all, these responses clearly indicate that our respondents saw the period of liberal reform as being over and being replaced by a period of retrenchment or even positive conservative reform.

Fourteen percent of our respondents saw the actions combining to form an investigation. These perceptions were probably left over from some months before, when there had been a series of investigations and attacks by the news media. In fact, the frequency of this response decreased during the six-month period from January to July 1976, when we were interviewing. Investigation is frequently a prelude to a change from control by liberals to control by conservatives, or vice versa.

We then moved to questions about how the three interest groups stood relative to each other in terms of priorities or goals, alliances, and power:

3. *Let's talk about how liberals, conservatives, and formal decision makers stand relative to each other.*

a. *Which of the following best describes the priorities of the liberals?*

26% 1. *New programs for youth more important than orderly administration*

61% 2. *An orderly system of liberal programs more important than more new programs*

13% 3. *Other*

100% Total

N = 90

b. *Which of the following best describes the priorities of the conservatives?*

38% 1. *Control of problem youth on the premises of the program more important than control of problem youth (including perhaps the same DYS youth) in the surrounding community*

50% 2. *Control of problem youth (including DYS youth) in the surrounding community more important than control of perhaps the same problem youth on the premises of the program*

12% 3. *Other*

100% Total

N = 86

c. *Which of the following best describes the priorities of the formal decision makers?*

56% 1. *Development of broad, policy-oriented constituencies more important than development of individual patronage constituencies*

38% 2. *Development of individual patronage constituencies more important than development of broad, policy-oriented constituencies*

6% 3. *Other*

100% Total

N = 79

d. *Which group, the liberals or the conservatives, can count more on the support of the formal decision makers at the present time?*

29% 1. *Liberals*

40% 2. *Conservatives*

31% 3. *Neither group more than the other*

100% Total

N = 70

e. *Do some of these three groups have more power and influence than others? Please rate each one of the three groups according to their power and influence on a scale of 1-10, with 1 being low and 10 being high.*

5.075 1. *Liberals* (N = 93)

5.728 2. *Conservatives* (N = 92)

7.698 3. *Formal decision makers* (N = 86)

Not surprisingly, the liberals had retreated from a priority on new programs to a priority on an orderly system of liberal programs. Instead of installing new programs immediately, as they did at the peak of the reform process, hoping that administrative, financial, and coordinating details would catch up, they now waited to put in a new program until such details could first be clarified. The conservatives maintained a priority on control of problem youth in the surrounding community, reflecting the fact that the system, despite its growing conservative strength, now primarily relied on community-based rather than institutional programs. Since the youth were largely in the surrounding community, that is where they created problems.

The surprising finding is that the priority of the formal decision-making group was still seen as the development of policy-oriented rather than individual patronage constituencies. This perception may have reflected raised hopes on the part of liberals when John Calhoun became commissioner in early 1976. Theoretically we would have expected a dominant patronage orientation trend as a result of alienation by the extreme tactics of the liberals as early as 1972; closer analysis over the six-month period from January through early July 1976 while these interviews were being conducted showed that the tendency to perceive the formal decision-making priorities as policy-oriented declined steadily to the point of no consensus at all by July. The validity and importance of the decline is further reflected in the fact that our respondents saw the formal decision makers as favoring the conservatives more than the liberals, although this perception did not reflect an overwhelmingly strong consensus. While the liberals had been more powerful earlier, by 1976 the conservatives were seen as slightly more powerful than the liberals, as reflected in mean power ratings, and the formal decision makers were seen as clearly the most powerful. We would not have expected, in a predicted conservative takeover, that the formal decision makers would be so *much* more powerful than the conservatives. Our next question pursued this matter further.

4. *The actions of the three interest groups are only a few among many factors competing, sometimes unsuccessfully, to affect the relative power and influence of the groups. Still, how do the actions or tactics of the liberals, conservatives, and formal decision makers* combine *or* interact *to affect which of the three groups will have more power and influence than others? Are the actions of some groups more important in this respect than those of others? Which of the following best describes the way the actions of the three groups are combining now to affect the future?*

13%   1. *To favor the liberals over the conservatives*

3%   2. *To favor the liberals over the conservatives and the formal decision makers*

16%   Subtotal

18% 3. *To favor the conservatives over the liberals*

22% 4. *To favor the conservatives over the liberals and the formal decision makers*

40% Subtotal

38% 5. *To favor the formal decision makers*

5% 6. *Other*

100% Total

N = 92

The first two response alternatives indicate that interest group actions combine and interact to favor the liberals, while the second two indicate that they favor the conservatives. The second and fourth response categories represent the extreme tactics that have precipitated turning points in the change process when the conservatives used them in the late sixties and again when the liberals used them in 1972. The fifth category reflects a favoring of the formal decision-making group which tends to occur as that group responds to the use of extreme tactics by the other groups. Here we see that in 1976, according to the single most popular response, the actions of the interest groups were thought of as combining to boost the power of the formal decision makers, although the combined proportion of respondents seeing the actions combining to promote the power of the conservatives very slightly exceeded the proportion seeing forces favoring the formal decision makers. Among those seeing the actions combining in favor of the conservatives, slightly more saw the combination as extreme, that is, favoring the conservatives over the formal decision makers as well as over the liberals.

To sum up, the overall pattern is clear. The liberals had backed off from change-oriented priorities to consolidate their gains; the balance of political action force had shifted in a conservative direction; and power balances now favored the conservatives. The tendency to see the formal decision-making group as nevertheless extremely powerful and as having policy-oriented priorities suggested an anomalous situation that, properly used, might conceivably prove helpful to the liberals.

We mentioned earlier that one group that was seen as part of the formal decision-making group was the DYS administrators. These officials had previously been perceived as liberals, and some still were. However, their movement into the formal decision-making group partially accounted for the increased power of that group and perhaps also for the tendency of the group to be perceived as having policy-oriented priorities. This tendency to see the group as having policy-oriented priorities was at its height just as a new commissioner took over the agency and identified himself as having both liberal and formal decision-making interests, and the policy responses may have reflected a hope during this commissioner's "honeymoon period" that he would make a dramatic difference in creating a resurgence of liberal policies.

While the liberal hopes reflected in these responses may well prove ephemeral, the pattern they suggest is worth exploring as a possible solution or response to the crisis produced by a conservative backlash. The suggested pattern, picked from the data as a secondary perception, is that instead of the formal decision-making group simply supporting a conservative takeover (having been alienated from the liberals in 1972), we are seeing instead the formal decision-making group being taken over by ex-liberals and rising to unexpected power. A strong minority of our respondents actually saw this group as favoring the liberals rather than the conservatives. This did not give the liberals power, but it could conceivably save their programs. It is like a tall man walking beside a short man. The tall man does not make the short man any taller, but he may protect him nonetheless. These trends, generated from the responses of DYS and program staff, are corroborated and illustrated, both in their facts and in their causes, by observation data. A particularly telling contrast is provided by looking at the strategies of the two commissioners who followed Jerome Miller.

After Miller had closed the training schools in Massachusetts, he left the state to try to undertake youth deinstitutionalization programs in Illinois and Pennsylvania. His deputy, Joseph Leavey, became acting commissioner and later commissioner. The new governor elected in 1974 did not confirm Leavey but retained him for about a year, after which he replaced him with the present commissioner, John Calhoun. Leavey was both a liberal and a formal decision maker. He was a liberal in his insistence on not adding more secure care, in his dismissal of the idea that more secure care was required, and in his attempt to build a constituency for the reforms among the probation officers, in order to head off the conservative judges. He was a formal decision maker in his natural concern for his own continually precarious job status, his attention to the job security of his co-workers, and his arbitration of disputes concerning the continuation of the contracts of certain programs. As a liberal, he gave priority to the maintenance of an orderly liberal system; as a formal decision maker, he gave priority to the development of decentralized concentrations of power within the DYS. These little empires could be justified as the bulwarks that would stabilize reform, just as similar bulwarks had stabilized the conservative system before.

Leavey's decision to follow a policy of decentralization was perceived by many as lack of leadership. People in the liberal coalition, sensing no guidance from Leavey or his staff, began to drift away. By the time of Leavey's resignation, the liberals were considered to be weak, and the shift of power toward the conservative and formal decision-making groups had begun.

Calhoun thus came on the scene when the formal decision-making group was powerful, and the liberals weak. He did not pursue liberal confrontative tactics, but rather focused his actions within the formal decision-making group. Within that group, however, his priorities were policy-oriented. A liberal leaning of the formal decision-making group in pursuing a policy orientation could possibly at that point have been more effective in achieving liberal goals, since the formal decision-making group was far more powerful than the liberals.

Calhoun and other DYS officials, some of them formerly active liberals within the DYS, some of them newcomers but with liberal credentials, had indeed been expressing concern about *how* decisions were made and who was involved in making them, rather than being solely preoccupied with the substance and outcome of the decisions themselves. They thus aligned themselves more fully with the interests of the formal decision-making group, and they did so aggressively, marshaling people together to consider the issues, making sure that everyone was heard. Calhoun formed a task force on problems of secure care, headed by an official from the attorney general's office and including correctional, welfare, and mental health agency personnel, judges, probation officers, and district attorneys, police, legislators, and members of private interest groups. He also set up another task force, similarly composed of a spectrum of interested persons, to study the issues of program evaluation and quality control monitoring. In this process the commissioner assumed the role of referee rather than leader of a clearly defined liberal or conservative interest group. While the legislature continued to consider bills that would increase the custodial character of the system, some money was apparently beginning to flow for community-based care, and the task force on secure care was firmly advocating that security requirements be decisively defined in a manner consistent with policies of community-based care.

These observations suggest some possibility that this secondary perception of our respondents was right. In spite of strong forces pushing the system in a conservative direction, there appeared to be strong counterforces which could possibly reverse that trend and preserve the reforms. On the other hand, this perception could be wishful thinking, encouraged by the confusion of having a new and untried commissioner with liberal credentials who obviously was concerned to get along with the formal decision makers. However, the perception appears to reflect fairly well the self-conscious strategy of the commissioner himself. It was a strategy which at this stage simply lacked the drive to promote major new liberal reforms. In fact, at this writing it remains to be seen how well Calhoun's strategy will succeed in protecting existing reforms.

We were also interested in learning what was happening to youth in the programs while all these complications were swirling in the political base that supports the correctional system. We asked first about relationships between the youth and the community:

5. *Let's shift now and talk about the relationship between the youth and the community during and after the youth's stay in the program. Which of the following best describes the standing of DYS youth in the community?*

11% 1. *Like other youth in the community*

75% 2. *Like a suspected criminal or dangerous person*

15% 3. *Other*

100% Total

N = 103

Our respondents were realists, not taken in by their own rhetoric of reintegration. Their sober estimate of the standing of youth in the community is corroborated by the fact that the recidivism rate for the state as a whole did not decline with the advent of reform, although there were declines in some regions, and the more open programs showed less recidivism than the more secure ones.

We asked about what the staff was doing about this relationship of the youth to the community, and what their explanation of the problem was:

6. a. *Among the many factors competing to influence the future relationship between the youth and the community are current actions by staff. Which of the following best describes these actions in general?*

71% 1. *Advocacy or support for the youth in the community with some supervision to protect the community*

23% 2. *Letting the rehabilitated youth find their own way in the community with some supervision to protect the community*

6% 3. *Other*

100% Total

N = 108

b. *Which of the following factors are preventing youth in the correctional system from making it in the community? Please rank the relevant factors in order of importance, 1 being most important.*

25% 1. *The state of the economy* (N = 108)

1% 2. *Lack of cooperation from the schools* (N = 104)

1% 3. *Fear or hostility on the part of employers* (N = 104)

1% 4. *Hassling by the police* (N = 104)

7% 5. *Lack of cooperation from the youths themselves* (N = 106)

13% 6. *Lack of support from the youth correctional system or its programs* (N = 107)

54% 7. *Bad family situations* (N = 109)

27% 8. *Other* (N = 26)

(Numbers to the left are percentages giving the response first rank. Ties were allowed, so the percentages add to more than 100.)

Our respondents claimed that the system was indeed providing advocacy for the youth in the community, despite their poor community standing. Observation and data from our cohort analysis support their claim. The largest percentage of our respondents gave first rank to family problems as the chief factor in preventing youth from "making it" in the community. Youth correctional staff in Massachusetts had seen family problems as the root of the difficulty since before the reforms. Interestingly, however, the state of the economy now began showing up as a major competitor with family problems. Massachusetts, like other states, has an unemployment problem and a severe shortage of public funds.

As implied by our earlier reporting of a few statistics on rewards, what goes on inside the programs between staff and youth is also important. First we asked about distributions of responsibility, power, and reward between youth and staff and among staff:

7. a. *What about relationships among people* within *the youth correctional system and programs that serve its youth? Which of the following best describes how power and influence are divided among youth and staff in individual programs or living units?*

22% 1. *Youth and staff share power, and youth feel responsibility to make each other confront personal problems*

32% 2. *Youth and staff share power, but youth do not feel much responsibility to make each other confront personal problems*

37% 3. *Power is concentrated in staff; responsibility of youth is for obedience*

9% 4. *Other*

100% Total

N = 106

b. *Which of the following is the greatest personal change for youth within the correctional system?*

3% 1. *New academic skills*

0% 2. *New vocational skills*

33% 3. *Better understanding of interpersonal problems*

0% 4. *More respect for authority*

49% 5. *Better self-image*

10% 6. *No real personal change*

4% 7. *Other*

100% Total

N = 69

c. *Please rate each one of the following three groups of staff according to their power and influence in the correctional system on a scale of 1-10, with 1 being low and 10 being high.*

4.515   1. *Staff in programs or living units* (N = 101)

6.432   2. *Staff in regional offices* (N = 95)

7.215   3. *Staff in central state office* (N = 93)

Again, our respondents were sober realists. In characterizing the social climates of the programs, they laid relatively little stress on the youths' feeling responsible to confront each other and laid more stress on the concentration of power in the staff and the simple demand of obedience from the youth. This lack of responsibility to confront one another is consistent with a community-based emphasis, which, as we have discussed elsewhere, differs from the isolated intensity of a therapeutic community. However, the emphasis on power and obedience indicates a plain failure to maintain the gains of the reform. These responses thus may reflect a disenchantment with the reform effort and, possibly, a perception of actual losses. Throughout the reform there have always been some instances of poor environments for youth. There is a possibility, judging from observation, that in the mid-seventies, with high unemployment, lack of public funds, public anger about crime, and the turmoil over secure care, more programs were degenerating into essentially custodial operations. This was certainly the case with a number of important secure programs.

Still, our respondents cited understanding of personal problems and self-image as the areas in which the youth changed the most personally, in contrast to the original conservative goal of academic or vocational skills or respect for authority. The data suggest then, that, though the system may have been slipping, it had not turned around.

One of the characteristics of service-oriented systems, as opposed to custody-oriented systems, is the concentration of power in a central administration. Our respondents indicated that power in the DYS was concentrated in the central and regional offices, as opposed to the programs.

We also asked, of course, about actions being taken currently that would affect all the relationships between youth and staff and among staff:

8. *Among the many factors competing, sometimes unsuccessfully, to affect future power and influence within the correctional system are actions by staff and youth within the system.*

a. *Which of the following labels best describes what staff and youth do that affect who will have more power and influence in individual programs or living units?*

39%   1. *Prevention of violence among youth in programs and emphasis on rewards in supervised, verbal confrontation*

44% 2. *Prevention of violence among youth in programs coupled with general, nonconfrontive support and rewards for doing well*

6% 3. *Reliance on punishment and physical restraint to ensure conformity to rules*

2% 4. *Mostly physical restraint of youth—temporarily "warehousing" them*

10% 5. *Other*

100% Total

N = 103

b. *Which of the following actions are frequently taken in the youth correctional system to affect youth skills? Indicate as many as apply.*

75% 1. *Academic education*

61% 2. *Vocational training*

92% 3. *Counseling*

0% 4. *None*

28% 5. *Other*

256% Total

N = 71

c. *Which of the following best describes current actions affecting the future power and influence of regional versus central state offices?*

30% 1. *Central office hires, fires, transfers, directs, and evaluates people in regional positions*

61% 2. *Regional offices make most of their own administrative decisions*

9% 3. *Other*

100% Total

N = 80

d. *Which of the following best describes current actions affecting the future power and influence of individual programs or living units versus the regional or central state offices?*

51% 1. *Regional or central offices control placement of youth and evaluate programs or living units regularly*

36% 2. *Individual programs or living units control their own intake of youth and are relatively free of outside evaluation*

13% 3. *Other*

100% Total

N = 102

It is interesting that the respondents claim in nearly equal proportions (a) that the program emphasis is on prevention of violence coupled with confrontation and (b) that the emphasis is on prevention of violence without confrontation. Confrontation is of course a characteristic of the therapeutic community, which was prominent in the early stages of reform but took a less important role as the community-based emphasis was developed. Still, our subculture studies suggest that the characteristic subculture of the therapeutic community is nearly impossible to develop in an open community context, not that the staff had stopped trying. On the contrary, there was a tendency, remarked upon by some of our observers, for the staff of the system to try to develop more professional-sounding clinical roles for themselves, despite the advocacy goals of the system. This therapeutic tendency may be what we are seeing in the claim that confrontation was encouraged, despite the fact that the youth did not feel that responsibility. Liberals might take comfort in the fact that only 6% of our respondents saw punishment or custodial techniques shaping up to affect the immediate future.

Our data on such activities as education and counseling suggest that all were pursued, but that the emphasis remained on counseling. This is consistent with the observations of the preceding paragraph.

Actions affecting the centralization of power among staff may prove more alarming. While our respondents clearly thought that these actions favored the central and regional offices over the programs (a structure consistent with the reform), they also clearly felt that these actions favored the regional offices over the central office. Their responses thus anticipated a possible movement away from the pattern of power distribution characterized in the answers to question 7c above. If these pressures toward regional power were to succeed in bringing about regional autonomy, an important feature of the reform could be lost, since the system could then drift in a custodial direction, partly in response to local pressures, partly for lack of central coordination. Lack of central coordination tends to result in more youth "falling into the cracks" and essentially being warehoused in a custodial environment.

Finally, we asked about the personal experiences of our respondents:

I. *What is your official position or occupation?*

II. *What do you actually do, relating to youth corrections?*

III. *What do you think of as the most important duties in your job? (List up to three duties, probing just once.)*

IV. *Thinking back over the last six months, what stands out as the most important thing you have done or the most important thing that has happened to you relating to youth corrections? Could you tell me more about that? (Probes: "Who, what, to whom, when, where, why," and "and then what?")*

We found that 43% of the respondents were youth workers and 57% were administrators, although many of the latter were actually also youth workers, particularly those who were administrators of programs. As their most important experiences, many simply told us of individual youth with whom they had been particularly successful, or they rejoiced at having secured more funding for program expansion. However, a few recounted harrowing tales of personal insecurity as they were caught in the reorganization of a program, or they expressed strong aspirations to achieve stronger decision-making roles. These responses seemed to reflect straightforwardly a continued centrality of the youth program, together with the stresses and strains of continuing change.

We are left with a picture of the reformed agency showing clear signs of difficulty and crisis in the political structure that supports it, and some suggestions of difficulty in its actual operations. On the other hand, there is some evidence suggesting a possible rescue by the formal decision-making group, now strengthened and influenced by liberal adherents.

What does all this say about the use of extreme tactics such as the ones back in 1972 which precipitated the process that led to this crisis in the first place? Of course it says that such tactics are risky, although not necessarily fatal. The way in which long-run defeat may be avoided seems complex, circuitous, and uncertain, and the aftermath seems to limit one's options, specifically ruling out the immediate continuation of a straightforward liberal movement, for example.

Should one use such tactics? Do they not invite unnecessary danger? That depends on whether one considers individual political survival or the ideological interests of one's interest group more important. In the Wisconsin correctional reforms of the early 1950s, after others had used extreme tactics in the attempt to suppress criticism, one key official simply joined the investigators and kept a place for himself in the reorganized system. He survived quite well by simply siding with the reformers who were successfully attacking his agency. Behn (1975) has suggested that conservative line staff in the DYS case in Massachusetts could have gotten through the reform with less discomfiture if they had yielded a little more to the winds of change, rather than resisting. Jerome Miller, the commissioner of the DYS at the time that the institutions were closed, certainly could have gotten along better with the legislature if he had not tried to dodge its authority. But to support the ideology of the interest group is another story. The official in Wisconsin, while protecting his own position, did little to support the conservative ideology of corrections which was being attacked. Thus it seems unlikely that the DYS line staff could have protected the custodial character of the system while bending significantly to the pressure for change. Furthermore, Miller would almost certainly not have produced a community-based system if he had not adopted extreme tactics to do it.

On the other hand, there does remain an intriguing question, one which must await comparative analyses of other reform situations for an answer. Miller's extreme tactics consisted both of closing the training schools to overcome resistance to change and of not only circumventing the interests of the legislators but actually offending them in his counterattack against an investigation by one particularly annoying legislator. Given both of these events, we cannot tell whether the closing of the training school alone was a sufficiently extreme tactic to bring on the current crisis, or whether the reformed system could have squeaked through without such a crisis had the commissioner not precipitated such a dramatic challenge to the legislative investigation.

In any case, the long-run dangers of extreme tactics are clear in the present crisis as well as in the earlier crisis of 1969 which initiated the reform. But of equal interest are the dynamics of the possible solution, involving a new realignment of some of the liberals within the formal decision-making group. One could not have created the earlier reforms by acting solely from within the formal decision-making group. A dominant liberal group was essential for that. But the consolidation of the reform may possibly be accomplished by a reconstituted formal decision-making group, given its greater power and its apparent responsiveness to liberal policy concerns.

NOTE

1. In individual cases, such as here and elsewhere in this chapter, the given lists of percentages may not add up to 100%. The apparent discrepancy is due to rounding.

REFERENCES

BEHN, R. (1975). "Termination: How the Massachusetts Department of Youth Services closed the public training schools." Working paper no. 5752, Institute of Policy Sciences, Duke University.

BLUMER, H. (1951). "Collective behavior." Pp. 167-222 in A.M. Lee (ed.), Principles of sociology. New York: Free Press.

COSER, L. (1956). The functions of social conflict. New York: Free Press.

DAHRENDORF, R. (1959). Class and class conflict in industrial society. Stanford, Calif.: Stanford University Press.

ETZIONI, A. (1963). "The epigenesis of political communities at the international level." American Journal of Sociology, 68(January):407-421.

GAMSON, W. (1961). "A theory of coalition formation." American Sociological Review, 26(June):373-382.

MILLER, A.D. (1976). "Knocking heads and solutions to functional problems: Components of change." Sociological Practice, 1(spring):40-55.

MILLER, A.D., OHLIN, L.E., and COATES, R.B. (1975). "Logical analysis of the process of change in human services: A simulation of youth correctional reform in Massachusetts." Unpublished manuscript, Center for Criminal Justice, Harvard University Law School.

——— (1976). "A theory of social reform: Correctional change processes in two states." Unpublished manuscript, Center for Criminal Justice, Harvard University Law School.

OHLIN, L.E., COATES, R.B., and MILLER, A.D. (1974). "Radical correctional reform: A case study of the Massachusetts youth correctional system." Harvard Educational Review, 44(February):74-111.

SMELSER, N. (1963). Theory of collective behavior. New York: Free Press.

THOMPSON, J.D. (1967). Organizations in action. New York: McGraw-Hill.

TURNER, R.H., and KILLIAN, L.M. (1957). Collective behavior. Englewood Cliffs, N.J.: Prentice-Hall.

Chapter 11

PRISONER MILITANCY AND POLITICIZATION: THE OHIO PRISONERS' UNION MOVEMENT

C. RONALD HUFF

The social and political struggles of the 1960s have significantly affected American prisons, as has been the case with virtually every aspect of American society involving ethnic minorities, the poor, and the powerless. One of the most important, but least studied, changes occurring among our vast—and growing—prison populations has been the increasing militancy and politicization of many prisoners.

This militancy and this politicization have caused great concern among correctional administrators and have drawn the attention of at least one congressional committee. During the summer of 1973, the House Committee on Internal Security conducted hearings on this topic in Washington and several other cities across the country. These hearings on "revolutionary activities directed toward the administration of penal or correctional systems" dealt with a wide variety of activities involving prisoners, ex-convicts, prison reform groups, and attorneys. Topics of discussion included prison gang violence, revolutionary political activities, the emergence of prisoners' union movements, and the activities of the National Lawyers' Guild.

Changes in the demographic characteristics, attitudes, and political consciousness of our prison populations have had a number of widely divergent manifestations. Although the House Committee on Internal Security, reminiscent of its congressional predecessor headed by Joseph McCarthy, tended to lump together the violent and the nonviolent, the highly political and the apolitical, its own witnesses frequently noted the disparate goals and tactics of prisoners' unions, gangs, prison reform groups, and individuals acting without the support of others. Rather than fitting a neat conspiratorial model of radical, revolutionary disruption of our prisons, available evidence suggests that each movement or other manifestation of prisoner militancy and/or politicization must be considered separately, paying close attention to its historical origins, its goals and tactics, and the functions it serves in the prison community and in the larger society.

While academic and professional observers almost uniformly condemn prison violence as a method of addressing grievances, there is less agreement on the merits of raising the political consciousness of our prisoners. Some, such as James Q. Wilson (1975:xviii), clearly are opposed even to avowedly nonviolent political action by prisoners:

> I regard as a major barrier to effective change in criminal justice the tendency for decisions in this field to be unduly influenced by the organized interests of those whose behavior is to be changed. . . . The *reductio ad absurdum* of this process has been the emergence of prisoner unions which insist on participating in decisions as to whether any changes are to be made in the purposes and methods of prisons.

Other authors, including Marvin Wolfgang and Seymour Halleck, view such processes as essentially healthy and potentially productive of meaningful social change. Specifically, Wolfgang (1975:9) has argued:

> Instead of becoming highly prisonized and taking on the old roles of prisoners of yesteryear . . . they now collectivize around a new political ideology. . . . They have become politicized and rally around the attack, not only on the correctional system but the entire social system that victimized them in the first place. Their previously designated idiosyncrasy in psychopathology becomes transformed into a politically meaningful behavior for them when shared by the inmates into whose propinquity they have been placed. Madness and the sick label are thrown off for the more palatable designation of radical. . . . Moreover, they no longer see themselves as bad, let alone sick.

> This activity is therapeutic and constructive because the groups have elevated the dignity of the individual. . . . I don't know where and how far this kind of prisoner politicization will lead, but the prognosis looks good.

Halleck (1975:46), writing in the same volume, cited the therapeutic utility of political consciousness-raising among prisoners:

> Currently, a number of violent men confined to prison have significantly changed their attitudes and behavior by developing a new awareness of how society has oppressed them. Black offenders in particular have gained a new sense of pride and identity that favors militant but often non-violent behavior. What would happen if instead of letting offenders develop a new

consciousness of their situation through covert and anti-establishment organization, the correctional system itself would seek to help offenders consider the extent to which they have been victimized? It is possible to conceive of a correctional system that would help offenders learn about the social and political as well as the psychological causes of their violence. Such learning, combined with efforts to teach legal forms of social activism, such as community organization, might be a powerful tool for diminishing future violence.

Despite such concerns, there has been a dearth of reliable information on these new forms of collective behavior in the prisons. Such studies have only recently begun to appear in the literature. Carroll (1974) and Davidson (1974) have focused on racial and ethnic factors influencing collective behavior among prisoners. Jacobs (1974) has systematically studied the functioning of prison gangs in Illinois and has documented the importation of street gang activities, hierarchies, rivalries, and ideologies into the prison social structure. This study of the Ohio Prisoners' Labor Union (OPLU) movement adds to that literature by providing information about one form of prisoner militancy.

DEVELOPMENT OF THE OPLU

Although the earliest prisoners' unions began in the Scandinavian countries (Marnell, 1974; Mathiesen, 1974; Ward, 1972; Jepsen, 1971), the first prisoners' union in the United States was formed in California in 1970 (Irwin and Holder, 1973). This union, which is now known as the Prisoners' Union, has since provided resources and consultation for other prisoners' union organizing efforts in the United States and has planned a national union for prisoners, based on strong local chapters in each state. The California union has a predominant outside base, with ex-convicts and others forming a coalition of outside support and guidance which is not subject to the strong retaliatory sanctions facing inmate organizers inside the walls. The centrality of the California organization among American prisoners' union movements in unmistakable. In addition to its national efforts, the San Francisco-based union has been relatively successful in lobbying the California legislature for prisoners' rights within the state. The Prisoners' Union has approximately 20,000 members, of whom about 4,000 are confined in the California prison system.

Survey research data concerning inmate grievance mechanisms used in American prisons (McArthur, 1974:44) and supplementary information obtained from the Prisoners' Union indicate that approximately half of all the states have experienced some attempt to organize their prisoners into unions. Of these attempts, one of the most significant and wide-ranging took place in Ohio and provided this author with the opportunity to conduct the first systematic, empirical study of a prisoners' union movement (Huff, 1974a).

During 1972-1974, thousands of Ohio prisoners, assisted by outside advisors and supporters, participated in a movement to form a prisoners' union. This movement, although it failed to sustain itself beyond 1974, stands out as the most significant attempt in the United States (and one of the most important such efforts in the world) to form an inside-based prisoners' union. Other prisoners' movements have been more successful at prolonging their organizational activity, exerting pressure on correctional administrators, or obtaining financial assistance; none, however, has surpassed the Ohio movement in building a large, grass-roots membership among inmates and attempting to get the prisoners, through their representatives, to assume responsibility for the direction of the movement.

Detailed accounts of the development of the Ohio Prisoners' Labor Union (OPLU) have been provided elsewhere (Huff, 1974a, 1974b). To summarize, the origin of the OPLU can be traced to two riots which occurred at the Ohio Penitentiary in 1968. Following those riots, inmate leaders requested the governor's permission to form a union which would provide a regular mechanism for bargaining and resolving disputes. The state officials did not grant permission to organize such a union, but prisoners continued to discuss this idea during the next two years. In 1970, Ohio elected a new governor who had made prison reform a key part of his platform and his image. He also had extensive support from organized labor and talked frequently of repealing the state law prohibiting strikes by public employees and of the state's duty to negotiate with groups representing labor. After his election in 1970, inmate leaders around the state organized several work stoppages and then, in 1971, notified the governor that the inmates of Ohio Penitentiary intended to form a union. This message was officially ignored, and no discussions or negotiations took place until March 1972, when a prisoner hunger strike developed into a virtual statewide shutdown of the adult correctional institutions. At that point, informal negotiations took place among inmate leaders, the warden of the Ohio Penitentiary, correctional officials, and representatives of the governor's office. Partly in response to the negotiations, the Division of Corrections formulated regulations specifying the "ground rules" by which inmate councils would be permitted. These regulations received a mixed reaction from the state's prisoners. At Ohio Penitentiary, the idea of an inmate council was unanimously rejected because of a belief that it would be state-controlled, not self-determined. It was felt that such a group would be powerless and ineffective. The prisoners at the London Correctional Institute, on the other hand, accepted the idea and formed the first inmate council in the state. However, after increasing dissatisfaction with the implementation of the inmate council, the prisoners at that institution held a series of meetings in July 1972, when they decided to form a prisoners' union. They requested, and received, advice and assistance from the American Civil Liberties

Union, the National Lawyers' Guild, and the Ohio State University Legal Aid Clinic.

In early 1973, Interim Executive Boards of the OPLU were formed inside each of the eight state correctional institutions. The OPLU intensified its organizational efforts and raised its visibility significantly during the first six months of that year. The first real encounter with prison officials took place at the London Correctional Institute, where the local prisoners' union chapter charged that cigarettes which were confiscated from prisoners were then resold in the institution's commissary. This charge was well documented, and the prison administration ordered that funds be transferred from the commissary account to the inmate welfare account to compensate the prisoners for the confiscated cigarettes.

In April 1973, a statewide conference of persons and organizations interested in the prisoners' union took place in Columbus. Later that month, two staff members of the California-based Prisoners' Union responded to a request from Ohio prisoners and organizers and toured the state, meeting with prisoner leaders, ex-convicts, and outside supporters. They offered advice, based largely on their experiences in California. Some of that advice, such as the need to train inmate leaders to ensure a succession of leadership in the event of transfers of original inmate leaders (known as "bus therapy" among prisoners), proved accurate and quite helpful. Other suggestions, especially those encouraging the OPLU to assume a highly visible stance early in its developmental history, were completely inappropriate, at least in retrospect.

On May 1, 1973, the OPLU opened a state headquarters in Columbus. On that same day, the governor's office was presented with approximately 1,500 petition signatures of inmates authorizing the OPLU to be their exclusive bargaining agent. At this point, OPLU had already claimed to have signatures for "over 60% of the state's prison population" (*Ohio Connections,* 1973a:2).[1]

In June 1973, a food boycott planned by inmate leaders at the Lebanon Correctional Institute was carried out by a substantial number of prisoners at that facility. The administration at Lebanon had received advance word of the action and immediately isolated a number of leaders. One inmate was cited with "conspiracy to create a disturbance," "union organizing," and "possession of union material and contraband" (*Ohio Connections,* 1973b:4). The superintendent had previously issued a policy statement on prisoners' unions, which was cited as the basis for this disciplinary action. That statement read, in part:

> It is the policy of this administration to prohibit a prisoner union or its equivalent or activities within the institution to organize such a union, and violators will be subject to disciplinary action or other appropriate action. [*Outlaw,* 1973:7]

Other inmates involved in the boycott also received disciplinary action. Many of them began a hunger fast and expressed their intention of continuing the fast until they received due process in the form of institutional hearings. Within two weeks, all of those who had been placed in isolation were either released or charged, and two were transferred elsewhere as a result of their union organizing activities.

An event which proved to be the "beginning of the end" for the OPLU occurred on May 24, 1973. On that day the Interim Executive Board of the OPLU at the Southern Ohio Correctional Facility (Lucasville) called for a work stoppage in support of the grievances of dining hall employees. This "wildcat strike" (it was neither organized nor called by the state office) lasted 11 days and led to a number of actions and reactions by correctional officials and by the OPLU. Hundreds of inmates who participated in the strike were confined to their cells 24 hours a day during and following the strike. In addition, the more militant inmates were kept confined in "correctional cells" for months following the strike action (*Columbus Dispatch,* 1973b:27B). OPLU attorneys, protesting that due process requirements had not been observed by state officials, filed a suit challenging the violations of inmates' rights. The isolation of inmates who participate in work stoppages and other expressions of inmate protest has been a common tactic used by correctional administrators in many locations around the world. Finally, with respect to the strike itself, it should be noted that the prisoners' grievances included more than just the problems of dining room employees. For example, at the time of the strike, the facility was still not totally completed, and the vast majority of inmates had little or nothing to keep them occupied all day.

On July 24, 1973, a correctional officer was killed by a prisoner at Lucasville, and a second guard died during an attempt to rescue hostages. The prisoner's action initially was linked by rumor to the OPLU, and he was described in the media as previously having been "confined to a maximum security safe cell because he backed a prisoners' union and refused to work" (*Columbus Dispatch,* 1973a:1). However, the official state investigation provided no link between the killing and union activity; it was concluded that the inmate in question had acted alone in murdering the guard and, furthermore, that a gun used in the incident had been smuggled in by another guard. Nevertheless, tensions at the institution were at an all-time high, and many guards assumed an attitude of generalized hostility toward inmates, reflected in events which occurred at Lucasville during the "shakedown" and lockup of prisoners following the killings. A number of prisoners were disciplined for their participation in the strike, and prison guards confiscated and, in some cases, destroyed the personal property of many prisoners. A federal court later awarded substantial damages to many inmates whose property had been destroyed.

In that same eventful summer of 1973, the aforementioned House Committee on Internal Security hearings were taking place. A portion of those hearings dealt with Ohio, and much of the material presented focused on the OPLU. The OPLU was characterized by a police intelligence officer as a "front" for the more "radical" Prisoners' Solidarity Committee, and its activities were depicted as radicalizing inmates and fomenting disobedience and rebellion in the prisons as part of a larger plan of revolution coordinated among several organizations (U.S. Congress, House Committee on Internal Security, 1973:1035-1052). This characterization of the OPLU, however, was not supported by the testimony of the director of the Ohio Department of Rehabilitation and Correction, who denied that the organization was either radical or revolutionary, even though he personally disagreed with the OPLU on "philosophical grounds" and believed that intimidation had sometimes been employed to coerce some inmates to join (U.S. Congress, House Committee on Internal Security, 1973:970-971).

There were other events involving the OPLU following the summer of 1973. However, crippled by the wildcat strike at Lucasville, the organization simply "went through the motions" in many respects until 1974. There was no sudden, dramatic end to the movement. In fact, many prisoners still support such a movement in principle. But the premature strike at Lucasville, combined with the power held by the Department of Rehabilitation and Correction over virtually every aspect of a prisoner's life, led to the gradual weakening of the union and culminated in the closing of the outside headquarters. The reprisals at the disposal of correctional officials were extremely effective in crippling the overt support and activity of union sympathizers in Ohio. To be confined in isolation for days, weeks, or months; to be confronted with denial of parole for activities "not in the best interests of the institution"; to be transferred from a minimum or medium security institution to one of maximum security—these and other sanctions within the discretionary power of correctional administrators are persuasive arguments against anything beyond token support for a prisoners' union. An exchange theory perspective is extremely useful in understanding the reluctance of prisoners to continue their support for the union following these developments.

Any movement of the OPLU's scope involves a number of components. There must, obviously, be leadership—in this case from both inside and outside the walls. It is essential that there be organizational goals which are broadly understood and supported. There are the physical requirements of survival: financial resources, a headquarters for both physical and symbolic reasons, a staff with the skills necessary to carry out the work effectively. It is essential that the propaganda of the movement be disseminated in the most favorable possible manner and reported as widely as possible. For the movement to attain its mission of forming a prisoners' union, there must obviously be substantial grass-roots support among the inmates; the union must be able to demonstrate that it does indeed represent the prisoners. Beyond the movement itself, the support of the citizens of the state is the ultimate necessity, especially in the face of opposition by influential persons in the corrections department and elsewhere. If citizen support cannot be won, then correctional administrators have, in a sense, carte blanche in dealing with the prisoners' union. The failure of the movement to deal effectively with any of these components necessarily limits its possibilities for success.

The Study

The Ohio Prisoners' Labor Union movement was studied for more than a year using several different research strategies to gather data. This author attended every regularly scheduled meeting of the Ohio Prisoners' Labor Union staff from the spring of 1973 until the collapse of the union. In addition to such observations, I was able to conduct in-depth interviews with key staff of the OPLU and with inmates and ex-convict leaders from around the state. Information gathered via these participant-observation and interview procedures was supplemented by data collected on 535 randomly chosen OPLU rank-and-file members and 13 key OPLU inmate leaders. Finally, documents emanating from both inmate and official sources were analyzed, and reports contained in the mass media were monitored as additional sources of information concerning the movement. Utilizing these procedures, I obtained data on virtually every aspect of the OPLU.

Since this was an exploratory study, the analyses and interpretations necessarily were limited by the absence of prior information and experience. Therefore, one of the primary functions of this study was to provide comprehensive, descriptive data which would help to generate hypotheses for further investigation.

Organizational Goals

It is extremely important to an organizing effort such as the OPLU movement that it be able to develop goals which are clearly articulated and widely supported by the membership. The OPLU consistently stated its goals as follows:

(1) Salaries: We believe that all workers should be paid at least the minimum wage set by law, and we should, ideally, be paid on the same basis as civilian employees. This is the goal of the OPLU: to see prisoners treated as the civilians they were and will be again.

(2) Legislation: We support and encourage all legislation beneficial to prison labor.

(3) We wish to develop apprenticeship programs that are meaningful to, and appealing to, the prison labor force.

(4) We support increases in institutions' (correctional institutions') staff salaries so that more qualified personnel can be hired.

(5) We aim for the establishment of self-help academies and vocational programs subsidized by the OPLU.

(6) We seek workmen's compensation for Ohio prisoners.

(7) We seek rehabilitation programs for the handicapped.

(8) We endeavor to protect the human, civil, and legal rights of prisoners.

(9) We seek to correct dangerous working conditions.

(10) We encourage private industry to come into institutions.

(11) We combat cruelty and injustice wherever found in the prison system.

(12) We seek to affiliate with outside unions.

This list of stated goals of the OPLU implies a predominantly labor orientation. However, my own observation of the functioning of this organization convinced me that the main thrust of the union had little to do with labor issues. It was, instead, very much a social movement whose goals were much broader than labor issues alone. Of the above list of 12 goals, the energies of the movement were most invested in numbers 8 and 11 and very little invested in the others. The staff apparently realized that the labor issues were subsumed, in a sense, under the broader goals reflected in numbers 8 and 11. So the OPLU, although calling itself a labor union, really never was one. Its ideology, in fact, did not really lend itself to the labor union model in any sense of the term. American labor unions have had, and continue to have, a "bread and butter" orientation which is quite different than the class-oriented, macrolevel appraoch implied in the ideology of the OPLU. The commonalities of the two types (the demand for improved wages and working conditions and the right to collective bargaining) were minimized in the approach taken by the OPLU, despite its stated goals. The OPLU, like nearly all prisoners' union organizations which have been in existence, approximated a civil liberties union model, rather than a labor union model.

Leadership

The leadership which emerged in the OPLU was, for the most part, charismatic and self-appointed. This was not unexpected, because it is widely known that social movements, or even entire nations, that are at a very early stage of development generally lack the traditional or legal bases on which to develop leadership. Therefore, the charismatic leader frequently plays an important role in such situations. This was the case with the OPLU throughout its brief history. Although a constitution was drafted by the inmates at one prison, the mechanism for approving and implementing it really was not functional. There was the obvious problem of how such an organization could hold open elections while its members were residing in prisons operated by an administration which did not recognize the organization and, in fact, strongly opposed its very existence.

To gain a better understanding of the types of inmates who became leaders of the OPLU, I first identified 66 persons who had, at one time or another, served in a leadership capacity for the union inside the walls. Then, through my own observations of which inmates were most relied upon and through interviews with the staff, in which they were asked to name the key inmate leaders, this list was reduced to 18 key leaders. Of these 18, I was able to obtain from the official state records complete data on 13. All 13 of these individuals were acknowledged by the staff of the OPLU to be in the top echelon of inmate leadership. These data make it possible to construct a profile of the inmate leadership which kept the union movement active inside the walls.

The inmate leaders were older, generally, than either the rank-and-file membership of the OPLU or the general prison population. The median age of the 13 leaders was 36, almost 10 years senior to the followers and to those in the general population.

Racially, the key leaders were disproportionately white. In a prison system in which a majority of the inmates (52.3%) were black, this leadership survey indicated that almost 70% (9 of 13) were white. In addition, there were no black full-time staff members, a fact which caused a significant amount of criticism on the part of black inmates that the OPLU was not representative of their concerns. Many black prisoners charged that the OPLU was a "white man's organization." As will be shown below, data on the rank-and-file membership of the OPLU demonstrate that its membership *was* racially representative. However, the leadership of the OPLU, both inside and outside the walls, was disproportionately white. During the course of this study, only two blacks served in any quasi-staff capacity, and neither of them was given any significant responsibilities. It should be noted that there were a number of strong black inmate leaders in Ohio's prisons at the time, but most of them were affiliated with other factions of the population, such as the Sunni Muslims.

As might be expected, data on these key leaders indicate that they tended to be better educated and more intelligent than the general rank-and-file prisoners' union members or the general population. The average (mean) educational attainment of the leaders was slightly above 12 years, compared to about 10 for the other groups. Even more notable, perhaps, is the fact that 8 of these 13 leaders had IQs in the above average (110-119) or superior (120+) ranges—an impressive 61.5% (compared to 28.6% of the OPLU membership and 22.9% of the general prison population).

The median number of adult convictions among these 13 leaders was nearly twice that of the rank-and-file members (5.0 to 2.7). In addition, the leaders had spent far more time incarcerated than had the members (a median of 93 months for the leaders, compared to 39 months for rank-and-file members). Like the rank-and-file membership of the union, the modal offense of the leaders was that of armed robbery.

These data, supplemented by field notes and other observations during the participant-observation study, suggest that the OPLU inmate leaders were distinguishable in a number of ways. The leaders were inmates who had served a lot of time, had a vested interest in the operation of the prison, were very intelligent, and were generally charismatic individuals with the intangible leadership qualities which typically accompany charismatic personalities. In terms of criminal value systems and other normative behavioral expectations which appear to be associated with types of criminal careers, the OPLU inmate leaders had offense patterns which were representative of a substantial number of OPLU members and other prisoners. In sum, because of the respect that they commanded under the prevailing normative system and because of the magnetism of their personalities, these inmates were able to get others to follow their lead.

What of the leadership exerted by the staff? Except for two attorneys, outside staff exercised very little leadership. The other staff continually depended upon these two attorneys for direction, policy, and general guidance; they frequently seemed unable to function autonomously. Given the scarcity of time that these attorneys had to donate to the union, the dependency of the staff upon them proved to be a crippling factor for the organization. The staff of the OPLU was a mixture of convicts, who generally had very few skills to offer other than the claim to a natural affinity with the inmates who comprised the membership, a few well-educated reformers, and a few people in between (with a little jail time and a little education). The problem with this mixture was that it represented an attempt to be both representative of the inmates and skilled enough to operate an organization which ostensibly was representing over 8,000 inmates in the sixth largest state in the United States.

In fact, it did neither. The OPLU never had the ex-convict presence on the staff required to be truly representative of the inmates, nor the skills requisite for operating the office effectively. The "middle class" skills associated with effective and efficient business operations were missing, as was the total trust of the inmates in a staff which was predominantly not "ex-con" and was

Table 1. SELECTED CHARACTERISTICS OF THE OHIO PRISONERS' LABOR UNION (OPLU) MEMBERS AND
THE OHIO PRISON POPULATION (OPP)

Variable/Attribute	OPLU	OPP
Mean age[a]	29.7	30.3
Race[b]	50.2% white, 49.8% nonwhite	47.6% white, 52.4% nonwhite
Urban/nonurban[c]	72.1% urban, 27.9% nonurban	74.4% urban, 25.6% nonurban
Sex[d]	97.9% male, 2.1% female	96.4% male, 3.6% female
Mean educational attainment[e]	9.8	9.8
IQ[f]	28.6% above 109 24.8% below 90	22.9% above 109 27.2% below 90
Current offense[g]	Homicide, robbery, burglary, breaking and entering = 54.6% Modal offense = robbery (26.0%)	Homicide, robbery, burglary, breaking and entering = 58.2% Modal offense = robbery (26.5%)
Security classification[h]	Maximum = 47.5% Medium = 46.6% Minimum = 5.9%	Maximum = 42.0% Medium = 48.4% Minimum = 9.6%

a. p < .05
b. p < .30
c. p < .30
d. p < .10
e. p < .01
f. p < .001
g. p < .50
h. p < .02

overwhelmingly white. Even those ex-convicts who were on the staff were not always able to win the trust of inmates. For example, when the union attempted to implement a dues system ($1 per month per member), some inmates sent word that they did not want the ex-cons outside handling their money. It is highly probable that prisonization produces more suspicion than solidarity, and this must be overcome if a prisoners' union is to be effective. It never was overcome by the OPLU.

The Membership

As noted earlier, one of the key questions to be asked about a prisoners' union is whether or not it is representative of the inmates. Obviously, if such a movement is promoted and supported by a fringe group with a narrow vested interest, then correctional officials and citizens can dismiss the movement as a highly atypical and unrepresentative expression of prisoners' views. But if, on the other hand, such a movement could back up its claims of representativeness, then it must be taken more seriously, especially if it has a large number of members and presses its goals aggressively.

To determine whether or not the OPLU did in fact attract a membership which was representative of the population of Ohio's prisons, a representative sample of OPLU members (n = 535, or 16.7% of the membership) was analyzed and compared with the general inmate population on a number of relevant characteristics. One cautionary note should be mentioned: the operational definition of "OPLU member" employed in this study consisted of a prisoner's signature on a form authorizing the OPLU to serve as his or her exclusive bargaining agent. Obviously, an inmate's signature on a petition does not constitute an infallible indicator of membership. Undoubtedly, many inmates will sign almost any petition, without necessarily indicating thereby a sincere commitment to the cause espoused. Also, many inmates who believed strongly in the union and who may have been involved in union activities, might have preferred not to sign their names to anything connecting them with the OPLU due to their fear of reprisals.

With these limitations in mind, but realizing that there were no demonstrably valid indicators available to use as alternative measures of membership, data were collected for this sample of 535 inmates and for the general prison population of 8,421 as of June 1974.[2] Table 1 summarizes some of the comparative data which emerged from this study. These comparisons suggest that the OPLU was fairly representative of the general inmate population. Perhaps this conclusion is not too surprising, since the OPLU's membership included nearly 40% of the entire prison population. In any event, these and other comparisons (based on data generated by the 45-item information sheet utilized in this study) clearly demonstrate that the OPLU membership did not comprise an atypical, fringe group of inmates.

OPLU members were slightly younger, on the average, than the general inmate population. Rank-and-file OPLU members, unlike the leadership, closely reflected the racial composition of the Ohio prison population. In terms of urban/nonurban distribution (based on county of commitment), one might expect that OPLU's members might disproportionately have represented the 11 large, highly urban counties of the state, since these counties would provide more opportunities for firsthand experience with labor unions and pro-civil rights movements. However, the data again demonstrate the representativeness of the OPLU membership.

Like all other states, Ohio has relatively few adult females residing in penal institutions. The OPLU's strength among these women was slightly, but not significantly, less than might be expected. The OPLU's representativeness on this attribute may be somewhat surprising, since socialization processes experienced by women typically have fostered neither unity nor activism, but rather have encouraged competition among themselves and passivity in political matters.

Insofar as educational attainment was concerned, the means of the two populations were equivalent. However, the proportion of OPLU members who had completed high school was considerably lower than the corresponding figure for the general population. The fact that the average inmate had completed the 10th grade indicates a significant improvement over the educational profiles of prisoners a decade ago. This development, along with the more impressive educational backgrounds and intelligence of the inmate leaders, supports the view that intellectually the inmate population is increasingly capable. Closely related to this is the finding that the OPLU's membership contained a disproportionately large number of prisoners with IQs in the above average or superior ranges.

The offenses which led to the most recent incarceration of OPLU members were very much the same offenses, in the same proportions, that precipitated the incarceration of the general prison population. This would appear to refute the idea that prisoners' union members might disproportionately reflect one or more criminal behavior system or offense categories. Finally, the OPLU clearly had more strength in the maximum and medium security facilities and was underrepresented, in varying degrees, in the three reformatories and in the prison which contained a high concentration of elderly male inmates.

Fear of Reprisals

One of the most significant factors serving to weaken the OPLU was the widespread inmate fear of reprisals, such as punitive transfers or changes in security classification, denial of parole, and physical assault by guards. Field interviews produced many verbal expressions of such fears, and the issue seemed important enough to justify more systematic inquiry. Therefore, 180 prisoners who were participating in a prerelease program were given a questionnaire which included four items relating to prisoners' unions. The responses of this group provided clear evidence that these men overwhelmingly endorsed the concept and principal goals of the OPLU: the right to form unions and to bargain collectively regarding prison labor and prison conditions (83.9% answered "strongly agree" or "agree"); the right to form *labor* unions (81.1%); and the right to receive at least the federal minimum wage for prison labor (87.8%). However, relatively few (38, or 21.1%) of these inmates had joined the OPLU. An analysis of their stated reasons for not joining the union indicated that fear of reprisals played a major part in inhibiting them.

Of these various fears of reprisals mentioned by respondents, those involving parole board discrimination against OPLU members were rather prominent. However, data on the sample of 535 OPLU members indicate that this particular fear was not warranted. In fact, nearly half (44.9%) of the OPLU sample were released within a year of the time that they joined the union; this rate of release certainly did not reflect discrimination against OPLU members. Nevertheless, fear of reprisals inhibited many prisoners from affiliating with the union.

For those interested in becoming active *leaders* in the union, such fears may have been justified. The comparable rate of parole of OPLU leaders was only 23.8%, and, while the relationship between union leadership and parole is complicated by sentence length and other factors, there was some evidence of discrimination against OPLU leaders. One leader's parole board file contained an article that he had written for *Prisoner's Digest International,* a publication featuring news of inmate organizing activities and prison conditions. Another example is this quotation from a parole board reviewing officer's work sheet:

> Recently testified at Ohio Civil Rights Commission (July 13, 1973). Inmate politician. Active in prisoners' union.

It is difficult to imagine that such notations and inclusions were intended as endorsements of the inmates' progress and support for their early release.

The Media and the Citizens

The OPLU was unable to attract the support of the media or the citizens of Ohio. These two important sectors are, of course, interactive and influence each other significantly. The mass media tended either to ignore the OPLU or to express opposition. In addition, most Ohio citizens probably shared this opposition. Questionnaire data collected from a random sample of 955 citizens showed that they were opposed to collective bargaining for prisoners (78.9% answering "strongly disagree" or "disagree"), did not believe that prisoners should have the right to form unions (77.9%), and opposed the payment of the federal minimum wage for prison labor (75.1%). Interestingly, the vast majority of respondents either had no idea what wages were paid Ohio prisoners (the modal response, given by 26.7%, was "no opinion") or overestimated inmate wages by five to 12½ times their actual average rate (10 cents per hour).

DISCUSSION

The formation of prisoners' unions has been surrounded by controversy. As yet, not enough experience has accumulated to permit confident predictions as to the full impact which prisoners' unions would have upon the administration of penal systems. While nothing that has occurred to date would provide grounds for serious apprehension, it is clear that the process of institutionalizing prisoners' rights in this manner is likely to be exceedingly difficult, regardless of the abstract merits of such unions.

There has always been a deep-seated fear of inmate power, whether it be in the earlier efforts to establish inmate councils or in the more recent attempts to unionize prisoners. Historically, expanded inmate power has provoked fears of increased violence. For example, Garson (1972) analyzed the disruption of prisons from 1863 to 1970 with the hypothesis that prison rioting was related to the establishment of inmate councils. He concluded that there was no statistical or historical connection between the two phenomena. Similar fears, however, have been voiced with respect to prisoners' unions.

Despite such fears, the fact is that inmates have always bargained informally with their keepers and continue to do so. Sykes (1958:53-58), in his classic study of inmate social structure, documented the "corruption of authority" which occurred via "deals" and "trades" between prisoners and guards. Similarly, Carroll (1974:58-59) recently quoted a senior captain at a large prison:

> It's gotten so that I cannot tell an officer things that I should be telling him. I can't tell him anything serious that I might think is going down because he runs right to the inmates. . . . I can't figure it out. But one thing I do know, most of 'em ain't working for me, they're working for the inmates.

The involvement of staff in such exchanges constitutes de facto bargaining. The principal difference between such traditional trade-offs and the institutionalized collective bargaining model is the greater visibility, participation, and formality of the latter. It may be that correctional administrators, faced with increasing intervention by the courts and the growth of guards' unions and prisoners' unions, will become more receptive to a formal model of bargaining. As Rutherford (1971) has suggested, the rationales for adopting a pluralistic perspective of the prison community also suggest the appropriateness of a formal bargaining model as a means of institutionalizing conflict. Private employers, despite their initial opposition, long ago learned to coexist with unions and collective bargaining. Recent negotiations between the Prisoners' Union and the California Department of Corrections suggest that at least some prison authorities are prepared to do the same.

NOTES

1. It is probable that this claim was an inflated one, since my own examination of the OPLU files and the inmate petitions which had been forwarded to California confirmed a total of 3,210 inmate signatures, out of a total inmate population of 8,189 at that time. It is likely that the OPLU never *officially* represented more than 40% of the inmates in Ohio. However, it should be pointed out that the record-keeping system of the OPLU staff was so inefficient that many signatures could have been lost. Nevertheless, it seems highly doubtful that a majority of inmates ever signed authorization forms, despite the union's claims, which ranged up to 90% of the population of some institutions. This does not, however, negate the fact that the union obviously did represent thousands of inmates in Ohio's prisons, a proportion of the prison population which has been unmatched by any other prisoners' union organizing effort.

2. Data on the entire state prison population were provided by the Corrections Data Center of the Ohio Department of Rehabilitation and Correction. Data on the OPLU sample were extracted from the Ohio Adult Parole Authority's inmate files.

REFERENCES

CARROLL, L. (1974). Hacks, blacks, and cons: Race relations in a maximum security prison. Lexington, Mass.: D.C. Heath.

Columbus Dispatch (1973a). July 26, p. 1.

––– (1973b). August 15, p. 27B.

DAVIDSON, R.T. (1974). Chicano prisoners: The key to San Quentin. New York: Holt, Rinehart and Winston.

GARSON, G.D. (1972). "The disruption of prison administration: An investigation of alternative theories of the relationship among administrators, reformers, and involuntary social service clients." Law and Society Review, 6(May):531-561.

HALLECK, S.L. (1975). "A multi-dimensional approach to violence." Pp. 33-47 in D. Chappell and J. Monahan (eds.), Violence and criminal justice. Lexington, Mass.: D.C. Heath.

HUFF, C.R. (1974a). "Unionization behind the walls: An analytic study of the Ohio prisoners' labor union movement." Unpublished Ph.D. dissertation, Ohio State University.

––– (1974b). "Unionization behind the walls." Criminology, 12(August):175-194.

IRWIN, J., and HOLDER, W. (1973). "History of the prisoners' union." Outlaw: Journal of the Prisoners' Union, 2(January-February):1-2.

JACOBS, J.B. (1974). "Street gangs behind bars." Social Problems, 21(3):395-409.

JEPSEN, J. (1971). "KRIM, KRUM, KROM." Prison Service Journal, 9(October). Quoted in D.A. Ward, "Inmate rights and prison reform in Sweden and Denmark." Journal of Criminal Law, Criminology and Police Science, 53(June 1972):249.

MARNELL, G. (1974). "Penal reform: Swedish viewpoint." Unpublished paper.

MATHIESEN, T. (1974). The politics of abolition: Essays in political action theory (Scandinavian studies in criminology, vol. 4). Oslo, Norway: Universitetsforlaget.

McARTHUR, V. (1974). "Inmate grievance mechanisms: A survey of 209 American prisons." Federal Probation, 38(December):41-47.

Ohio Connections: Journal of the Ohio Prisoners' Labor Union (1973a). 1(March):2.

——— (1973b). 1(September):4.

Outlaw: Journal of the Prisoners' Union (1973). 2(May-June):7.

RUTHERFORD, A.F. (1971). "Formal bargaining in the prison: In search of a new organizational model." Yale Review of Law and Social Action, 2(fall):5-12.

SYKES, G. (1958). The society of captives. Princeton, N.J.: Princeton University Press.

U.S. Congress, House Committee on Internal Security (1973). Hearings: Revolutionary activities directed toward the administration of penal or correctional systems (93rd Congress, 1st session). Washington, D.C.: U.S. Government Printing Office.

WARD, D.A. (1972). "Inmate rights and prison reform in Sweden and Denmark." Journal of Criminal Law, Criminology and Police Science, 53(June):240-255.

WILSON, J.Q. (1975). Thinking about crime. New York: Basic Books.

WOLFGANG, M. (1975). "Contemporary perspectives on violence." Pp. 1-13 in D. Chappell and J. Monahan (eds.), Violence and criminal justice. Lexington, Mass.: D.C. Heath.

Chapter 12

SOCIAL CONTROL IN HISTORICAL PERSPECTIVE: FROM PRIVATE TO PUBLIC RESPONSES TO CRIME

STEVEN SPITZER and
ANDREW T. SCULL

The rising costs of crime control are among the most refractory of the problems facing modern capitalist states. In the United Kingdom, for instance, the costs of justice and law more than doubled between 1951 and 1973, increasing from 0.6% to 1.4% of the gross national product (Gough, 1975:60). From 1902 to 1960 expenditures on local police in the United States increased more than 30-fold—from $50,000,000 to $1,612,000,000 (Bordua and Haurek, 1970:57)—and had reached a level of $3,803,000,000 by 1970 (U.S. Bureau of the Census, 1975:416). Moreover, in the United States since 1942, expenditures on corrections by state-run systems have at least doubled every decade, moving from $14,000,000 in 1902 to $1,051,000,000 in 1970 (U.S. Bureau of the Census, 1975:416).

The rapid escalation of these costs, which has been paralleled by a massive expansion of other forms of state activity (Gough, 1975), has contributed to the "fiscal crisis of the state" (O'Connor, 1973). In an effort to alleviate this crisis, the state has struggled to divest itself of at least some of its most expensive control functions. One strategy has been to encourage, on at least a limited scale, the "privatization" of police and correctional services—thereby both reducing social expenses and stimulating investment in the private sector. (On the police, see Kakalik and Wildhorn, 1971; Klare, 1975. On corrections, see Griggs and McCune, 1972; Rutherford, 1973; Bailey, 1974; Scull, 1977, chapter 8.) This development has been part of a broader process through which the spheres of public and private activity have become progressively less distinct.

The interpenetration of public and private services is, of course, not without historical precedent. In fact, the notion that the state should be considered solely responsible for the control of crime and other "public" services was not really established in England and America until the latter part of the 19th century. Prior to that period, social protection and services were frequently offered as part of an explicit contractual arrangement between two interested parties. Radzinowicz (1956:259), for example, noted that "the enlistment of Police Officers in private service in the form in which it flourished in the eighteenth and early nineteenth centuries transformed the Police Offices into police markets." Well into the 19th century the English policeman was "a member of a liberal profession, whose fortune and standing in life depended on the goodwill of his private clients" (Radzinowicz, 1956:255). Until 1835, the handling of the poor in England also took on many features of a profitable business. Sidney and Beatrice Webb (1927:412) described the "adoption of the plan of dealing with the nuisance of destitution very much as with the nuisance of town dung, namely by handing it over at a fixed price to the speculator who saw his way to make the largest pecuniary profit from the contract." Among the varieties of "poor farming" were "contracting for the maintenance of all the persons having any claim on the Parish; contracting merely for the management of the workhouse; contracting for infants and children; and, in the latter decades, contracting for lunatics" (Webb and Webb, 1927:412). The last arrangement evolved into a "trade in lunacy" (Parry-Jones, 1972), wherein a system of private profit-making madhouses became the dominant form of institutional provision for the mad in England until 1850. This relatively "pure" form of private enterprise may be compared with the operation of 18th century English gaols which, although public in name and operated under official auspices, were actually almost universally administered as the private profit-making concerns of the gaolers. According to the Webbs (1922:5), "so completely was it assumed and accepted that the keeping of the gaol was a profitable business that it was exceptional for any salary to be attached to the post; and, down to 1730, this unsalaried office was even made the subject of purchase and sale."

The examples outlined above present us with a fascinating research question: How can we explain *both* the emergence of profit-making control arrangements during the period between the end of the 17th and the beginning of the 19th centuries, and the subsequent movement from private to public forms of "deviance management" in the modern era? In order to shed some light on these developments we will concentrate on the process through which crime control was "privatized" and then "socialized" in England. The decision to embark upon an historical investigation of changes within English rather than American society was dictated by three considerations: (1) the privatization and socialization of crime control occurred first and most comprehensively in England; (2) the historical materials on England are far superior to those available on America; and (3) the reforms introduced in England not only predated, but in many cases provided the model for, similar innovations in the United States. (On the police, see Reith, 1952, chapter 6; Richardson, 1970; Rubenstein, 1973. On gaols/jails and prisons, see McKelvey, 1936; Lewis, 1965.)

Before beginning our discussion, we will try to eliminate any conceptual confusion by identifying what we take to be the essential characteristics of private and public varieties of crime control. It should be noted, however, that these characteristics are rarely, if ever, found in pure form in the societies we have studied. Instead, they represent end points in a theoretical continuum along which responses to crime have been and continue to be organized and carried out.

By public crime control arrangements we mean those which are characteristically supported by taxation, organized on a bureaucratic basis, and operated directly by full-time employees of the state. Private forms, by contrast, are predicated on a market or contractual relationship and may be distinguished from services and arrangements offered voluntarily or through some sense of community obligation on the one hand and from modes of control that are organized and directly implemented by a single monopolistic entity (i.e., the state) on the other. In their simplest form, private arrangements may involve the offer of a monetary reward, fee, or gratuity by a private individual, group (corporation), or the state to *anyone* who will perform specific services (protection, apprehension of offenders, recovery of stolen property, etc.). When efforts to achieve crime control take this form, those paying for and those providing services are normally unknown to each other in advance of the transaction, and their relationship tends to be fortuitous and temporary rather than regularized and stable. Postings of rewards by the state or private individuals are examples of this form. At a more developed level these arrangements may involve an independently negotiated contract between a single party (individual or corporation) and a specific individual or organization willing to provide services on an exclusive basis. Personal bodyguards, private investigators, and corporate security forces are examples of this pattern. Finally, in the advanced stages of capitalist society, when private profit making and public services are most intertwined, the state may underwrite or contract out for the private provision of public services on an ongoing basis. The state, in this instance, serves as an intermediary between those offering control services (corporations and agencies) and those consuming them (the "public"), and the provision of services which have come to be defined as the responsibility of the state (including crime control) provide yet another opportunity for private profit.

It should be clear from this discussion that it is not the source of funding in itself that defines crime control as public or private, but the character of the *relationship* between those seeking and those supplying services. If the services are supplied by "public servants" as part of their routine responsibilities as agents of the state, the services are public. On the other hand, if these services are furnished through the workings of a competitive, profit-oriented market, they are private. It is only when the enforcement of the law and the punishment of criminals takes place exclusively within the domain of public bureaucracies at public cost that we can say that socialization of crime control is complete.

THE NATURE AND DEVELOPMENT
OF PRIVATE CRIME CONTROL

It was not until medieval institutions of collective responsibility began to decay that the control of crime could become a profitable undertaking in English society. The ancient Saxon and Norman institutions of hue and cry *(hutesium et clamor), posse comitatus* (the sheriff's power of calling out every man between 15 and 50 years of age), collective fines, outlawry, and the frankpledge were predicated upon the feasibility of collective, informal, unitary, and spontaneous reactions to crime. The character of this system is suggested by Pollock and Maitland's (1968:578-579) description of how thieves were expected to be handled prior to the 13th century:

> When a felony is committed, the hue and cry . . . should be raised. . . . The neighbours should turn out with the bows, arrows, knives, that they are bound to keep and besides much shouting, there will be horn-blowing; the "hue" will be "horned" from vill to vill. Now if a man is overtaken by hue and cry while he has still about him the signs of his crime, he will have short shrift. Should he make any resistance, he will be cut down. But even if he submits to capture, his fate is already decided. . . . He will be brought before some court (like enough it is a court hurriedly summoned for the purpose), and without being allowed to say one word in self-defence, he will be promptly hanged, beheaded or precipitated from a cliff, and the owner of the stolen goods will perhaps act as an amateur executioner.

Although "civic responsibility" for the apprehension and punishment of evildoers was not always a sufficient spur to action (fines were frequently invoked for nonperformance),[1] as long as the suppression of crime was a community affair and could be accomplished without specialized agents and facilities there was little opportunity for profiteering from its control. When specialization initially occurred—as in the establishment of the office of constable in the late 13th century (Critchley, 1972)—officials went without pay, their duties to be discharged out of civic rather than pecuniary motives. But as feudalism declined and England was transformed from a series of relatively homogeneous and tightly integrated communities into a differentiated and loosely articulated society, the informal and voluntary system of social control became increasingly suspect. In a society where interests were becoming more distinct, associations more transitory, relationships more fragmentary, and public order more fragile (see Beloff, 1938), it made less and less sense to rely on the alacrity and spirit of the people to secure obedience and tranquillity. Rather than appealing to something as unreliable as "public spirit," emphasis was increasingly placed on personal needs. Private interests thus came to replace social obligations as the mainspring of the control system. By the 18th century the system had reached a point where the architects of legal control were beginning to ask "private individuals for no higher motive than self-interest, and were confident that they could, by a system of incentives and deterrents —rewards and punishments, bribes and threats—so exploit human greed and fear that there would be no need to look for anything so nebulous and unrealistic as public spirit" (Pringle, 1958:212).

The twin spurs of fear and greed were thus intended to work hand in hand. Fear was nourished by the extension of capital penalties to a wide range of offenses,[2] while greed was appealed to through a burgeoning network of incentives and rewards. Of the two motivating forces, the latter proved to be more determinative, because, in the absence of an effective prosecutorial agency and regular police, some means had to be discovered to inflict punishments (whatever their intensity) on those who violated the law. Because of the long-standing view of police as a "system of tyranny; an organised army of spies and informers, for the destruction of all public liberty, and the disturbance of all private happiness" (J.P. Smith cited in Thompson, 1963:22) and because of the inadequacy of "spontaneous enforcement," any concerted attempt to regulate crime had to be undertaken "from a distance."[3] It was generally assumed, therefore, that the regulation of crime could best be achieved by manipulating the latent conflicts of interest and aspirations for gain within both criminal and "respectable" segments of society. The initiative of the law-abiding and the depravity of the "dangerous classes" were to be harnessed as a single force—a force that could function in lieu of direct official intervention. At least in theory, society would be disciplining itself, and the incentives provided by private citizens and the government were no more than a convenient stimulant to proper action.

It was within this context that a system of privately organized crime control could emerge and begin to flourish by the middle of the 18th century. The incentives that evolved during this period were explicitly designed to induce collaboration of the citizenry in the suppression of crime. Private interests were seen as the key to the system, and, if these interests could be skillfully adjusted to the interests of the criminal justice system, they were expected to act, in the words of one reformer, "with the certainty of gravitation" (Chadwick, 1829:288). In some cases, inducements involved no more than the reduction or elimination of civic obligation. One such measure was the so-called "Tyburn Ticket," which entitled anyone bringing a certain class of felons to justice to a lifelong exemption from the burden of serving "all offices within the parish or ward where the felony was committed" (Colquhoun, 1806:391). In other instances there were categorical pardons for accomplices, statutory and ad hoc rewards offered by government, as well as special rewards and gratuities announced by private individuals, insurance companies, prosecution societies, property owners associations, and groups of residents. Informing was encouraged by the promise of pardons and shares of any goods seized by the authorities, and those who informed soon became known as "voluntary police" who were "always on the alert to discover any infringement of the law which might prove a source of profit to themselves" (Radzinowicz, 1956:146).

The long-range and indirect nature of the incentive arrangements fostered a system of payment by results. In consequence, many crime control services took on the character of *piecework* rather than work for wages. One commentator of the period argued that constables should not be "compelled day after day ... to go in search of some atrocious ruffian" (Allen, 1821:29), only to be informed that he had merely done what was expected. "Extra remuneration for extra service" was considered far preferable to a general increase in salaries. Similarly, because keepers of gaols were paid through fees rather than wages, they too were more like independent purveyors of services than salaried employees.

The changing character of the private system and the reasons for its transformation can be grasped most clearly if we consider two of its specific features—policing and imprisonment. Policing for profit had its origins in the office of the constable. Although this office traditionally "rested on the principle of unpaid performance of duty by members of the community as their turn came round" (Tobias, 1975:106), it gradually took on pecuniary potential as (1) citizens chose to pay deputies to perform these disagreeable services in their places, (2) constables were able to demand rewards and portions of recovered goods in exchange for their services, and (3) private individuals and organizations began to contract those with experience in law enforcement for specific protective or investigative duties.

The growth of deputization was such that by the first decades of the 19th century "there were few parishes in which the office was not filled by a deputy" (Radzinowicz, 1956:278). Hart (1951:24) reported that, "as the duties of constables increased in volume and perplexity, the office became more and more unpopular. The middle classes in particular regarded it as a waste of their time, and disliked having to assume for a whole year an unpaid, arduous office which might entail enforcing unpopular laws. They therefore took to paying deputies to do the job for them." Eventually, according to Radzinowicz (1956:278), "by taking bribes, by frauds and extortions, they [the deputies] made such a profitable trade of their offices that many were prepared to serve for nothing." When salaries were attached to the office, they remained quite low (less than £100 a year in 1822). Nevertheless, profits could be gained privately from rewards and forfeitures and publicly from such routine duties as serving warrants and serving as a witness for the prosecution and by claiming a wide range of "operating expenses." In some cases, magistrates even "ordered a fine when otherwise they might have sentenced an offender to imprisonment; for if they sent him to prison, then the officer would get nothing 'for his pains' " (Radzinowicz, 1956:242).

The reluctance of authorities to raise salaries as well as the growing opportunities for enterprising constables did much to promote the appearance of specialists in police services. "An officer who had risen high enough in his profession to become personally known could aspire to more than occasional remuneration for petty services. The next step in his career would be to obtain a number of well paid special employments consisting of permanent or temporary duties, for which he might be hired by any one willing and able to pay" (Radzinowicz, 1956:257). Wealthy individuals, merchants, the Bank of England, theaters, and other places of entertainment were frequent employers of police.[4] But services of this type were not only arranged through private agreement; they could also be secured through the mediation of police offices themselves. At the beginning of the 19th century, it was common practice for the police offices to "send officers from London at the request and expense of private individuals," and officers who received nominal stipends from the parish were encouraged to accept "additional gratuities from interested persons" (Radzinowicz, 1956:261).

When the provision of private police services received the countenance of official authority, the stage was set for the growth of what became the apotheosis of the incentive system—the Bow Street Police Offices (Pringle, 1958; Fitzgerald, 1888). As a marketplace for the trading in police services, this office became " 'a pecuniary establishment to itself,' the headquarters of a closely knit caste of speculators in the detection of crime, self-seeking and unscrupulous, but also daring and efficient when daring and efficiency coincided with their private interest" (Radzinowicz, 1956:263). At about the same time (the beginning of the 19th century), the first large-scale collective sponsorship of policing was undertaken with the founding of the Thames River Police. This force, consisting of twice as many officers as employed by all the Metropolitan Police Offices, was charged with suppressing threats to maritime commerce. The West India Merchants, a group whose interests this experimental force was directly intended to serve, absorbed 80% of the initial operating costs (see Colquhoun, 1800). In 1800, two years after it began operation, the Marine Police Establishment was established as a publicly authorized and supported force "for the more effectual Prevention of Depredations on the River Thames and Vicinity" (House of Commons, 1799-1800:723).

Paradoxically, this first venture in organized policing, although private in origin, provided the springboard for the development of policing as a publicly administered and financed service.[5] The Thames River Police were to be the model for the subsequent development of the Metropolitan Police in 1829 and the progressive socialization of policing throughout the 19th century.

Prior to the reforms of the 19th century, imprisonment (much like policing) frequently afforded an opportunity for private gain. But to understand the peculiar history of incarceration in England, one must keep in mind that imprisonment was always among the most costly forms of punitive control. This fact provided a strong disincentive to its use as a routine form of punishment in the premodern era and led to efforts "to enforce a line of conduct on a defaulter by pledges of payments rather than by detaining his body" (Pugh, 1968:2). However, with the weakening of collective responsibility, some form of custodial imprisonment became essential, if only to secure a defendant's appearance for trial or a condemned man's presence for infliction of sentence. By the Middle Ages, the primitive lockups which served such functions were also being used to some extent for coercive imprisonment, in the first place "as a means of securing the payment into the Exchequer of debts due to the Crown" (Pugh, 1968:5) and later as a sanction against all types of debtors. While the expenses of the first gaols sometimes came out of the royal purse, the Crown increasingly "relieved itself of such expenses, together with the costs of maintenance, by requiring a subject to keep a gaol in return for land, or by selling a right to do so in return for cash" (Pugh, 1968:5). All gaols remained nominally the king's, but in practice they were in a wide variety of hands—the possession of local landed magnates, of ecclesiastical potentates, or of town corporations under royal charter, each of whom "clung to them as income-yielding properties" (Webb and Webb, 1922:3).

As this overview suggests, the distribution and administration of gaols was haphazard and fortuitous. Some attempts were periodically made to ameliorate this situation: for example, the 1532 Gaols Act placed nominal responsibility for gaol management on the justices of the peace and endeavored to rationalize the distribution of gaols; but such efforts met with little success (Pugh, 1968:343-344). From the late 16th century on, these medieval gaols were supplemented by a number of houses of correction, for the most part modeled on the London Bridewell (1557) and supposedly under the direct administration of the justices of the peace. Originally, these places were intended to serve as a deterrent to the ablebodied idler and vagrant and, under mercantilist principles, to add to the national wealth by setting the poor to work. By the end of the 17th century, however, the distinctive features of the houses of correction had all but disappeared, and they were essentially used interchangeably with gaols as places of pretrial detention, as a punishment for various minor offences, and as a means of keeping debtors in custody. Since neither church dignitaries nor landowners nor local justices were in the least inclined to busy themselves with the sordid day-to-day business of administering gaols or houses of correction, such places were used simply as sources of income, being leased out to those desirous of speculating in this form of human misery. Thus, "both institutions were, in effect, run as private ventures of their masters or keepers" (Webb and Webb, 1922:15).

Such businesses were conducted in a multitude of settings. Of the 518 gaols that John Howard surveyed in 1777, six (all in London) were relatively sizable establishments, each containing 90 or more prisoners; but in the provinces, only seven housed as many as 50 inmates, and well over a hundred confined fewer than 10 (Webb and Webb, 1922:131). Small operations like these could scarcely afford to provide specialized accommodations, and few of the gaols of the period were purpose-built. Many, indeed, consisted of little more than a room or two in a tavern or gatehouse, more or less ill adapted to serve as a place of confinement. At West Wycombe, for example, the "gaol" consisted "of two small rooms in the back court of the keeper's public house, about seven feet by three, and six feet high: apertures in the doors: ... the windows are almost closed up by strong planks nailed across for security" (Howard, 1792:282). In small, often decaying structures of this sort, prisoners were thrown together in a single heterogeneous mass: "Debtors and felons, men and women, the young beginner and the old offender, ... idiots and lunatics" (Howard, 1792:8)—all subject to the depredations of entrepreneurial gaolers, "low-bred, mercenary and oppressive, barbarous fellows, who think of nothing but enriching themselves" (*Gentleman's Magazine,* 1767).

Like other "deviant farmers" of the period, gaolers extracted their living from those whom they kept confined, a practice which obviated the need to pay them a wage and hence kept demands on local taxpayers to a minimum. "Every incident in prison life, from admission to discharge, was made the occasion for a fee" (Webb and Webb, 1922:5), and tables of legitimate charges were often ratified by the local justices at quarter sessions. For an appropriate additional payment, prisoners could obtain better food and accommodation "on the master-side" with the gaoler's family (Howard, 1792:238). Similarly, "the tap for the sale of beer was a recognized and legitimate source of profit to the keeper. ... There was a public house in every prison. ... In the King's Bench [prison in London] there were at one time no less than thirty gin shops, and in

1776, 120 gallons of gin were sold weekly besides other spirits and eight butts of beer a week." So profitable was this trade and so anxious were the keepers to further it that not infrequently "the treatment of the prisoner depended upon his consumption of liquor" (George, 1965:291).

Even the physical decrepitude of many of the gaols were turned to advantage. To guard against escapes, prisoners were chained: but "if they have the money to pay, their irons are knocked off, for fettering is a trade by which some gaolers derive considerable emolument" (W. Smith, 1776:12; see also Pugh, 1968:178-180). So long as the gaol required but minimal subventions from local taxpayers, most magistrates were only too willing to turn a blind eye to the keepers' methods—a willingness accentuated by the physical hazards of the alternative. Howard (1777:379) reported that a standard response among the gaolers whom he questioned about magistrates' tours of inspection was, "Those gentlemen think that if they came into my gaol they should soon be in their graves." And in view of the massive prevalence of typhus or "gaol fever," such an attitude was scarcely unrealistic. There was tacit agreement to leave undisturbed any arrangements from which both parties apparently benefited.

THE TRANSFORMATION OF PRIVATE INTO PUBLIC CONTROL

Although the system of profit-oriented crime control seemed to address the needs and mirror the priorities of 18th century English society, its dominance and appeal were relatively short-lived. Like most social arrangements, it was transformed by pressures operating from both within and without.

When we examine the internal structure of 18th century private controls it is clear that the very principles upon which these controls were founded contributed to their demise. While unbridled self-interest may serve as a powerful stimulus to action under certain conditions, it must always be articulated within a collectively oriented system if that action is to serve social rather than personal ends. The problem with the arrangements that evolved during this period was that they failed to integrate opportunities for gain within a coherent administrative framework. Without this integration, an effective link could not be forged between individual and collective interest. As long as the market in crime control services remained diffuse and decentralized, the activities of independent profit-seekers could only be imperfectly coordinated at best. Moreover, since the spurs to action tended to be ad hoc and provisional (rather than part of a centrally conceived and directed plan), a net of incentives was woven which, instead of trapping the "criminal classes," grew ever more tangled and porous. Finally, it may be argued that the method of payment-by-results upon which the system was so firmly established actually encouraged the very behavior it was designed to eliminate.

The irrationality and inefficiency of the "trading in justice" may be illustrated by a few brief examples. At its very foundations the administration of justice was corrupted by structurally generated pressures to turn "offices of burden" into "offices of profit" (see George, 1965:23ff.). The justice of the peace or magistrate "was the product of the system which aimed at making the administration of justice self-supporting by exacting a fee for every act that was performed. These fees were individually small in amount, and they could only be made to yield an income to magistrate and clerk by a perpetual flow of business which it thus became the interest of both of them to promote" (Webb and Webb, 1906:326). Consequently, "the transition from 'encouraging business' to a corrupt or oppressive use of magisterial authority in order to extort fees or levy blackmail was, to a Trading Justice, seldom perceptible" (Webb and Webb, 1906:326). Pringle (1958:57) even noted that "to keep up the flow of business some magistrates employed barkers and runners to tout for customers and when business was slack the magistrates even allowed credit, issuing warrants and summonses on easy terms."

In a similar fashion, because of their position in the structure of rewards, constables were encouraged to instigate crime. Thief-takers were turned into thief-makers by the opportunities for lucrative bargaining and piecework.[6] This pattern took two major forms: (1) consorting with organized thieves in the commission of an offense and then acting as a go-between (for a fee) to effect the return of the stolen property and (2) trapping innocent victims into crimes to obtain rewards. The first practice was "encouraged by the great banking-houses, who were eager to recover their property, or a portion of it, on any terms" (Fitzgerald, 1888:141). Thief-takers were more likely to compound the felony than bring the felon to justice because "when a sum like £20,000 had been stolen, and perhaps half of it might be recovered by negotiation, the statutory reward of £40 per robber became too trivial to be considered" (Pringle, 1958:161). The second practice was perpetuated by constables and others who were willing to stage offenses and then falsely accuse novices or young offenders. "Thief-makers were ruthless . . . not shrinking ever from 'swearing away' the life of an innocent, and their trade prospered in proportion to the progressive multiplication of rewards" (Radzinowicz, 1956:327).

The system of rewards as a whole led to a "horrible trade in blood demands" and was linked to an increase in crime "fostered and cultivated by the very persons set to watch over and prevent it" (London *Times,* 1817, cited in Radzinowicz, 1956:338). Informers were part of this trade and were taken to task by reformers of the day because they did not take, "nor wish to take measures to prevent parties infringing the law, but merely to entrap them in order to get the penalty" (*Parliamentary Papers,* 1834:1). The practice of pardoning felons was likewise scored by critics like Edward Sayer (1784:25), who argued that it created "an asylum opening itself for the reception of offenders into the bosom of Justice herself."

The organization of incarceration for profit reflected, in yet another way, the internal contradictions of privatized control. For example, in 1701 the House of Lords refused to pass a bill "regulating" the overcrowded King's Bench and Fleet Prisons on the grounds that, if the number of prisoners fell, "the profits thereby accruing will not be proportional recompense to the officers to attend the Courts, so that the king's four Courts at Westminster will be without prisons and without officers to assist them" (House of Commons, 1701). Moreover, since "mere parsimony could not . . . make the gaol yield a profit . . . many eighteenth century gaolers . . . varied the squalid misery of prison life by deliberate torture for the purpose of extortion, and . . . a whole system of skillful extortion under the pressure of wanton discomfort and physical pain, and the sale of licentious indulgence to those who consented to pay, prevailed in the majority of contemporary prisons" (Webb and Webb, 1922:21). Whether the purpose of incarceration was deterrence through proportional punishment or rehabilitation, these arrangements were palpably counterproductive. But even more inconsistent with effective control were the habits of prison wardens who were willing to sell the "right to escape to such [debtors] as could afford their terms" (Webb and Webb, 1922:28).

The *external* changes promoting the abandonment of private and the adoption of public means of crime control form part of and are predicated upon a much larger movement toward rational management in public administration, finance, and economic policy—indeed, of social life as a whole. On the most fundamental level, such rationalization was compelled by competition: in the private sector, between firms for markets; at the level of state administration, between states for political power (Weber, 1961). And the process was a progressive and self-perpetuating one: that is, increased rationalization in one sector reacted back on and reinforced pressures toward rationalization in the other, fueling a sustained and cumulative advance in the direction of the increased systematization of human activity.

We might trace briefly just a few of the connections. Beyond a certain point, further developments of markets and long-distance trade were hindered by a locally based, arbitrary system of law enforcement, which was effective as a means of sustaining and reinforcing the authority and social position of a rural landed class[7] but which was highly inefficient as a means of guaranteeing the kind of stable, predictable, orderly environment that alone permits sophisticated forms of markets to flourish. Private, localized, and personal forms of control entailed the scarifice of efficiency and certainty in the enforcement of the law and thereby also of a measure of public order and tranquillity. Indeed, "the English propertied classes in the eighteenth century were prepared to put up with a level of casual violence from their inferiors which would lead to martial law and the suspension of civil rights were it to occur today" (Stone, 1976:26). Moreover, such a system necessarily weakened the safeguards of *some* forms of property—"the property of men in trade, and manufacture and farming" (Hay, 1975:60). But the landed elite, who had "large numbers of personal servants to guard their plate and their wives" and who "as M.P.s ... passed a mass of legislation which allowed them, as J.P.s, to convict ... pilferers of their woods and gardens ... without the trouble of legalistic indictments or tender-minded juries" (Hay, 1975:59), suffered no equivalent disabilities. On the contrary, *their* interests were threatened by a rationalization of the criminal law, which promised to substitute central for local authority and to remove perhaps the strongest single support of the social order over which they presided—all for the sake of benefits which would largely accrue to another class.

For the bourgeoisie, on the other hand, a rationalized crime control apparatus had a quite different significance. Although the factory system had allowed them to achieve greater control over such internal sources of disorder and loss as employee pilferage, dishonesty, and so forth (indeed, in the early stages of the Industrial Revolution this was perhaps its most significant advantage over the putting-out system), it did nothing to solve the pressing problem of external disorder—the ill-regulated, at times almost anarchistic, social context within which business was perforce conducted. Yet such an uncertain and unpredictable environment was at least as severe a limitation on the growth of a sophisticated exchange economy as the more obvious problem of effective control over the conduct of one's employees.

Riot was tolerated by the English ruling class in the 18th century; in fact, it formed an important channel of communication between the masses and their masters, a quasi-legitimate means of securing redress of grievances (Hobsbawm, 1959; Thompson, 1971). But "in the nineteenth century breaches of the peace, if committed by armed crowds, were deemed an incipient rebellion and an acute danger to the state; stocks collapsed and there was no bottom in prices. A shooting affray in the streets of the metropolis might destroy a substantial part of the national capital" (Polanyi, 1944:186-187).

"The market system was more allergic to rioting than any other economic system we know" (Polanyi, 1944:186). A stable public order was a precondition of rational calculation on the part of industrial capitalists, and in the absence of such calculability the development of all sectors of the market system—investment, production, trade—was held within strict limits. This problem of the establishment and maintenance of external order was, moreover, save in unusual circumstances,[8] something not amenable to private solutions. In the first place, with the growth of national and international markets, the geographical area which required pacification was simply too extensive, and the number and diversity of the actors whose interests and activities had to be combined and coordinated were simply too great. Even more serious, while capitalists as a class required a hitherto unprecedented degree of social order, it was in the interests of no one of them, *as an individual,* to provide or to contribute to its provision; for those who "irresponsibly" refused to do so would continue to enjoy the benefits of a more stable operating environment while giving themselves a competitive cost advantage. As a "collective good," order had to be collectively provided.

Even as the growing political power of the commercial classes brought with it a decreasing tolerance for disorder, the type of society that those same classes were busily creating was systematically undermining traditional sources of restraint and threatening the stability of the social system itself. Vertical linkages in the stratification order were first weakened, then in many cases destroyed, as the market undercut the significance of purely local ties and allegiances and as traditional bonds of obedience and deference to one's "natural superiors" gave way before the calculating impersonality of the wage labor system. This breakdown of the paternalistic foundations of society and the traditional institutions of control coincided with the sharpening of class antagonisms, heightening the dangers associated with perpetuating the 18th century reliance on the army as the ultimate protection against disorder. For the use of the military entailed "an alternation between no intervention and the most drastic procedures—the latter representing a declaration of internal war with lingering consequences of hate and resentment" (Silver, 1967:12).[9] Then, too, industrial capitalism promoted "what was taken at the time to be the virtually universal deterioration of family life. The stupendous social dislocation had affected this most fundamental of social institutions, and if anything was calculated to alarm the middle classes into a consciousness of possible social disaster, it was the notion that the most stabilizing of social maintenance systems was imperilled" (Marcus, 1974:211).

At the same time, however, the development of industry and markets had already proceeded sufficiently far to force the development of more efficient managerial techniques and a trained managerial class (Pollard, 1965), as well as the development of a much higher level of economic activity and a greater monetarization of the economy. These latter developments had massive effects on the possibilities for effective state action. The changing structure and trend of the economy offered the state "ever-increasing possibilities of action, not only because greater production affords more extensive levying of taxes, but also because a more highly developed exchange economy allows one to establish taxes with greater accuracy" and to raise them with greater ease (Ardant, 1975:166). And the new administrative techniques and the emerging class of administrators and managers permitted the state to make effective use of its new fiscal muscle. Thus, those controlling the state apparatus found themselves pressed toward and capable of a far more effective and thoroughgoing intervention and control of social life than had hitherto been feasible; and, as these possibilities became realities, the resulting increase in the orderliness and predictability of social existence prompted further rationalization of economic life.

As a whole, then, the rationalization process clearly corresponded to the needs and aspirations of the commercial and manufacturing bourgeoisie, while it undermined the basis of the authority of the old rural aristocracy. The very entrenchment of the peers and gentry in the local political apparatus and their consequent ability to resist efforts to bring into being a more "rational" criminal justice system through permissive legislation placed further pressure on the bourgeoisie to opt for a national approach. Practically speaking, the administrative "reforms" of the English political system—the shift from a system based on (local) judicial and legislative power to one increasingly dominated by executive power and staffed by salaried professional workers (see Webb and Webb, 1963)—had their structural roots in the growing political power of the middle class, an increased power not so much produced as recognized and ratified in the 1832 reform of Parliament.

The rationalization of crime control consisted of a number of separate but closely interrelated changes. The control system increasingly came to be predicated on *instrumental* rather than *symbolic* methods: gross and capricious terror attended by the ceremonial trappings of authority (as in the public hangings at Tyburn) were replaced by a system which (at least in theory) was designed to work uniformly, evenhandedly, and with machinelike precision. The rise of imprisonment as the dominant response to crime brought to the fore a form of punishment precisely suited to uniform administration, allowing the infliction of a standardized penalty of graduated intensity which could be adapted to match the gravity of the crime. In a caricature of marketplace rationality, it made possible the exaction of an infinitely variable "price" which the offender had to "pay" for his crime. Control was increasingly tied to certainty rather than severity of punishment, for Sir Samuel Romilly and other English penal reformers were convinced that "the occasional terror of the gallows would always be less effective than sure detection of crime and moderate punishments" (Hays, 1975:59). Hence the necessity of a professionalized police, for without adequate police, there could be no certainty of punishment and, therefore, at best an imperfect deterrent. With an organized police force there accrued still another advantage: instead of merely reacting to crime after the fact, crime might even be prevented. In parallel fashion, once the criminal had been caught, imprisonment in its newly emerging forms promised—vainly as it turned out—not simply to punish but also to rehabilitate him.

The rationalization of the system incorporated a wholly new emphasis on impersonal forms of control, with an associated decrease in the arbitrariness with which laws were enforced. Traditional responses to crime had been permeated by personal considerations. In a social order premised upon the fusion of political, economic, and social domination, squires, parsons, and wealthy landowners directly and personally supervised the apparatus of politico-legal coercion. At all levels, the law was used to reinforce the structure of personal ties and dependencies. The very discretion which the reformers condemned so vehemently played a crucial role in this process. The system of private prosecution, for example, allowed the gentry to become the arbitrators of the criminal's fate, for they could prosecute or not, as they chose. Likewise, the free and frequent use of the pardon, while undermining the certainty of the law, "helped create the mental structure of paternalism" (Hay, 1975:42). For pardons more often than not depended upon the intercession of propertied men in behalf of the condemned, and such acts were both the product of and a powerful reinforcement of personal ties running vertically through the stratification order. A similar reliance on deference and personal dependency was evident in the standard use of the yeomanry—a cavalry force largely composed of small landowners—for police purposes in times of civil disturbance and riot. Such tactics reflected the conviction that "the people would in many instances be debarred from violence by seeing those arrayed against them to whom they were accustomed to look up to as their masters" (an English MP of 1817, cited in Silver, 1967:9). And, of course, the actions of gaolers, thief-takers, and private police were usually fairly directly motivated by their personal (rather than impersonal) interests.

But the underlying structural supports of this "irrational," personalistic response to crime were slipping away beneath those who sought to defend it. At an ever-increasing pace, the market dissolved away local and communal ties, replacing the master-servant relationship with the cash nexus—the conviction that the employer "owed his employees wages, and once these were paid, the men had no further claim on him" (Mantoux, 1928:428). A social system whose notion of reciprocity did not extend beyond the wage contract could not long sustain paternalism as its reigning ideal. Moreover, the laborer was becoming, as Adam Smith, David Ricardo, Thomas Malthus, and other political economists recognized, no longer a human being but a thing—a "factor of production" along with land and capital, responding to market imperatives, not personal ties.[10] And on yet another level, the rise of a single national market to a position of overriding importance in English society was steadily undermining the rationale of a fragmentary, locally based response to crime.

One of the central achievements of capitalism as a system of domination was that "into the center of the historical stage it has brought a form of compulsion to labour for another that is purely economic and 'objective' " (Dobb, 1963:17). Just as the invisible hand of the marketplace provided an unequaled means of mystifying control over the work force, so the class character of the legal order could be masked by appearing to place that order firmly beyond the influence of human agency. The rise of the bourgeoisie to a position of cultural and political hegemony thus corresponded to a growing emphasis on impersonal forms of social control. For, through impersonal control, the newly dominant class could ideologically separate the enforcement of "constitutional" authority from its own social and economic ascendance; that is, it could present the surface appearance that society was now subject to "the rule of law and not of men." Here, then, was yet another support for a system of crime control with quasi-automatic regularity, uniformity, and efficiency and with as little evidence of human activity as possible. The public execution—that elaborate morality play with its individual performers—was replaced by the gray passionless prison—a mechanical "mill for grinding [anonymous] rogues honest and idle men industrious" (Jeremy Bentham to Jacques Brissot in Bentham, 1843:226). Without the necessary sentiments of deference among those to be controlled, "the use of social and economic superiors as police exacerbated rather than mollified class violence" (Silver, 1967:10), and manufacturers who noted this effect sought to depersonalize police operations by placing them in the hands of trained professionals. As with the transformation of the self-interested, profit-oriented gaoler into the salaried employee of a publicly financed prison system, the bureaucratization of police work placed day-to-day operations of the control system in the hands of faceless agents of the state, men who no longer operated in their own self-interest, but (presumably) in the general interest, and who discharged their responsibilities "according to *calculable rules* and 'without regard for persons' " (Weber, 1946:215, emphasis in the original).

It was through this process, therefore, that the management of crime was rationalized and transformed into a responsibility of the state. But because these changes occurred within the context of class struggle and required the dissolution of long-standing social arrangements, they were not effected at the same rate throughout English society. There were many pockets of resistance to the standardization of the criminal law, the establishment of a preventive police, and the assimilation of prisons under state control. Resistance was strongest in areas where the grip of the landed gentry and their paternalistic institutions were most secure. Although the consolidation of crime control under a single national system was heralded by a series of legislative and administrative reforms between 1828 and 1835, "an extensive social reform is not effected overnight by the mere passage of a bill through Parliament. The administrative process by which it is implemented commonly stretches over a number of years, and resistance is encountered at every turn from those who have a vested interest in frustrating the measure" (Mather, 1959:112).

The metropolitan experiment in preventive police was undertaken swiftly and on a massive scale, but "police reform outside London was gradual, patchy and unspectacular compared to what happened in the Metropolis" (Hart, 1951:31). Despite the establishment of the London police in 1829, at least 53 boroughs (29% of the whole) possessed no police force in 1839, and as late as 1848 at least 22 corporate towns (12%) remained in this position (Mather, 1959:112). While efforts to establish a nationwide police force were given impetus by the industrial violence of the 1830s and 1840s, "the organization of the new police on a county basis meant that the rural districts of a county, remote from industrial unrest but heavily rated on account of the large amount of landed estate situated within them, would be footing the bill for the maintenance of public order in the relatively distant manufacturing towns and villages, where property of highly rateable value was more scarce" (Mather, 1959:131). Thus, although the introduction of salaried police into rural areas could not be completely halted, it could at least be delayed by magistrates who, "as the principal landowners of the county, had a vested interest in keeping down the rates" (Mather, 1959:131).

By the same token, uniform, centrally directed, and bureaucratically organized prison practices could be completely implemented only when the last vestiges of parochial power had withered away. The compromised character of legislative activity at the end of the 18th and first half of the 19th century offers one indication of how the struggle between bourgeois and landed interests evolved. The Prison Act of 1791 was drafted to apply the principles of projected national penitentiary to all places of confinement in England and Wales. Nevertheless, the act "could not decide to make the gaoler simply the salaried servant of the Justices, and, because it shrank from explicitly commanding the levy of a rate, it failed to abolish his fees, or the profit-making character of his post" (Webb and Webb, 1922:41). In 1823 an act was passed "for consolidating and amending the laws relating to the building and regulating of certain gaols and houses of correction in England and Wales" (Webb and Webb, 1922:74). But the act did "not contemplate . . . the appointment of Government inspectors to insist on the law being obeyed, nor did the Act provide any machinery for compelling negligent or recalcitrant local authorities to comply with its requirements" (Webb and Webb, 1922:75). Moreover, the act applied to only 130 prisons and did nothing to reform the debtors' prisons or the gaols and bridewells in local districts. The system of inspection was intended to standardize and regulate the conditions of confinement, but "it was not until the passing of the Prisons Act of 1865 that the inspectors . . . could rely on anything more than 'the uncertain weapons of persuasion and publicity, backed by the imponderable authority of a Secretary of State' " (Moir, 1969:139). With the passage of that act, central control was strengthened significantly, and "all 193 local prisons were forced into the uniform regimen prescribed by the Home Office, and the local variations in diet, treatment and discipline which had resisted with such vigour the attempts of the inspectors were at last ironed out" (Moir, 1969:139).

While the commitment to personally administered, privately organized, and locally based crime control was not overturned without opposition, by the last quarter of the 19th century its fate was sealed. As the 20th century unfolded, social control was increasingly organized and carried out as a public effort —coordinated, financed, and implemented by the state.

CONCLUSION

The historical transformation of social control arrangements has seldom received systematic attention. Most of the accounts that we do possess are largely descriptive. To the extent that "explanations" *are* offered, they appeal to a number of factors, singly or in combination: some accounts emphasize the spread of humanitarian ideas and the activities of charismatic reformers; others postulate a crudely deterministic relationship between what is alleged to be a dramatic upsurge in crime rates and the adoption of more effective methods of control; while still others claim that reactions to crime are shaped by the conditions attending the emergence of an industrial and urbanized society.

In contrast to these accounts, we have argued that the privatization and subsequent socialization of crime control was conditioned by historically specific changes in the political and economic structure of English society. Taken together, these changes were to prove decisive for the development of what we know today as the "crime control establishment"—an establishment which both reinforces the priorities and reflects the problems of the modern capitalist state.

NOTES

1. For an illustration of how the principle of collective liability was resurrected in the 18th century see Thompson (1975).

2. Radzinowicz (1948:4) estimated that the number of capital statutes in England grew from about 50 to over 200 between the years 1688 and 1820. But as Thomson (1950:65) suggested, "the policy of mere terror did not deter; for so long as detection and capture were so uncertain, and juries were reluctant to convict where conviction meant disproportionate penalties, these offences continued in abundance."

3. The character of objections to the establishment of a preventive police may be gauged from the conclusions of an 1822 commission: "It is difficult to reconcile an effective system of police with that perfect freedom of action and exemption from interference which are the great privileges and blessing of society in this country; and Your Committee think that the forfeiture or curtailment of such advantages are too great a sacrifice for

improvements in police, or facilities in detection of crime, however desirable in themselves if abstractedly considered" (cited in Thomson, 1950:66).

4. Outside incorporated towns, private police were frequently hired by railway companies and industrial concerns to maintain order among "large bodies of unruly workmen" (Mather, 1959:80).

5. It is significant that the success of the Thames River Police experiment depended on a renunciation of the desultory incentive (piecework) system in favor of established wages. The instructions to the first officers were clear: "you are to receive no fee or gratuity from any person whatsoever, for any duty you perform" (Colquhoun, 1800:642).

6. For a similar account of how police in New York were more "private entrepreneurs than public servants" and the abuses of the fee system, see Richardson (1970:23-50).

7. See the superb analysis in Hay (1975), to which we are indebted here.

8. One such exception was the entrepôt trade centering on the Thames River, in which a limited number of actors dominated a form of economic activity essentially taking place within a geographically circumscribed area. This unusual situation permitted the development of a collaborative private solution to the problem of pilferage and thievery at the docks; and, not surprisingly, we find here one of the earliest (and privately supported) moves toward professionalized policing—the Thames River Police (see Colquhoun, 1800).

9. For a discussion of the politically disastrous consequences of relying exclusively on military force to maintain domestic order, see Thompson (1963, chapter 15) on the Peterloo Massacre. For a consideration of how direct, personalized enforcement tends to intensify class antagonism, see Mather (1959, chapter 5).

10. Compare, for example, Adam Smith's comment (1776:183) that "the demand for men, like that for any other commodity, necessarily regulates the production of men; quickens when it goes slowly, and stops when it advances too fast."

REFERENCES

ALLEN, L.B. (1821). Brief considerations on the present state of the police of the metropolis. London.

ARDANT, G. (1975). "Financial policy and economic infrastructure of modern states and nations." Pp. 164-242 in C. Tilly (ed.), The formation of national states in Western Europe. Princeton, N.J.: Princeton University Press.

BAILEY, R.H. (1974). "Can delinquents be saved by the sea?" Corrections Magazine, 1(September):77-88.

BELOFF, M. (1938). Public order and popular disturbances, 1660-1714. London: Oxford University Press.

BENTHAM, J. (1843). Works (vol. 10; J. Bowring, ed.). Edinburgh.

BORDUA, D.J., and HAUREK, E.W. (1970). "The police budgets's lot: Components of the increase in local police expenditures, 1902-1960." Pp. 57-70 in H. Hahn (ed.), Police in urban society. Beverly Hills, Calif.: Sage.

CHADWICK, E. (1829). "Preventive police." London Review, 1:252-308.

COLQUHOUN, P. (1800). A treatise on the commerce and police of the River Thames. Montclair, N.J.: Patterson Smith.

——— (1806). A treatise on the police of the metropolis. Montclair, N.J.: Patterson Smith.

CRITCHLEY, T.A. (1972). A history of police in England and Wales. Montclair, N.J.: Patterson Smith.

DOBB, M. (1963). Studies in the development of capitalism. New York: International Publishers.

FITZGERALD, P. (1888). Chronicles of Bow Street Police-Office. Montclair, N.J.: Patterson Smith.

Gentleman's Magazine (1767). July.

GEORGE, D.M. (1965). London life in the eighteenth century. Middlesex, Eng.: Penguin.

GOUGH, I. (1975). "State expenditures in advanced capitalism." New Left Review, 92(July-August):53-92.

GRIGGS, B.S., and McCUNE, G.R. (1972). "Community-based correctional programs: A survey and analysis." Federal Probation, 36(June):7-13.

HART, J.M. (1951). The British police. London: George Allen and Unwin.

HAY, D. (1975). "Property, authority and the criminal law." Pp. 17-63 in D. Hay, P. Linebaugh, J.G. Rule, E.P. Thompson, and C. Winslow (eds.), Albion's fatal tree: Crime and society in eighteenth century England. New York: Pantheon.

HOBSBAWM, E.J. (1959). Primitive rebels. New York: W.W. Norton.

House of Commons (1701). Journals (May 15).

——— (1799-1800). Journals, 55:723-784.

HOWARD, J. (1777). The state of prisons in England and Wales. Warrington.

——— (1792). The state of prisons in England and Wales (4th ed.). Warrington.

KAKALIK, J.S., and WILDHORN, S. (1971). The private police industry: Its nature and extent (vol. 2). Santa Monica, Calif.: Rand Corporation.

KLARE, M.T. (1975). "Rent-a-cop: The boom in private police." Nation, 221(November): 486-491.

LEWIS, W.D. (1965). From Newgate to Dannemora: The rise of the penitentiary in New York, 1796-1848. Ithaca, N.Y.: Cornell University Press.

MANTOUX, P. (1928). The Industrial Revolution in the eighteenth century. London: Cape.

MARCUS, S. (1974). Engels, Manchester and the working class. New York: Vintage.

MATHER, F.C. (1959). Public order in the age of the Chartists. Manchester: Manchester University Press.

McKELVEY, B. (1936). American prisons: A study in American social history prior to 1915. Chicago: University of Chicago Press.

MOIR, E. (1969). The justice of the peace. Middlesex, Eng.: Penguin.

O'CONNOR, J. (1973). The fiscal crisis of the state. New York: St. Martin's Press.

Parliamentary Papers (1834). "Report from the select committee on police of the metropolis." 16:407-421.

PARRY-JONES, W. (1972). The trade in lunacy. London: Routledge and Kegan Paul.

POLANYI, K. (1944). The great transformation. Boston: Beacon.

POLLARD, S. (1965). The genesis of modern management. Middlesex, Eng.: Penguin.

POLLOCK, F., and MAITLAND, F.W. (1968). The history of English law (vol. 2). Cambridge: Cambridge University Press.

PRINGLE, P. (1958). The thief-takers. London: Museum Press.

PUGH, R.B. (1968). Imprisonment in medieval England. Cambridge: Cambridge University Press.

RADZINOWICZ, L. (1948). A history of English criminal law and its administration from 1750 (vol. 1). London: Stevens.

——— (1956). A history of English criminal law and its administration from 1750 (vol. 2). London: Stevens.

REITH, C. (1952). The blind eye of history. London: Faber and Faber.

RICHARDSON, J.F. (1970). The New York police: Colonial times to 1901. New York: Oxford University Press.

RUBINSTEIN, J. (1973). City police. New York: Ballantine.

RUTHERFORD, A. (1973). "Youth corrections in Massachusetts." Pp. 283-297 in S.L. Messinger, S. Halleck, P. Lerman, N. Morris, P.V. Murphy, and M.E. Wolfgang (eds.), Crime and justice annual. Chicago: Aldine.

SAYER, E. (1784). Observations on the police or civil government of Westminster with a proposal for a reform. London.

SCULL, A.T. (1977). Decarceration: Community treatment and the deviant: A radical view. Englewood Cliffs, N.J.: Prentice-Hall.

SILVER, A. (1967). "The demand for order in civil society: A review of some themes in the history of urban crime, police and riot." Pp. 1-24 in D. Bordua (ed.), The police. New York: Wiley.

SMITH, A. (1776). The wealth of nations (A. Skinner, ed.). Middlesex, Eng.: Penguin.

SMITH, W. (1776). State of the gaols in London, Westminster, and Borough of Southwark. London.

STONE, L. (1976). "Whigs, marxists, and poachers." New York Review of Books, 23(February):25-27.

THOMPSON, E.P. (1963). The making of the English working class. New York: Vintage.

——— (1971). "The moral economy of the English crowd in the eighteenth century." Past and Present, 50(spring):76-136.

——— (1975). Whigs and hunters: The origin of the Black Act. New York: Pantheon.

THOMSON, D. (1950). England in the nineteenth century. Middlesex, Eng.: Penguin.

TOBIAS, J.J. (1975). "Police and public in the United Kingdom." Pp. 95-113 in G.L. Mosse (ed.), Police forces in history. Beverly Hills, Calif.: Sage.

U.S. Bureau of the Census (1975). Historical statistics of the United States: Colonial times to 1970. Washington, D.C.: U.S. Government Printing Office.

WEBB, S., and WEBB, B. (1906). English local government: The parish and the county (vol. 1). London: Archon.

——— (1922). English local government: English prisons under local government (vol. 6). London: Archon.

——— (1927). English local government: English Poor Law history: Part I, The old Poor Law. London: Longman's Green.

——— (1963). The development of English local government. London: Oxford University Press.

WEBER, M. (1946). From Max Weber: Essays in sociology. New York: Oxford University Press.

——— (1961). General economic history. New York: Collier.

ABOUT THE AUTHORS

RICHARD A. BERK is Professor of Sociology at the University of California, Santa Barbara. He has published widely in the fields of collective behavior and evaluation research, and is the coauthor of *The Measure of Justice: An Empirical Study of the Changing Criminal Law* and *Prison Reform and State Elites*.

ROBERT B. COATES is Research Associate and Associate Director of the Center for Criminal Justice, Harvard University Law School, and is engaged in the center's study of reform in the Massachusetts Department of Youth Services.

ROBERT E. DORAN received his Ph.D. in sociology from the University of California at Davis and is Deputy Superintendent of the California Rehabilitation Center at Corona.

SCOTTY EMBREE is Assistant Professor of Sociology at Brooklyn College, City University of New York. She is now analyzing the history of the American Public Health Association and its relationship to imperialism.

DAVID F. GREENBERG is Assistant Professor of Sociology at New York University. He is the author of *Mathematical Criminology* and coauthor of *Struggle for Justice* and *University of Chicago Graduate Problems in Physics*.

C. RONALD HUFF is Assistant Professor of Sociology at Purdue University. He has held professional positions in correctional and psychiatric settings and has been a research consultant.

DREW HUMPHRIES is an Assistant Professor of Sociology at Rutgers University, Camden, New Jersey. She received her doctorate from the School of Criminology, University of California, Berkeley, in 1973.

JOHN IRWIN is an Associate Professor at San Francisco State University. His publications include *The Felon* and *Struggle for Justice,* the latter coauthored with other members of an American Friends Service Committee Working Party.

JAMES B. JACOBS is Assistant Professor of Law and Sociology at Cornell University. He is the author of *Stateville: The Penitentiary in Mass Society* and of numerous articles on prison organization and penal policy.

ALDEN D. MILLER is Research Associate and Associate Director of the Center for Criminal Justice, Harvard University Law School, and is engaged in the center's study of reform in the Massachusetts Department of Youth Services.

LLOYD E. OHLIN is Director of Research of the Center for Criminal Justice, Harvard University Law School, and Roscoe Pound Professor of Criminology. He is engaged in the center's study of reform in the Massachusetts Department of Youth Services.

PETER H. ROSSI is Professor of Sociology and Director of the Social and Demographic Research Institute at the University of Massachusetts at Amherst. He has taught at Harvard, Chicago, and Johns Hopkins. His recent monographs include *Prison Reform and State Elites, Reforming Public Welfare,* and *The Roots of Urban Discontent.*

ANDREW T. SCULL is Assistant Professor of Sociology at the University of Pennsylvania. He is the author of *Decarceration: Community Treatment and the Deviant: A Radical View* and is currently working on a book on the social organization of insanity in 19th century England.

RICHARD SPEIGLMAN has taught at the University of Lowell and the Massachusetts Correctional Institution at Walpole and now teaches a class on crime at an alternative junior high school. He is writing a text on prisons with a collective in the San Francisco Bay area.

STEVEN SPITZER is Associate Professor of Sociology at the University of Northern Iowa (Cedar Falls) and has written in the areas of deviance and criminology. He is currently completing a book on *Deviance and Control in American Society* and is beginning a study of the development of police systems in the United States.

FRANKLIN E. ZIMRING is Professor of Law and Director of the Center for Studies in Criminal Justice at the University of Chicago. He is coauthor of *Deterrence: The Legal Threat in Crime Control* and *Firearms and Violence in American Life.*